SOCIAL THEORIES
OF THE MIDDLE AGES

SOCIAL THEORIES
OF
THE MIDDLE AGES

1200–1500

by

BEDE JARRETT, O. P.

New Foreword by
JOHN C. MÉDAILLE

✣ Angelico Press

Angelico Press reprint edition, 2012
This Angelico edition is a republication of the
work originally published by Ernest Benn, Ltd., London, 1926
New Foreword © John C. Médaille, 2012

For information, address:
Angelico Press, 4619 Slayden Rd., NE
Tacoma, WA 98422
www.angelicopress.com

ISBN: 978-1-887593-39-7

Cover Design: Cristy Deming

FOREWORD
to the
ANGELICO EDITION

We are currently in the midst of many troubles. We seem to go from crisis to crisis, and have few ways to deal with the complexity of our social systems. So is this a time to be looking backwards at the Middle Ages? Is this not an exercise in pure nostalgia, an escape from the problems of the moment? It is certainly appropriate to ask such questions on the occasion of republishing Dom Bede Jarrett's *Social Theories of the Middle Ages*, but I would like to assert that this is indeed the perfect time for the republication of this important work. For our problem is that, having no grounds for comparison, we have no way to critique our society. We have only the vocabulary our age provides, that is, the sort of thinking that arises from the very system we are trying to critique. After all, as Albert Einstein noted, "you cannot solve a problem at the level of thinking that created it."

What marks the modern age is a fracturing of human life from human thought. We have divorced science from art, commercial life from family life, the moral realm from the physical, the political realm from the economic, and so on. All such divisions can be summarized, I believe, as consequences of the division between faith and reason. In contrast, what characterizes the Middle Ages is the *unity* of all these sunderings. This is why the Middle Ages provides so salient a counterpoint to our current situation.

The great problem in looking at the Middle Ages, however, is that in the popular imagination this period is barely distinguishable from the Dark Ages. And even if we grant this civilizational epoch some measure of progress, we still view it as a time when faith triumphed over reason, superstition reigned over science, and religious myths suppressed artistic imagination.

The picture of the Middle Ages that emerges from Jarrett's work is however that of an age of reason, of science, and of art. But more than this, it is an age in which all three of these were seen as interconnected, in which the fracturing tendency characteristic of the modern age was not indulged. Faith was not then something opposed to science or to reason—it was the firm foundation upon which these things stood. Now, one may agree or disagree with this view of the relationship between faith and reason, but in disagreeing it is important to first look at and consider an age that offers a completely different point of view. And if our disagreement should then still continue, we will at least have established a clear basis for comparison.

The medieval view of society was based on a wholly different view of man. According to this view, man was a creature who could reason, who could act, and who could make things. In reason such men sought the truth, in acting they sought justice, and in making things they sought usefulness and beauty. Note that although these are three distinct things, they are not really three *separate* things. The end of knowledge was action, the point of action was creativity, and the purpose of both was a more complete and concrete expression of the truth.

Whereas medieval science was inclusive, modern science derives its power precisely from being limited to weight and number. Although modern man will to some degree acknowledge the existence of the humane sciences, they are accorded a lesser status. To have any prestige at all, these humane sciences are forced to ape the methods of the natural sciences. But to do this, the nature of man must first be distorted. The human mind must be treated as a machine, as an economic calculator; and the family and community as mere utilities aimed at getting what is wanted rather than at seeking what we really need and giving back to others what we can.

To make things clearer, we might envision medieval science as a pyramid: at its base are the sciences that deal with the pure search for truth; in its upward-tapering mid-region are the action-oriented practical sciences, and at its pinnacle art, the science of making things. Art, then, was for medieval man not something opposed to science, but something that stood at the pinnacle of human knowledge. Nor was it something subject to a narrow moralism. It is quite true that in the latter part of the age—as the unity of the medieval vision was breaking apart—firebrands such as Savonarola did view art as a profanation of divine things. But, as Jarrett notes,

> A scholastic would have told Fra Girolamo that his own St. Thomas, whom he quoted so frequently, would have refused him the right to speak as to what was good and what was bad in art. He was a moralist, a preacher; his virtue was prudence, and prudence may not judge art. Prudence might be more truly a virtue than art insofar as it made men good simply, but art was more truly a virtue than prudence insofar as it was more scientific and had more of the intellectual splendor of an authentic *habitus*, and "life in accordance with thought is better than life in accordance with man."

In contrast to the medieval view, the modern tendency to reduce all science to questions of weight and measure has been particularly problematic in the humane sciences, such as economics. Whereas the scholastic age was able to make a distinction between *œconomia* and *pecunativa*—the former having as its end the material provisioning of society, while the latter dealt with the purely private pursuit of wealth—the modern age has lost this distinction. Indeed, it has reduced all of economics to *pecunativa*, in the naïve belief that the private pursuit of wealth will be to the greatest common good. But certainly our current economic situation provides grounds for calling that belief into question, and for searching out another model.

By the conclusion of the 15th century, the end of the period of Jarrett's study, the unity of the Middle Ages had begun to break apart under the hammer blows of nationalism, secularism, and conciliarism. But it is enough, for our present purposes, to know that there had been a unity, and that what held true then can be rediscovered. Not, indeed, in the same form, because the modern age does represent real advances. It is not true traditionalism, but mere antiquarianism, that attempts to do no more than reproduce the past rather than transform the present. It is precisely this task of transformation that is now forced upon us; and so it is a truly opportune moment to look to an age that achieved a certain unity—however imperfectly it may have been achieved—which we have lost.

JOHN C. MÉDAILLE

INTRODUCTION

Any reader of this book may realize the difficulty that its composition has involved: the cutting down of three hundred years of active social theorizing to the compass of three hundred pages. Nor has the difficulty been lessened by the knowledge that to other writers have been assigned the Political and Economic Ideals of the period. It was right and scholarly that this should be done; nevertheless, it entailed the separation of what in practice was never separated.

Again it has been difficult to select from the mass of material those theories precisely most worth while considering—namely, such as influenced the world generally from 1200 to 1500. The rest—and their name is legion—had perforce to be ignored. For every work cited a dozen others have had to be omitted. My effort has been to present only those typical of their age or of their school.

Since my task—more pleasant in what I was led to read than in what I have tried to write—has been solely that of an historian, I have not attempted to criticize the theories I have recorded, nor to award praise or blame. Moralists and theologians and preachers have that for their province; not historians. I have tried to understand what these people aimed at saying and to explain to those who really wish to know. To introduce any reader to any medieval theorist and to enable him to understand what that theorist meant is all I have attempted. That he shall approve of the theorist, or not, though I may have my doubts and my hopes, is his affair, not mine.

CONTENTS

CHAPTER I

LAW

In dealing with mediæval social theories it is not possible to avoid the difficult and delicate task of endeavouring to discover, describe, and set in order the development of the mediæval theory of law. Difficult and delicate the task must be, even in spite of the many master minds already at work disentangling it. Both historians and lawyers [1] have devoted a good deal of patient attention to it ; philosophers even have not considered the subject to lie outside their cognizance. It is not then for lack of material, nor for lack of sufficiency of theory to explain that material, that the task remains forbidding ; rather is it the curious conflict dividing historians and lawyers and philosophers into different schools that makes the matter one of such considerable delicacy.

Nevertheless the task must be attempted.

It is clear that the first thing to emerge out of the collapse of a civilization, or the intrusion into it of another civilization, is law. Other arts have to wait for its emergence before they can find scope for their own enlargement. Perhaps architecture alone of the arts has some chance of existence in lawless society, and then only in the form of architecture built for offence and defence. All else is too unsettled, life too " nasty, brutish and short." Civilization then can become evident only as society settles down, and as it settles down organization appears and law begins, for law is the reign of order. Law implies the acceptance by a group of people of certain common regulations ; it presupposes that these people have already been made co -scious of their unity ; it presupposes too their submission not only to a ruler but to rule.

Law, which is not however to be identified with mere words of command, marks, therefore, a stage in the development of a society. Law, truly so called, cannot yet be considered to exist where tumult is apparent and into which breaks some giant

---

[1] A. J. Carlyle, *A History of Mediæval Political Theory in the West*, 1903, and C. T. Flower, *Public Works in Medieval Law*, 1915.

I

wielding a club. Mere force in possession is not law. The leader of a war party enforcing his strategy and his directions by means of compulsion is not a lawgiver, though he may become a lawgiver. Mere order and coercion do not constitute law. Law would seem to denote something more than these—a settlement, customs, a common consciousness, and ordered unity.

But once a people accepts law, it enters history. Before that it is prehistoric. After that it takes its place in "the pageant of man."

Law, moreover, does not merely show us that the people who possess it are now "historical"; it itself shapes their history. The laws of a people begin by being the expression of that people's life and thought, and thereby they show us at every stage of its history where that people has reached, and indeed its character and habit of thought. Beyond this, moreover, they even deflect the history of that people. The national characteristics are evinced by its laws, and these in turn become themselves moulded by those laws, which thus react to individualize the people themselves.

This is evident, indeed, in the thirteenth century, the date from which this volume begins to consider, and attempts to describe, the social theories of Christendom. All dates of the growth and development of a theory are necessarily arbitrary, none the less for practical purposes they are inevitable. The dates of a monarch's reign are often as useful for marking history into periods as any other method, particularly if that monarch, by the strength or weakness of his character, left a considerable impress on the government of his people, and this is probably true of nearly every mediæval monarch. The historian who undertakes to write the history of the English people, for example, may think fit to ignore as landmarks the reigns of its kings, may dismiss monarchs as figureheads that appeal merely to the imagination of simple and romantic historians, and may elect to be guided by movements and tendencies. Yet as a matter of sober fact all the movements and tendencies of English history were developed or thwarted or deflected by English kings, in their moments of strength when they guided, in their moments of weakness when they let go, the government of their people.

The mediæval kings fix, therefore, better than centuries the stages of their nation's development. But when a historian deals with Christendom he is at once at a loss. He has no single state by whose kings he can mark the successive stages of development. Even the Papacy, the unique central fact in Christian history, cannot be so put to use. Its princes did not in this sense determine the fate of the Christian people, except in certain rather isolated instances. Consequently the only possible measurement left is the admittedly crude system of dating movements and theories by centuries. We must use it therefore, for there is no other.

Yet, in beginning from the thirteenth century to describe the social theories of Christendom, we have a rough date which is sufficiently satisfactory; for by the thirteenth century the fumbling in the dark was over, the latch had been found, the door was already at least ajar.

The old Græco-Roman inheritance into which the barbarians had succeeded was indeed only gradually acquired. The barbarians, who had in some cases impinged only on the borders of the Empire and had in others actually been admitted within the Empire, had succeeded to Imperial titles, customs, coins and social organization. The instances of these are too many to be quoted; nor do they need quoting. The fact is generally admitted: the *tufa* of the Saxon Bretwalda, the gold coins minted under Alfred in Oxford and London, the villa and beneficium, that later became the manor, are no longer in dispute as showing how the old civilization was taken over by the new.

Nevertheless, new wine poured into old bottles is not thoroughly at home in its straitened circumstances. It effervesces and bursts its narrow limits. There is no " give " left in the old skins, which have long since been expanded to their uttermost. The cannibal chief will make himself comfortable with the hat of the late missionary: the hat, however, that suited the missionary may have suffered a little in the process of becoming suited to its new wearer. It loses its shape when it becomes a crown.

3

It is not sufficient to recognize that the barbarians took over the old civilization unless it is recognized also what a change they very promptly made in it. First notice that it was considerably damaged in the process of handing over. The Roman remains frequently show signs of having been fired ; they are often enough rather ruins than remains. Moreover when taken over they were not always put to the use that had previously been made of them. They were adapted to new uses ; sometimes they were treated worse than that : they were " restored." That is a word which experience has taught us to regard as bearing a grim meaning. The old Roman ruins were terribly " restored."

The Saxon gold coin bears some resemblance to the old coin of the Empire, yet how corrupted in the transformation ! The quadriga has drifted from its wheels, the ears of the wheat have deserted their parent stem. The Bretwalda may still wear the insignia of the old Imperial governor, but he has only a very shadowy semblance of his predecessor's power. Even the villa, however persistent here and there its life till it became the manor, did in process of time become the manor, and cease any longer to be a villa at all.

The Imperial development was entirely altered by its being redirected by another race, with other ideals, other memories, and other preoccupations. For one thing, the Empire fell apart. That in itself was a change of immeasurable effect. Politically the unity of Europe was gone. Had there been no other link left between the various provinces, anarchy would have set in almost beyond recovery, the unity of Europe would have been irretrievably lost. Fortunately the Faith of Christ had by that time been accepted by the Empire, and the act of Constantine which made that Faith common to every part of the Empire saved civilization. The Church replaced the Emperor, the Faith saved man.

Imagine then to yourself the barbarians encamped on the Roman lands, wearing the captured spoils of Roman greatness, administering the broken territories of Rome nearly always from some half-destroyed Roman city. But as the civil toga of a Roman had to be cut to suit the figure of the warring barbarian, so equally had Rome's political theories and her social theories to be adapted too. They had to be cut away to fit a more youthful figure, more war-like, more athletic, more full of hope.

But the Church of the West was a Latin Church. For at once the Empire governed from Constantinople had fallen apart, and the Exarch of Ravenna alone remained to represent, and that timidly, the dominion of Byzantium. Its Latin tongue meant a survival of Latin phrases, however barbarously massacred, and this particularly made recoverable the old civilization of Rome. For the point to be noticed is that all through Christian history the Christian people are perpetually and consciously going back on their past. They renew themselves deliberately out of their old greatness. From time to time the classical languages are forgotten and despised; new advances are made which dwarf " the greatness that was Rome." But these advances in turn suffer violence and disorder, and are in danger of producing anarchy and decay. Christendom, sometimes led by the Church, sometimes against the dominant party in the Church, goes back to its origins, and renews itself. Note that this renewal is an appeal to antiquity, and that the antiquity appealed to is sometimes sacred and sometimes profane; note also that, like all appeals to history, it is as often as not made by those whose knowledge of history is extremely inaccurate; note finally that in spite of this inaccurate history and false antiquarianism the recovery of Christendom has always been achieved.

The eleventh century and the twelfth century saw the appeal made to the past; the thirteenth century witnessed the recovery.

The real Dark Ages, dark because our knowledge of them is fragmentary and gloomy, fell just before and after the meteoric career of Charlemagne; and the recovery from them was effected by means of religion. Cluny and Cîteaux stand as the results of the dawning of the light which was breaking over the darkness. They were not the light, but bore witness to it.

In this dawn comes, brighter than all, the beginnings of the University of Paris, from which radiated the glories of the thirteenth century; and Paris was an appeal to the past. Paris seemed by way of Metz to continue the traditions of

5

Charlemagne's culture, and Charlemagne himself deliberately went back for his inspiration to old Rome. His literary revival, particularly through monasticism, was an attempt to rediscover antiquity. Its survival was noticed by Abelard, accepted by St Bernard. John of Salisbury, without being respectful to it, was yet encompassed by it, and, however much he might think that the spirit of Christ and the spirit of Aristotle were antagonistic, he himself had inherited from both. St Bernard considered that he stood for Christ and that Abelard was Aristotle reborn : logic busied with the mysteries of faith. The thirteenth century—accomplishing what the Council of Sens could not do—incorporated both St Bernard and Abelard, producing at its close a commentary on the Canticle of Canticles, dictated on his death-bed by St Thomas Aquinas, wherein the *Sic-et-Non* only makes crisp and clean the mystic lyric note. Both sides in the dispute appealed to antiquity. Christendom went back to its origins ; civilization began to renew itself.

First and foremost came the recovery of law ; society was settling down to live.

The law and the theory of law that the thirteenth century inherited had, therefore, a double origin. It inherited naturally Roman law, but not the original law of Rome, for this had been made to fit all sorts of new conditions and was barely recognizable. It was eked out by customs that were wholly at variance with it ; its saws and wise sayings were repeated as sacrosanct, yet were interpreted in a way that would have astonished the legists of the Empire. Throughout mediæval times these proverbial sayings were bandied about, but, like the majority of legal tags that come into common use, they were misunderstood.

Further, the Church had continued its own separate law, the outcome of various General Councils, the decisions of popes or of local assemblies of bishops, whether authentic or legendary, genuine or forged. Sometimes these decisions ran counter to the Imperial tradition, sometimes followed it surprisingly, occasionally struck out an entirely new line of their own. Before Gratian made his famous redaction the collections of these decrees were too imperfect to allow of a general codification of them, so that until 1142 the Church lawyers are halting and contradictory in their attempts to give us the bare principles of law.

As regards the civil courts there were also various collections of laws, as in England, with its Kentish law, Northumbrian law and Mercian law, with later on the laws of Edward the Confessor, and later still the laws of King Henry, which Cardinal Langton was supposed to have discovered at the beginning of the thirteenth century among the charters of Canterbury and to have produced to the assembled baronage, assisting them in consequence to formulate the demands which they incorporated in the Great Charter. Again, both in the Empire and in France, there were the capitularies of the kings, which were many, confusing, contradictory, and uncertain in origin.

Roman law filtering through barbaric custom, Church law that included local decisions in East and West, personal formularies of individual kings or such as acquired traditional prestige from being linked to a royal name, these were themselves sufficiently confusing, but they were in addition crossed by increasingly influential principles for which feudalism, as we call it, was responsible. For feudalism was neither Roman nor Teutonic, neither ecclesiastical nor royal. It opposed all of these in turn, and was in perpetual opposition to one or other of them. Kings, like Henry II., imposed checks on the feudalism of their subjects, yet made use of feudalism to obstruct the policy of their equals or superiors. Historians, like Freeman, hold that it cannot come from Rome, or, like Fustel de Coulanges, that it cannot have its origin in barbarism. Truly, it was the result of none of these, squared with none of them, and was used but sparingly and without consistency, since it was always a double-edged blade, cutting backwards as well as forwards, and wounding alike Pope and king and subject in the house of their friends. No wonder the far-sighted Innocent III. preferred to let it alone, and told Philip Augustus and Richard I. that he had no intention of judging feudal matters. It was quite evident to him that Philip and Richard were handling explosive material, as likely to injure the one who used it as the one against whom it was used.

Feudalism complicated then the medley of law which the thirteenth century inherited. It even complicated itself. By binding together the tenants and their lord feudalism gradually organized, as well as armed, the kingdoms of Europe under their kings as the apex of that wide-based triangle the commonalty, yet while it created a national weapon it was itself an international force. In a real sense there was more fellow-feeling between the baronage of England and the baronage of France than between the baronage and the commonalty of either country. Simon de Montfort and his party, it is true, opposed the foreign Poitevin nobility which came in with Henry III.; nevertheless, Simon himself was a foreigner, as were also not a few of his fellow-nobles.

But the thirteenth century began its experiment by endeavouring to make quite clear to itself the meaning of law. As it proceeded in its search, and as its work continued till the end of the fifteenth century, we may note how lively was the interest in, and how vital the elaboration of, the theory of law. For us this interest and elaboration are of peculiar value, for they display the keenness with which social problems were then being discussed, and explain the solutions propounded by successive thinkers.

We are not here, it will be realized, considering law from its legal but from its social aspect. The courts of law reveal indeed the practice of their age, but the theories of the courts reveal its ideals.

First the mediæval schoolman found himself confronted with an inheritance of patristic learning—the mind of the great Christian traditional thought at work on the facts of the world. By what right was there law at all? By what right did one Christian impose his will on another, since by the teaching of Christ each soul was equal under the Fatherhood of God? Was law, that is compulsion in the name of order, justifiable? Was it not rather a mere inheritance of paganism, to be rejected in the new Christian commonwealth? The Fathers had debated all these points and had reached their own conclusions, which were more or less commonly accepted in the cultured society of Christendom, when our period opens. Alexander of Hales (*d.* 1245) is but summing up common opinion when he states as his thesis (*Summa Theolog.*, quest. 47, m. 1, a. 1): "That one man should be ruled by another is just, not owing to a condition of nature but owing to inequality of merit." Very carefully he explains that by this he means that man for man we are all equal, but that rulers are chosen because of their greater capacity to rule, their greater virtue in ruling. The purpose of dominion is to coerce the evildoer: "Natural law ordains the equal freedom of all in the state of original nature (*naturæ institutæ*); but according to the state of fallen nature (*naturæ corruptæ*) it ordains that subjection and lordship are necessary for the constraint of evil." Thus, as Alexander of Hales (who was one of the great English schoolmen, and in some ways the master not only of his own Franciscan body of theologians but even of certain of the Dominican thinkers) saw it, the justification of law springs from sin and the corruption which sin begat in humanity; law is itself instituted to restrain sin. He looked, therefore, on sin as the origin of authority, in the sense that the existence of sin in the world produces the necessity for authority—namely, to keep sinners in order.

This attitude is not merely Alexander of Hales' personal view. Gerald de Barri (Giraldus Cambrensis, 1146-1220), in the opening chapter of his *De Instructione Principum*, suggests the same line of thought: "Princely power is necessary for men, since where there is no government the people will come to ruin."

Again, a similar view is found in Vincent de Beauvais (*d. circa* 1270), the Dominican friend of St Louis IX., who wrote for the guidance of the young French princes *Tractatus de morali principis institutione* (cap. 3): "If man had not ruled man, the human race by the absence of justice would have slaughtered itself to extinction." [1]

St Bonaventure (1221-1274), a good disciple of Alexander of Hales, not only echoes the teaching of his master, but is careful to give the name of him who originated it: "Freedom is in man by nature, but the power of lordship is destructive of

---

[1] *Cf.* Friedrich, *Vincentius von Beauvais als Pädagog nach seiner Schrift De Eruditione filiorum regalium*, Leipzig, 1883.

freedom ; therefore lordship would seem not to be from nature."
This was the problem as he saw it. He defines freedom as " the
natural power in every man to do what he likes," and states that
" subjection has been introduced on account of sin, as in many
places Augustine says." As a matter of fact he is giving us here
as much Peter Lombard as St Augustine. In his answer to the
problem he has enunciated he distinguishes, on the one hand,
the power of precedence (*potestas præsidendi*)—namely, the
power of father over son and of husband over wife—which he
admits would have existed even had sin never come into the
world, on the other hand the power of lordship (*potestas
dominandi*), the existence of which is due entirely to our fallen
nature (*On the Sentences*, Bk. II., dist. 44, art. 2, quest. 2).
Further on (art. 3, quest. 1) he states more explicitly the limits
of this power of lordship : " Christians are bound to their
earthly lords, not, however, in everything, but only in those
things which are not against God. Nor even is this the only
limit, for further it is to be accepted only in those things
which are reasonably ordered according to right custom, such
as tribute, taxes, and other such things."

In his *Commentary on Ecclesiastes* St Bonaventure expands
his teaching on the position of authority in the same sense as
Alexander of Hales, as being due to sin : " For some are worse
and more evil than others, and so the just judgment of God
makes them and their children subject to others " (cap. 8);
moreover otherwise everyone would do what he liked, and so
there would be " the schism of iniquity." Here, notice, we have
the notion, borrowed vaguely from Aristotle's theory of the
origin of slavery, that sin is the cause of authority in the sense
that the worse must serve the better. It is not difficult to see
how easily this was to become in the hands of Wyclif (1324-
1384) the theory of the " Dominion of Grace." Authority is
lawful because the evil are to be constrained, says Bonaventure ;
therefore, argues Wyclif, goodness is the test of authority and
the sinner may not rule.

St Bonaventure himself saw the danger of his own theory
and went to much trouble to explain (cap. 10) how a ruler
might be an evil man and yet compel his subjects to obedience :

"A prelate may be just or evil in three different ways: one is unjust in himself [lives an immoral life] but succeeds to his dominion justly and justly exercises it. Such a one can rule just subjects nor sin in so doing, and justly should these subjects obey him. Another, however, has unjustly usurped his authority and exercises it in an unjust manner; he is not just in his office nor may one justly obey him. In a third way a ruler may be unjust, for, though he has justly succeeded to his office his administration is unjustly carried out by afflicting the good and promoting the evil. To him it is right to be subject in what he commands that is lawful, but in what he commands that is contrary to God no man may obey him; moreover, since he who abuses the power committed to him has deserved to lose this power, he may be rightfully removed from it, although he is rightfully in possession of his authority." He adds "that evil men who rule well should be in authority is no evil to the State; but that those who rule badly should be in authority is not due to their justice, but to the divine justice which has appointed them to rule on account of the sins of their people."

Vincent de Beauvais the Dominican, who, like Giraldus Cambrensis, wrote a treatise of advice to princes, *De Eruditione Principum* (sometimes ascribed to Guillaume de Perault, *cf.* p. 9, n. 1), goes further than Alexander of Hales and Bonaventure, and sees in law not a mere coercive force but something higher, more positive: "The prince ought to urge his fellows to a love of justice, which implies first that they should injure no one, and secondly that they should promote the common good" (Bk. IV., cap. 2). We are approaching that view of law which finally flooded with such idealism all the later Middle Ages. Dante is at white heat of enthusiasm with it when he pens his *De Monarchia*; Ockham (1280-1340) is flaming with it, and Pierre du Bois (1255-1322). But the one mainly responsible for the lighting of the flame, and who inspired this burning enthusiasm, was Aquinas. The study of him was crucial in Dante's life, and his name receives honour where one would least expect to find it—namely, in the *De Recuperatione Sancte Terre*.[1]

---

[1] Edited by Ch. Langlois, Paris, 1891, p. 53.

St Thomas had a mind that was essentially orderly. His treatise *De Legibus*, incorporated in the First portion of the Second Part (quest. 90-97) of his *Summa Theologica* (1268-1270), is especially a triumph of masterly arrangement, which deals with all the theories of law as exemplified in the many definitions of law, shows the value of each and the truth contained in all, and finally gathers up the whole into a consistent body of doctrine that has continued to impress lawyers as well as theologians, and that certainly to the end of the Middle Ages influenced and almost entirely controlled public opinion. To have guided the minds of Dante (1265-1321), du Bois (1255-1322) and Richard Rolle of Hampole (1300-1349) is no inconsiderable tribute to the combination of sound sense with mystic idealism in this treatise of Aquinas.

Right or law is a rule or measure ; that is its simplest significance and its most universal. It measures actions. The law will vary with that which it measures, for the actions to be measured must include those of stars as well as of men. In this general sense then law is a rule measuring action ; but when law is considered in particular, in so far as it deals with rational nature a further notion is found to be contained in it, or perhaps only to grow out of it—namely, that a man by reason of some law or rule is found to have acquired thereby a right. Hence St Thomas, like a thoroughly well-taught student of trivium and quadrivium, with his love of mathematical exactness and order, decides to speak of law as " a measure " and of right as " that which is measured " and therefore as commensurate with law. Truly we are in the thirteenth century with its scientific passion for exactness and its Pythagorean belief in numbers and figures. Architecture, painting, music and thought are looked upon as built upon order, and beauty as that order when splendidly arrayed.

When a law is purely natural the rights which it confers will be commensurate—that is, will be purely natural too. But all law must be in some way natural, either fixed by nature or at least not opposed by nature, so that right is always natural, at least in the general sense that it is not opposed to nature. Nature is our only master (for reason is but nature's child, part of nature) in that all law and all right must be directed by or allowed by nature. To oppose nature is to hurt it. Law must never do that. It must not hurt nature since its function is to regulate nature, for law is measurement. Red tape, perhaps, Aquinas would have urged, is not a regulation of nature, but its strangulation. Law then must at the least be according to nature.

We can go further than that, for we can lay down the principle that law must be concerned with some good end. It must be busied with man's good, since it must suit his nature and what is good for him will be according to his nature, though that good may at times be the mere negative good of preventing harm. If law be natural, law will be good or ethical in its motive. Hence the first principle which directs ethics will also direct law—namely, good is to be pursued and evil avoided.

There you have morality in its simplest terms, and there also you have the restraining and inspiring influence of law. It has a twofold purpose: negatively, as Vincent de Beauvais said, to save from injury, positively to promote the common good. It will be noticed, therefore, that though scholasticism is dry it is not barren : you see a field of bones, but the bones live.

At once St Thomas (1225-1274) takes a wide vision, for he has to fit into his theory not only the law of Christ and the laws of faith but the Roman law and the *Decretum* of Gratian. He is confronted with a text of Ulpian : " the law of nature is that which all beasts follow." This is made the centre of a famous article (I. ii. 92, 2),[1] which describes all the good which man's nature pursues till it is found to include whatever as a mere substance he inclines to—for example, the preservation of his existence ; whatever as an animal—for example, the instinct for procreation ; whatever as a man—for example, the instincts to be rid of ignorance or not to offend his neighbour.

Because man, however, is a reasoning animal, his nature must tend principally and especially to a reasonable good. His laws must deal above all with this, his pursuit of rational good.

---

[1] This and following page references to the *Summa Theologica* of St Thomas Aquinas refer to the *English translation* by the Dominican Fathers of the English Province (Burns, Oates & Washbourne Limited).

From this St Thomas, by a keen analysis of man's experience, arrives at the conclusion that just as reason has its first principles, the law of contradiction and the like, so also there are first principles of morality, known absolutely to man, to be found everywhere, universal; others which are known only to the wise; others again which are of a much higher order and of which only revelation and faith make us cognizant. These universal absolute principles, in which amongst others the commandments of the Old Law are included by him, cannot be wholly lost, though they may, one or other of them, be lost here and there. As an instance, Cæsar's *Commentaries* are quoted as proving that to the Germans theft was not considered dishonourable, for St Thomas holds himself that the commandment " Thou shalt not steal " is an absolute first principle of natural law. He would seem, however, to hold that the only principle of natural law impossible to be forgotten is : " Do to others as you would they should do to you." The principles known only to the wise can on the other hand be wholly obliterated from the thought of man : " To do honour to grey hairs " is the example he quotes.

These primary principles are indirect teaching from nature, as also are the secondary principles ; the difference between them is that the first can never wholly be obliterated from man's heart, while the second can be wholly obliterated.

From both these principles conclusions can be drawn. But first it must be recognized that since the principles come direct from nature's teaching they are immutable in themselves, for nature is a constant force. We can be ignorant of both primary and secondary principles, we can be blinded to them by passion ; but the principles themselves are immutable.

On the other hand, the conclusions drawn even from primary principles are mutable, not in the sense that they can be diminished but that they can be added to. We cannot remove them, we can develop them in greater detail.

For St Thomas, let us repeat, law is the measurement of nature's action ; it must at least, therefore, accord with nature. Nature herself is to be considered not as a vague force urging the world to its fulfilment, but rather as an instinctive force or tendency driving each man to the fulfilment of his own purposes. These purposes must be good for man, since (here St Thomas discovers a phrase of Aristotle which he loves as much as Sir Thomas Browne seems to do) "Nature does nothing in vain." Since, therefore, man is eminently rational, the good he pursues must above all else be rational. Nature, therefore, dictates certain laws to him, certain measurements of action, fundamental in their origin. Some of them he knows without much exercise of thought : these are primary ; some only after prolonged thought : these are secondary. From these two sets he can deduce further conclusions, not directly taught by nature but arrived at from nature's teaching "by way of conclusion." These are not to be identified with the secondary principles, for they are not principles at all. They are argued to from principles.

These conclusions are usually discovered by man's experience of life, and are confirmed by positive enactment and made part of his civil governance. However, some are so universal and so instinctive as never to be found in any code, but to be earlier than all codes, to be discovered wherever man is, to be treasured by him in every stage of his growth, so powerfully tangled with his nature that even though he may deliberately discard them he must return to them or he will die. These last he calls the findings of the law of nations.

By this law of nations he does not mean what Grotius has taught us to mean—a law between nations—but a law so instinctive, so forced on man by his experience everywhere, as to be found in every nation the world over. No code, he urges, establishes the necessity of a government, or the law of property, or the need of one man to work for another. No code again is required to insist that agreements are to be kept. These things are so tangled with the roots of our being as to be discovered from the sheer process of life and to follow inevitably from it. Again there are other universally accepted principles which regulate the relationships not only between man and man but between group and group, such as the safe-conduct always granted to ambassadors, the observance of treaties (*Commentary on the Nicom. Ethics*, V., lect. 12. Cf. *Summa Theologica*, I. ii. 95, 2, not to murder; 95, 4, treaties to be observed and ambassadors respected. See also I. ii. 71, 3, ad 3 m, and II. ii. 40, 3; II. ii. 57, 3, private property; also 12, 2). These last are mentioned among the *jura gentium* not because they belong to international relationships but because they are arrived at from experience and found everywhere, as conclusions flowing from the principles of natural law.

Lastly there are the conclusions derived from and decided on by the civil authority : a senate, a parliament, a people or a king. Like the *jus gentium*, this *jus civile* is positive or conventional ; unlike the *jus gentium*, it requires to be put on the statute-book to carry force. It is not a direct conclusion of natural law but a conclusion reached by a distinct legislative body and having its force from that body (*ex sola lege humana vigorem habent*). Always indeed it must be in accord with nature ; though it need not be dictated by nature it must never be opposed by nature : " Every human law has as its condition of being a law that it shall be derived from a law of nature. . . . It is of the essence of a human law that it should be derived from the law of nature (*Omnis lex humanitus posita in tantum habet de ratione legis, in quantum a lege naturæ derivatur. . . . Est de ratione legis humanæ quod sit derivata a lege naturæ*) " (*Summa Theologica*, I. ii. 95, 2).

All this is, of course, very elaborately staged by St Thomas, broken up into all sorts of questions, and dealt with in far fuller detail than we have here been able to give. Every point is repeated in many ways and from many different standpoints, as though St Thomas considered all he had to say to be so important and so vital that he would leave nothing to the risk of being misunderstood.

Nor was he misunderstood till very much later than his period. Right to the end of the fifteenth century his careful and patient analysis of law and its significance, his delicate divisions of it, the specific value of each of these divisions, its majesty, its restraint, the inspiration it can afford, the curb to tyranny it must establish, are all notions that must spring to the consciousness of each subsequent writer on law, are remembered and, finally, are fitted into every theory of law. Even his definition of law we find repeated from his time onward: "Law is an ordinance of reason, for the common good, promulgated by him, who has care of the community" (I. ii. 90, 4). If any so-called law lack so much as one of the four conditions contained in this definition, it is not law at all, he says, but violence, the negation of law. It is an explosive test. Law must be reasonable, must be for the common good, must, by competent authority, be duly promulgated.

It would be unhistorical to think that St Thomas can write only dryly and by way of syllogism. The *Summa Theologica* is a text-book for beginners: so St Thomas styles it in his preface. It is indeed a very prince of text-books, but its purpose is only to set in order and with economy of language the barest principles of thought. It needs the infusion of a teacher's inspiration to give life and movement to its mere outlines. It is a note-book rather than a literary heritage; but if the purpose of literature be to express in fitting language thought worthy of expression, then the simple wording of the *Summa* embodies a masterpiece of clearness, tact and terseness.

To illustrate how St Thomas can write, and to give our readers the practical effect of his teaching as above set forth, we may take a passage from his treatise on the *Governance of the Jews*, addressed in 1269 to the Duchess of Brabant in reply to a letter from her setting out some of her difficulties in the way of just rule:

"But since your bailiffs and officials have only temporal power committed to them I see no reason why you should not sell them their offices so long as those to whom you sell them can be presumed to be capable of their work and so long as the price to be paid for the office be not so high as to necessitate to the buyers excessive exactions from your subjects to make it possible for them to recoup themselves for this initial expense. None the less it is not expedient to dispose of these offices by sale. First because often enough those most fitted for them would be too poor to buy them, or were they already rich the best of them would not seek office in order to make money out of it. Hence those of your subjects who seek for office by payment would be the worst, the most ambitious, the most covetous.

nor would these be likely to refrain from oppression or to fulfil their duties faithfully. Therefore it would seem to be the best for you to choose the most capable of your subjects for places of rule under you, and even to compel these to accept them, for their goodness and industry would benefit both your people and yourself far more than would the money obtained by the sale of offices.

"Then you ask whether it is lawful for you to tax your Christian subjects. Here you must consider that the princes of the earth are instituted by God not to seek their own gain but the common good of their people. . . . Hence land-dues were introduced to protect the people from spoliation. . . . Sometimes it happens that the revenues of a prince may not suffice for the defence of his realm or for the other purposes for which he would be reasonably expected to provide. In this case his subjects may be taxed to enable him to provide for the common good. Hence, by ancient custom in certain lands the lords collect fines from their people, and this is certainly lawful so long as these fines be not excessive. So that a prince may lawfully raise money by means of his ordinary revenues, or, if these be depleted or insufficient, by collecting from his individual subjects in order that he may provide for the common good from the common goods. This would also be lawful if a sudden emergency made exceptional demands on him as, for instance, in the event of foreign invasion. Here he would be at liberty to make special exactions above his customary dues, but these must not be for his private pleasures nor for any disordered or immoderate expenses. That would be altogether wrong."

A son of the house of Aquino knew from experience that "by ancient custom in certain lands the lords collect fines from their people," and his comment on it is just indeed: "This is certainly lawful so long as these fines be not excessive."

It is in this spirit that Bracton (*d.* 1268) (*De Legibus*, ix., §§ 2, 3)[1] writes of the king as "God's vicar and minister on earth," yet says, "The king must therefore limit his power

---

[1] *De Legibus et de Consuetudinibus Angliæ*, ed. G. E. Woodbine, Newhaven, 1915, vol. ii., pp. 19-28.

by the laws, since nothing better becomes authority than that
it should live by the laws " (xvi., § 3), and that Vincent de
Beauvais (*De Mor. Princ. Inst.*, cap. 12) urges that " The king
ought to place in posts of command only those of whose
capacity he has already made trial, and not to proceed to make
trial of the capacity of those whom he has placed in posts of
command."

We see again the very ideals of law that St Thomas has
sketched inflaming the spirit of that nameless Franciscan who
wrote the *Song of Lewes* (about 1270):

[1] " Nor is he [the king] made a servant when by law
restrained."

The theory of law elaborated by St Thomas was his in the
sense that he had schemed out the relationship of definition
with definition, and had taken into consideration every kind of
law that he had met or could read of. Not, however, as a new
view but as an orderly arrangement of what was already accepted
did the treatise of St Thomas become dominant in mediæval
schools. To go through any of the numerous writers of the
fourteenth and fifteenth centuries is, in every case that we
have examined, to light upon traces of his words and thoughts.
If, as very rarely happens, he is not actually quoted by name
his words are nevertheless used, and used in such a way as to
imply that they are a definite and familiar statement of the case.
Almost more perhaps than as a philosopher did the influence
of Aquinas as a canonist last throughout our period, especially
in his treatise on law.

Turning to the Empire, we find a careful distinction made
between laws and royal decrees, for it was the tradition both of
Rome and of the barbaric races that law issued from the people
and not from the prince. It was indeed within the province
of the emperor or king to issue capitularies, but these were
recognized as having in themselves no binding force beyond
that of the monarch by whom they were actually issued, and
they dealt—at least in principle—with administration rather
than with law, though they might become law by the action
of the people who consented to them. To what extent this

---

[1] Edited by C. L. Kingsford, 1890.

consenting power of the people gave force to law is extremely difficult to determine, but those German historians, who have maintained that under the Empire the assent of the people was essential to the validity of law, have certainly marshalled a convincing array of evidence in support of their theory.

Long before the thirteenth century the emperors had to admit, notwithstanding the authority conferred on them by the sense of insecurity and the need of a strong hand, that the law-making power lay not with them but with their people. A passage in the Carolingian capitularies collected by Ansegisus, Abbot of St Wandrille, in 827 (820, § 5) runs : " We admonish all in general that the capitularies which last year *by the consent of all* we decided should be added to the Salic law are now no longer to be called capitularies but only law, and indeed are to be held as law " [1] (Boretius, i., p. 295). This is but one of many quotations which go far to strengthen the contention that the people's consent was essential to the validity of law.

Nor should this occasion any surprise. The definition of Aquinas laid down as an essential condition of law that it must be issued by competent authority, and the principle was universally admitted in the Middle Ages that the prince was a lawgiver only in virtue of his being chosen and accepted by the people. The Archbishop of Milan in 1158 is reported to have said to Frederick Barbarossa : " Know that all the right of the people in the making of laws has been granted to you. Your will is law, as it is said ' *Quod principi placuit legis habet vigorem.*' " It may seem strange that the very principle so often used to defend the greatest acts of tyranny should be thus justified to Barbarossa himself by a reference to the essentially popular source of his power. But this, curiously enough, is to be found generation after generation, century after century, in the writings of those who defended the Temporal Power ; Ockham and his fellow-pamphleteers, who in the fourteenth century, half-way through our period, championed Louis of Bavaria against Pope John XXII. (1316-1334), based themselves on this very same

---

[1] Cited by H. A. L. Fisher, *The Medieval Empire*, London, 1896, vol. i., p. 159, n. 1.

argument—namely, that the Emperor had absolute power because it had been given him by the people.

It is in this way that we must understand the curious idea common in the Middle Ages that law is personal to the man. Law is created by a people. It is limited to that people. It is also the privilege of that people. Wherever any of that people may go this law clings to him. It " adhered to his bones." The law was promulgated on the soil of the people from whom it issued, but it was valid in every person of that people. The writ ran in the person of those who were the nationals of that law in the name of whose majesty the writ was issued : wherever an Englishman was to be found, there was a spot " that was forever England." Hence when Henry VII. (son of Frederick II.), King of the Romans, outlawed some Bavarians in 1222 the sentence contains the clause " notwithstanding that we are not in the Bavarian land." The author of *The Medieval Empire* (H. A. L. Fisher), who cites this quotation (vol. i., p. 175), gives also (*ibid.*, p. 173, note) a passage from Grimm's *Deutsche Rechtsaltherthümer* illustrative of the persistence of personal law : " According to a *Landgerichtsbrief* of 1455, the Nuremberger judge must stand on Frankish ground, beyond the bridge on the Neuenstadt Road, when outlawing a Frank ; on Swabian ground, beyond the stone bridge on the road to Onolzbach, when outlawing a Swabian ; on Bavarian ground, before the Frauenthur, if he be a Bavarian. If it be a Saxon, before the Thiergarthenthur on the road to Erlangen." Note the implication : the judge must stand on the land of the law, but the criminal is subject to the law wherever he may be.

To turn from the Empire to France is to discover the same underlying principle. It cannot therefore be regarded as merely Teutonic in origin. It would seem to be, as far as the thirteenth century understood it, the theory of Rome.[1] From Roman tradition came that mediæval passion for legality. St Louis, at the beginning of our period, is a fine example of it : he who, in his thirst for justice, surrendered to the English Crown districts which had fallen to the French because he could not be convinced of his right to retain them. When the Empire claimed

---

[1] Vinogradoff, *Roman Law in Medieval Europe*, 1909.

rights over him, or when the Pope claimed rights over the French bishops, St Louis,[1] at once laying aside personal feeling, neither assented nor denied until the legality of the claims had been settled for him by his judges. He refused to admit national feeling, he was determined only to discover national right. Had the Western kingdom *de facto* surrendered to Pope or Emperor what Pope or Emperor claimed? That was the only question he put to his legal advisers. Whatever might be their decision he would abide by it. To the uttermost he would accept or maintain, as the case might be, the obligations or the rights of the people of France. He was the source, therefore, of a national sense of right and justice begotten of this very love of legality. He was not only a maker of law but the instrument of law. To him drew that band of legists whose work for France is to be noted in subsequent French history : Philip of Navarre, John and James D'Ibelin, Peter des Fontains, and Philip de Beaumanoir.

The principle of the participation of the people—at least by consent—in the acts of the Crown is to be seen in the growing practice in the thirteenth century of summoning representatives of other classes than of the nobles and prelates to the Great Council, a practice leading up to those convocations of the nation under Philip the Fair (1285-1314) in which may be traced the beginnings of the States-General. Summoned at varying periods, and even earlier than the thirteenth century (Lavisse, *Hist. de France*, tome iii., part 2, p. 259), and differing in composition in accordance with directions emanating from the Crown, these general assemblies yet reflected that principle of government by consent the memory of which was never entirely obliterated though overlaid. As late as the sixteenth century, when the religious revolution had conferred on the civil power an absolutism the mediæval monarchy might

---

[1] His confessor tells a story of St Louis, illustrative of his punctilious sense of justice, that on one occasion, listening to the sermon of a preaching friar in the cemetery of the parish church of Vitry, and being prevented hearing by the noise going on in a neighbouring tavern, he inquired carefully in whose jurisdiction the place lay, and only after being assured that it was within his own would he send his servants to stop the nuisance (Lavisse, *Hist. de France*, tome iii., part 2, p. 38, n. 1.).

exercise but dare not claim, there were French writers still to be found who declared that though the king might appoint the legislators it was nevertheless the people who made the law (Paul Viollet, ii., p. 205).

Certainly the Crown retained practical control of those whom it thus summoned nominally to take counsel with, actually to receive the orders of, the king; only in the local assemblies where the carrying out of the orders was discussed and agreed to did any show of independence ever display itself. In 1254 St Louis prescribes to the Seneschal of Beaucaire how he is to act, what counsel he is to take, of whom his Estates shall be composed: it is to consist of prelates, barons, knights and burgesses of the "*bonnes villes.*" The determination of Philip the Fair to have the national feeling behind him in his struggle with Pope Boniface VIII. was responsible for the summoning of the Great Assembly of 1302, which had practically the character of a national referendum, and to which the king had again resort in 1308 to settle the question of the Templars, and again in 1314 on the eve of his death; the Assembly of 1303 was not of the same full composition, for which the king excused himself on the ground of urgency. The practice of convoking these general assemblies was subsequently replaced by a tendency towards consulting each order—and the orders of each of the great provinces—separately, in order to avoid giving occasion for malcontents to form the combinations which had recently shown themselves in the leagues of 1315 and 1316 (Langlois, *Medieval France*, ed. A. Tilley, 1922, pp. 116-117). But whatever precautions prudence might dictate the declaration of Hugh Capet to the Archbishop of Rheims remained the fundamental principle: " We settle all the affairs of the State in consultation with, and by the judgment of, our liege subjects (*in consultatione et sententia fidelium nostrorum*) " (Gasquet, *Precis des Instit. Pol. et Soc.*, vol. i., p. 33).

Though the centralizing power of the French Crown was more effectively developed than that of any other of the Western monarchies, and though peasant revolts in the middle of the fourteenth century following the Black Death made the nobles, the merchants and the lawyers afraid of the people whom they considered represented by themselves, the king was forced to acknowledge grudgingly the claims of the commonalty. The important dates were 1355 and 1356 and 1357. The right of fixing prices was abolished, forced loans were surrendered, officials were to be reduced in number : in 1355 nine persons were appointed to audit the royal accounts. But this, it must be admitted, was largely due to the personal ascendancy of Etienne Marcel, the great leader who saved for France the Third Estate. After his assassination the States-General surrendered to the king. But the theory of the participation of the people in government and of their consent as the basis of royal authority remained always latent as a centre and rallying-point to the people. It remained a traditional expression of the social theory that law ultimately issues from them.

Thus the Treaty of Troyes (1420), between Charles VI. of France and Henry V. of England, and the Treaty of Etaples (1492), between Charles VIII. of France and Henry VII. of England, for additional security were confirmed by the Three Estates of the two realms (A. F. Pollard, *The Evolution of Parliament*, 1920, pp. 70, 260). But the king contained in his person the greatness of his people, and it was as the representative of his country that he was great. Froissart relates in his *Chronicles* how Philip VI. of Valois after the battle of Crécy (1346) came in flight to the castle of Broyes : " The gate was closed because it was by that time dark ; then the king summoned the captain who came to the walls and asked : ' Who is there at this time of night ? ' Then said the king : ' Open your gate quickly for this is the fortune of France.' " The king was " the fortune of France " because he represented the nation, and not because he was its master. The royal summons to the Great Assembly was indeed so worded as to imply that mastership, " to hear the commandments of the king," but instances are on record of the refusal of representatives to grant supplies because they had not previously obtained the assent of their districts, in this way placing a check on royal encroachment. The two privileged orders, like the members of the Upper House in England, received a personal summons and could be present by proxy, but the commonalty were elected. There appears to have been no uniform method of election followed throughout the kingdom. Some of the districts must have enjoyed practically universal suffrage : at Ferrières in the Touraine in 1308 women voted. In other places the representative was nominated by the mayor or by the royal commissioner, but in such cases sufficient evidence has been found to justify the conclusion that this nomination was followed by an appeal—perfunctory and for the most part purely formal—to the people for confirmation. Country districts, as a rule, were the least well represented, sometimes they were not represented at all, or only by a representative who, at the same time, acted as proxy for one of the nobles of the district. Again, the candidates might all be elected at the same time—that is, the representatives of the clergy and of the laity might be voted for in a block. In Lyons in 1468 there was such an arrangement, " one cleric and three laymen." Under Charles VIII. occasionally all three orders elected their representatives together, the two lay orders electing two deputies from the clergy besides their own representatives. But the Church would not allow this as a permanent method, and was able to enforce its claim to elect its own representatives independently. Under the great French monarchy the tradition of popular participation in government by representation in national assemblies was maintained throughout the whole of our period, from the thirteenth to the fifteenth century. It would, of course, be impossible to claim much practical importance for the principle, but it was sufficiently often acknowledged by the Crown, the Church and the nobility to prevent the fact of its existence being ever wholly lost. At times of national crisis—that is, in moments when it was of the utmost import—it was solemnly and in effect proclaimed.

In Italy we pass over to an entirely different set of conditions. There were indeed the republics of Venice, Florence, Pisa and the rest, with their solemn assemblies and democratic traditions, but in all of these we have nothing comparable to the national assemblies of Western Europe. The city-republics of Italy bore more resemblance to the city-state of Aristotle's *Politics*, where the voice of a herald could make itself heard by all the citizens, than to the national states with their representative institutions. Where the Empire and its principalities, where France and

England, had to be content with assemblies composed of representatives of the people, the Italian political groups were very nearly assemblies of the whole people. We have to make use of the qualification " very nearly," for the growing ambition of each of these city-republics was to enlarge its borders : it was not by choice that it remained of a manageable Aristotelean size. It was only reluctantly and against its will, if at all, that it was able to hear from edge to edge the voice of a single herald. Incessant wars of aggression mark the history of each of them. Their political troubles moreover were complicated by the presence of a foreign element, the bequest of Imperial conquests, often enough Teutonic in origin, or Gothic, or Vandal, the aristocrats who sought always to impose their will on the city, and who, overpowered and forced to make way for factions, returned in the shape of tyrants to govern the city with absolute power. Further, Italy could never forget that beyond the Alps there was the Emperor with his persistent claim to lordship over the whole peninsula, which at any moment he might attempt to enforce.

It seemed therefore practically beyond the bounds of possibility to ensure that the law-making power in Italy should rest with a democracy ; nor indeed was the democratic control of law achieved any more in Italy than elsewhere. But it is not the political democracy so much as the social democracy that concerns our study, the law-making power and the theories that vested it in tyrant or oligarchy or democracy. Yet despite curious checks and counter-checks, a confused medley of voting and cross-voting, of groups electing other groups who in turn elected the ruling group, a method based on no principle of representation but adopted for the purpose of securing some sort of fairly honest government and at the same time avoiding the jealousy of the different interests involved, the Italian cities did on the whole admit the theory of law that Aquinas considered to be its real philosophic justification.

Besides the free cities, there was Milan, in the north of the peninsula, hardly ever free from the domination of some ruling family ; there was Naples, in the south, known as the Kingdom of the Sicilies, which, coming first into the possession of Frederick II., passed from his descendants into the grasp of Charles of Anjou, the unsaintly brother of Louis IX., and after him of all sorts of claimants, including that earliest figure of the Renaissance queens—the friend of St Catherine of Siena, yet the least Christian of rulers—Joanna; between Milan and Naples, alternately expanding and contracting, sprawled the Papal States, under the temporal governance of the popes or, in their Avignon days, of their more feared and disliked vicars.

With all these to include and to harmonize, it is no easy matter to discuss or to determine what may be called an Italian theory of law. The names of Dante (1265-1321), of Nicholas Roselli (1314-1362), of St Antonino (1389-1459), and of Savonarola (1452-1498), occur obviously to the mind as men who moulded Italian thought, names drawn from each century of our period; there are the schoolmen, like Aquinas and Egidio de Roma (*d.* 1316) and Tolomeo de Lucca; again there are the popes, like Innocent III. (Migne, *P. L.*, vols. 214-217)[1] and the Bonifaces VIII. and IX. The difficulty is certainly greater here than in England or France, or even the Empire, to find a consistent story. Dante, for example, looks over the mountains to the Emperor to re-establish the freedom of Italy. He had been intoxicated with the eloquence of Livy and supposed the historian to be a divine prophet. On the miracles that attended so often the protection of Roman greatness he built the fabric of his dream: "*Romanum imperium de fonte nascitur pietatis*" (*De Monarchia*, Bk. II., cap. 5): from the springs of faith began the rule of Rome. But though Dante forgot Rome's cruelty and remembered only her greatness, yet in his scheme of government he found a place for a theory of law that would save his country from the tyranny of Imperial power. He had himself suffered too much from loss of freedom not to make efforts to ensure its presence in the scheme of life as he wished it lived. His reply to Can Grande, be it only a legend, is made natural to those who read his *De Monarchia*.[2]

But by the end of our period one thing seems to have made itself clear to those who sought freedom for Italian cities. It is

---

[1] Luchaire, *Innocent III.*, vols. i.-vi., 1906-1911.
[2] Edited by E. Moore, 1916.

certainly remarkable that both Guicciardini (1483-1540) and Savonarola, despite their several disagreements, join in rejecting representative assemblies as instruments of freedom. In the *Discorsi* (vol. ii., p. 299) Guicciardini writes : " To maintain firmly this form of government it is requisite firmly to observe the law against parliaments, for these only serve to destroy the life of the people : since they who summon them compel the people by terror and force of arms to consent to all they propose and then make them believe that all that has been done has been done by the will and pleasure of the whole people." Savonarola, as becomes his decisive style, reached and described the same conclusion with decision and brevity : " Know that the only purpose of parliament is to snatch the sovereign power from the hands of the people."

But it is well to remember that both Guicciardini and Savonarola are speaking in reference to Florence, where there was hardly the same need of a representative assembly as existed in the larger states, that were politically one but geographically several. And even with Florence ever-present before his eyes St Antonino, its archbishop—who had died just before Savonarola joined the Preaching Friars, and who linked together not only the fourteenth and the fifteenth centuries but the Eastern and the Western Empires, who had seen the Emperor of Byzantium and the Emperor of Across the Alps, who had spoken within his Dominican cloister at Florence to a Patriarch of Constantinople and a Pope of Rome—was yet able to consider with impartial justice the claims of government and the force of law. Discussing the power of law he decides that the splitting of dominion, the severance of lordships, the break-up of the Empire, were all of them occasioned by the decrees of the people concerned, and that the same justice that allowed them to separate by their own will would equally allow them again to federate (*Summa Moralis*, Bk. III., § iv., Verona, 1740, p. 182). To him the omnipotence of law in all social

---

[1] Audin de Rians, Florence, 1847, *Trattati circe il regimento e governo della Citta di Firenze.*

[2] *Cf.* Guicciardini, *Istoria d'Italia*, Bk. II., cap. i. ; Savonarola, *Prediche sui Dalmi*, Serm. 26, 28th July 1495.

matters seemed essential to justice, and the making of law he held to be the prerogative of the prince, the appointment of the prince to lie with the people.

St Augustine in his *Confessions* (Bk. III., cap. 8) set down a statement of historic fact which was much quoted by mediæval writers : " There is a universal agreement in human societies to obey their kings." The mediæval theory was not indeed—like the theory of Rousseau—that of a social contract amongst the people themselves to pool their rights in society, but of a contract between themselves and their prince that he should rule them and they obey. Like all other contracts it was bilateral, and contained conditions. As long as he ruled them " according to their customs " they swore him fealty, not until he had agreed to that would the presiding bishop place on his brow the crown. Even now the same condition is put to the English king before the shrine of the Confessor in Westminster. Only when he has undertaken to abide by these customs, " The laws of good King Edward," is he formally accepted by the English race.

The decision as to whether or no he had observed his coronation oath lay with the Pope, since oaths, like all other sacred things, were considered to come under the jurisdiction of the Church. No deposing power, strictly so-called, was considered within the competency of the Pope, but only the power to sit in judgment on the observance of the oath solemnly sworn between the king and his people. Should the Pope decide that the contract had not been duly observed the claim of the king to his people's obedience automatically lapsed. The Pope did not depose : his was a declaratory power to decide whether promises had been kept or whether by non-observance of his promise the king had thereby himself released the people from their allegiance to him.

A generation after our period Reginald Pole (1500-1558), already a cardinal, not yet archbishop, steeped in the old traditions and full of the memories in which he had been nurtured, a witness almost from the bosom of English royalty to the traditions of England, wrote in his treatise *De Unititate* an appeal which seems to breathe " the last enchantment of the Middle Age " :

" Englishmen before now when they were oppressed have divided the State against the king ; they have brought him to account for reckless expenditure, have set him aside for the violation of the constitution. In bestowing the crown, they reserved the right to preserve their old freedom and to keep an eye on the administration. Who maintains that all property is the king's? Thou, O my country, art all ! The king is only thy servant and thy instrument " (Bk. III., cap. 7).

We cannot be sure that he would have maintained this doctrine as stoutly against Mary as against Henry, but had he done so he would certainly have had behind him the judgment of the Middle Ages in the writings of the schoolmen, the lawyers and the pamphleteers.

Are not his words but the rhetoric of the Renaissance enveloping in fuller phrase the simple and direct definition of Aquinas —itself derived from Isidore of Seville and from Gratian— that law is something rational, relating to the common good, promulgated by that competent authority who has the care of the community ?

CHAPTER II

EDUCATION

EVEN more than in its laws, the social theories of an age can be seen in its education, in the ideas thus held up to it for motive, in its form, in the things it studies, the hope it gives. For this reason social theorists have always written books on education, and laid great stress on the type and character of the education which they wished to introduce. In order, therefore, to understand the growing development of the concurrent theories of social economics it is essential to watch the development of education in Christendom from the thirteenth century to the fifteenth.

Vincent de Beauvais, in his *De Eruditione Principum*, insists on the education of princes as necessary to the due government of the peoples to be entrusted to their care; especially so, since the lives of kings are not as laborious and toilsome as those of other men and the only escape from idleness in a prince is a love of learning. The greater their responsibility, and the more leisurely their lives, the more insistent is their need of education (Bk. V., caps. 2, 3). He is writing for the royal sons and daughter of St Louis a practical treatise, therefore, dealing with conditions he knows.

Another reason given for a good education is that all knowledge implies self-knowledge, and that all education teaches man more about himself; says Humbert de Romans (1194-1277): "For whosoever knows most, the better in consequence he will know himself, which is of the greatest usefulness to man" (*De Eruditione Prædicatorum*: Bigne, *Max. Bib. Vet. Pat.*, Lyons, 1677, vol. xxv., p. 484. Sermon: *Ad omnes litteratos*). In his sermon for "students in logic and the liberal arts and philosophy" Humbert notes also the other advantages to be obtained by increase in knowledge: "Note that the study of liberal arts and of the philosophic sciences avails much in Christendom. It avails for the defence of the faith . . . it avails to the honour of the Church. For great is her honour when are found in her not only men learned in law and theology but even in philosophy" (p. 488). And he adds that "the devil

31

endeavours by means of pagans, heretics and false Christians to hinder knowledge lest there should be learned men in the Church who might provide us with spiritual weapons in our warfare. . . . Note that the studium for the liberal arts was originally in Athens, was afterwards transferred to the city of Rome, was then in the time of Charles moved to France, and thence has spread to other places." Of the fever of learning in that age, from the days of Abelard to Aquinas, we have very full evidence. But after another hundred years it had begun to burn out.

" The English," writes Holcot somewhere about 1390, " accuse the French of being nurtured too delicately and too luxuriously, and of being also too luxuriously and delicately clothed, contrasting with it their sparer diet and harder lives. But this is only due to their necessity, for when they eat at the expense of other people they are gluttons indeed. Thus it happens too with these latter-day clerks, because if anyone better than they expounds new interpretations of Scripture they quickly quote against him, ' Seek not the things that are too high for thee and search not into the things above thy ability ' (*Ecclus*. iii. 22), not because they really mean it but because they are ashamed of their own ignorance. So their own words damn them " (*In Proverbia Salamonis*, Paris, 1515, lect. clix., fol. cxciii.*b*). The *Philobiblon* (of which one manuscript bears Holcot's name) is also famous for the criticism it gives of the lack of learning of the clerks of that day.[1]

Even earlier there was some ignorance amongst religious : " Some there are who long have studied in the schools of their Order to little profit or to none, either because of laziness or the trivialities in which alone they are interested or of the worse things to which they are addicted, like the evil-living Paris students (*De Romans*, p. 461). But learning was honoured and demanded for all sorts and kinds of men :

(KNOWLEDGE says :)

" Everyman, I wyll go with the and be thy gyde
In thy moost nede to go by thy syde." [2]

---

[1] *Philobiblon* (The King's Classics), 1903.
[2] A. W. Pollard, *English Miracle Plays*, Oxford, 1914, p. 88.

EDUCATION

Tolomeo de Lucca,[1] a pupil of St Thomas for thirteen years, gives us in *De Regimine Principum* the scholastic argument in favour of education. It starts with the assumption, which underlies so much of mediæval reasoning, that man always seeks happiness, is always driven by this irresistible impulse, unconsciously, blindly, but without fail. False happiness lured him as well as true happiness, but true happiness was his final perfection when it was reached at last; and since each faculty of man had this thirst for happiness, that alone could be true happiness wherein every power was satisfied and at rest. Each faculty of man must, therefore, be developed, the three great groups of them—intellectual, moral and material—each taken into account and of importance, each having a place in the hierarchical organization of a man's soul, and therefore of a man's education.

At the summit lies contemplation, above the energy of discursive reason, as reason lies above sensation. The desires of men should be, therefore, under their free will, as their wills should be under reason, and reason itself based upon truth. Virtue, therefore, or the perfect exercise of reason, will and desire, properly ordered and duly motived, is the full happiness of man. This, says Tolomeo, the old philosophers understood, only being without the help of divine revelation they thought that the highest act of man was some human virtue, the love of wisdom, or for the Stoics and Cicero the love of humankind. They missed as the queen of virtues charity or the love of God.

On princes especially was virtue incumbent, perfect virtue, for as they were so would their people be; what gives heat to others must needs be hotter than that to which it gives its heat. A prince must, therefore, be a philosopher, he must reach out to contemplation, must enliven action with charity and justice. Yet he cannot be a solitary dweller, no man may; he needs a family, a city, the world. A family looks simple yet is really complicated, implying a triple relationship—husband and wife, parents and children, master and servants. These relationships are to be governed by reason according to nature.

---

[1] D. König, *Tolomeo von Lucca*, 1878, Harburg.

The material element of the family relationships would of itself lead to the *venere incerta* of Horace; but since we accept also moral and intellectual relationships, we look on the wife as a " helpmate " for man. The link between husband and wife cannot be dissoluble, for love thinks in terms of eternity; only if pleasure were the sole guide of life could the bond be dissolved. Moreover children imply the stability of married life, since they demand the responsibility of both parents. Even separation between husband and wife, allowed for grave reason by the law of Christ, will not be resorted to by His followers; in the name of their children they will mutually forgive.

The wife must be chosen for her virtues, for her appearance also, and her figure; she is not her husband's slave but his helpmate.

The obligations of both to the children extend throughout childhood, in the first seven years rather their material nurture, in the second seven years their intellectual nurture by the cultivation of memory and reason, in the third the completion of both; while moral education in gradual development is to be attended to all the time.

In point of fact we know that a boy's life, according to the ideal mediæval plan, was divided into groups of seven years— from one to seven he remained at home, from seven to fourteen he was a page or at school, from fourteen to twenty-one a squire or at the university, at twenty-one a knight. In his knightly days he was expected to have completed his accomplishments of riding, swimming, archery, fencing, hunting, rhyming, chess or even, later, whist.

The division of the school or university teaching of seven years was into the trivium and quadrivium, in which the subjects undoubtedly varied as the instruments of knowledge grew. At first the trivium meant grammar, chiefly the *Doctrinale* of Alexander de Villa Dei [1]; rhetoric, including letter-writing, a knowledge of legal documents and " the art of using secular discourse effectively in the circumstances of daily life " (Rabanus Maurus); and dialectic, which was almost synonymous with

---

[1] Edited by Reichling in the *Mon. Germ. Pædigog,* xii., 1893; *cf.* L. J. Pætow, *The Arts Course in Medieval Universities,* 1910.

logic. The quadrivium consisted of arithmetic, then worked in Roman numerals; geometry, by the thirteenth century from the text of Euclid; astronomy, covering such sciences as the physics and astrology[1] which the age then knew and the reckoning of Easter, etc.; and music, on which there were many treatises and the traditions of Charlemagne's school at Metz.

It must, however, be recognized that the amount of correct information imparted in the education of the thirteenth century was not very great, nor even of much concern either to the teacher or the pupil. Rather what each considered more important was the quickness of intellect which logic or dialectic would bring. The purpose of the training consisted principally in teaching accuracy of word and thought, and swiftness of argument, so as to produce the ready speaker, and not so much the learned man. Learning came indeed to be the pursuit of scholars, the endless procession of *Summæ* and *Specula* show that; but education was not given so much with the object of producing these as to effect the sharpening of wits. Abelard's method (earlier of course than 1200) was adopted, he tells us, not in order to show error or to oppose authorities, but "to provoke young readers to take the greatest care in the search for truth and to make them the keener for their pursuit" (*Prologue to the Sic-et-Non*, Migne, *P.L.*, 178, p. 1349).

"Time," says Aquinas, "is the great discoverer and collaborator in the unfolding of knowledge" (*Ethics*, I. ii.). It was a lengthy process then this "unfolding of knowledge," and it "went gradually from the imperfect to the perfect" (*Summa Theol.*, I. ii. 97, 1). Usually the method adopted was the method of commentary : the text of a masterpiece was taken and elaborated, and then discussion was invited on the more formal disputation. The text, the elaboration by the master, the disputation, these are the three stages of mediæval lecturing, and they express the mediæval concept of the way truth was to be reached.

"With a double purpose," writes Aquinas in his own commentary on the *De Anima* of Aristotle (Bk. I., lect. 2), "we should study the opinions of antiquity, to utilize what they

---

[1] T. O. Wedel, *Medieval Attitude to Astrology*, 1920.

have said truly, and to avoid errors into which they have fallen."

Again in the *Metaphysics* (Bk. II., lect. 1) the same thought appears : " In two ways we can be helped by those who have preceded us in the search for truth ; first directly, using the results of those who in whole or part have found the truth and who have thereby become of great aid in the construction of knowledge for subsequent investigators, then indirectly in so far as we can discern the least errors of our predecessors and can proceed more seriously and rigorously to new ideas."

" It is necessary to know the opinions of other authors in the clearing up of questions and the solution of doubts : for, as a judge cannot give judgment without hearing both parties, whosoever is occupied with philosophic problems can the more easily form a judgment truly scientific when he knows the opinions and doubts of different authors " (Bk. III., lect. 3). " In accepting and rejecting opinions no one should be led by love or hatred but only by the greater certainty of truth " (Bk. XII., lect. 9). He praises pathetically an older day " when ardent faith and Christian life flourished " (*Summa Theol.*, iii. 80, 10, ad 5 m).

Siger of Brabant and the unorthodox professors of Paris tried to use Aristotle as an authority, but Aquinas patiently put aside authority in philosophy—" Not who said it but whether it was true " (*In Cælo et Mundo*, I. xxii.) ; and Albertus Magnus made mock of those to whom " Aristotle was a god " (*Phys.*, VIII. i. 14).

Naturally a boy was not given this mature teaching at first ; it was only gradually that knowledge could be unfolded, but youth did not lose by being immature for it had gifts of its own to give : " The service rendered God in youth is more precious to Him than that of old age, for youth offers to God the best of life, the flower, the vigour ; an old man has but spent energies left " (*De Eruditione Principum*, Bk. V., cap. 5). Boys have even natural virtues—virginity, innocence and humility (cap. 6) ; these fit them also for the life of study. They are changeable creatures, mercurial, up in the sky one moment and the next in the depths of hell (cap. 48), timid and easily frightened, yet only conscious of their troubles at the moment, easily forgetting the next moment their fears. They speak without forethought, words tumble out of their mouths, they are interested in useless knowledge very often, and hardly trouble about life. They will lend money without difficulty. Yet they have their vices too. Pride and luxury and lasciviousness are as naturally theirs as are the opposite virtues. They are also very lazy (*ibid.*, cap. 48).

"Boys in grammar school when they are told 'Learn your lesson, because otherwise if you do not know it on Saturday you will be beaten,' will sometimes answer : 'I will learn my lesson to-morrow, or another day, but I shall play now and as long as I want. If I am beaten, good! That one beating will get me off hours of horrid study, get me off my lesson ; even I might be able to play truant on Saturday or pretend I am ill and so escape lesson, beating and all" (Robert de Sorbonne (1201-1274), *Opusculum : De Conscientia*, Bigne, p. 347). Saturday was evidently the day of terror : "The headmaster when he hears the lessons of his pupils on Saturdays, if it should happen that the boys do not know their lessons and if he should discover that the form-master was the cause or occasion of this because he neglected his work or taught badly, he would beat the boys but the form-master even more" (p. 351). So Saturday might bring its compensations after all.

Holcot, speaking of laziness, thinks immediately of boys at school. He adds moreover that they were taught declensions of many words together, "lazy" was declined with "a horned ox" in a long line,

bos cornutus mugiens et mutus niger et piger,

a difficult matter of memory but "a symbol alas ! of the horned or mitred prelates of our day who should be oxen in the Lord's yoke, keeping their possessions under governance to God's service, and who are far too lazy, lowing like oxen indeed but lowing only when their passions are on them or they hunger for rich food" (*In Proverbia Salamonis*, Paris, 1515, lect. xlv., fol. lviii.).

Boys are untidy too and uncleanly (*De Eruditione Principum*, Bk. V., cap. 48) ; but they have a gift for making friends. They should be taught the virtues of friendship—namely, fidelity, never lying to a friend, never revealing his secrets, never hurting what belongs to him, not leaving him even when all goes ill with him ; good-tempered, always kindly and prudent and in the same happy spirits ; constant, seldom changing old friends for new (cap. 43).

Yet it is difficult to lay down laws for teaching boys, for they are very different from each other. Some are to be lured on and others are to be driven. Threats are better than beatings for most boys because of their natural fear. Discipline they need in gesture and in laughter : " Rarely should there be laughter in this world " with reference to the rich man in St Luke vi., discipline in speech and eyes, in food and drink and dress (caps. 11-22). For boys are by nature undisciplined, rushing at things, reading indiscriminately, whereas they should be taught to study slowly and methodically, learning from every source of knowledge, not troubling over literary quarrels but discussing all that they read with other boys, giving attention to the Scriptures and not to fables or luxurious books (cap. 10). Like their reading should be their food, not precious viands which imperil the lives of them that seek for them, do harm to the boy's body, and by their extravagant price outrage the poor (cap. 22).

Humbert de Romans (Serm. lii., p. 482) has much the same to say about girls and their need of discipline, and sees in this discipline the hope that one day they may become nuns. He hardly seems to consider girls at school in convents without the prospect or intention of their entering religious life when they are of canonical age.

The children for whom education would have thus been available were never the mass of the people, though there is a statute of Henry IV.[1] giving absolute freedom to everyone to send their children where they wished. But the *Modus Tenendi Cur. Baron.* dated 1510, though in this largely a republication of a form itself centuries older (published by the *Manorial Society*, 1915, p. 4), shows how villeinage still prevented freedom of education : " Also yf there be ony bonde men of blode that putteth his sone unto the schole to make hym a preest or

---

[1] *Rot. Parl.*, iii. 602.

a prentyse or set hym to crefte or maryeth his doughter without leve ye shall do us to wete."

The thirteenth century had clear ideas as to what should not be taught to children as well as to what should be taught : " The study of letters can be good or bad. It can be bad because of what is studied as if anyone should study the book *Ars Amandi* and in others of the like sort. Therefore, is it forbidden to Christians to study the fantasies of the poets, lest the mind under the attention of these fables should be inflamed with evil passion ; and the same reason forbids the study of black magic and whatever else leads men to sin " (De Romans, Serm. lxii., p. 487, *Ad omnes Scholares*).

The positive side of study is no less forcibly stated : " Students in grammar who for the most part are boys and youths are to be exhorted to study of their own accord. And since this is of little purpose without a virtuous life they are to be warned to lead a good life, and because many do not know in what this consists they are to be instructed in what is needed for it. On this point it should be noted that every part of education concerns either mechanics—which is the affair of the body— or letters—which is the affair of the soul— and for this reason is the more excellent in proportion as the soul is more excellent than the body. Concerning this very excellence Socrates said : ' to know is as glorious as to rule.' Also it should be noted that this education is the entrance to all knowledge. For without knowledge of letters, no divine wisdom, whether prophetic or human, can be fully understood. But wisdom is of such usefulness that ' with her come all good things ' (*Wisd*. vii.). Also it should be noted that in the learning of mechanics is immense labour but in the learning of letters is immense consolation. Says Cicero : ' What is sweeter than literary leisure ! ' Says Pythagoras : ' Men should take familiarity with literature as the viaticum of old age.' Says Plato : ' Literature to a foolish soul is like crutches to the sick body.' And these three things give great consolation " (*Ad Scholares in Grammatica*, Serm. lxiii., p. 487). That no mere pouring in of information sufficed, or mere memory work, is clear from the words of Robert of Sorbonne : " To read and not to understand is to neglect " (*legere et non intelligere, negligere*) (*De Conscientia,* Bigne, p. 350).

It is difficult to gauge the precise standard of education in the thirteenth and following centuries [1] ; but it cannot have been low if it is fair to judge the capacity of the audience by the sermon-notes of the mediæval preachers that have survived to us. The promptuaries for preachers, particularly developed from the fourteenth century, are crowded with learning. But is that a fair test of the capacity of the congregation? Certainly it is not an absolute test. Yet it has to be taken into consideration when the historian endeavours to estimate the mediæval mind and its familiarity with the thought and illustrations which the preacher was advised to employ. Humbert de Romans, writing for the ordinary friar, lays it down (i., cap. 8., p. 433) : " First the preacher must know the Scriptures, for they are to be the substance of his preaching. . . . After a knowledge of the Sacred Books must come knowledge of creatures, for God has hid in them secret lessons of wisdom. St Anthony the Hermit has told us that creatures are a book for whosoever knows how to read them, profitable and full of thought. . . . Then should come a knowledge of history, for history both sacred and profane is full of examples, precious to the preacher who can use them deftly . . . knowledge of the laws of the Church is necessary, knowledge of the mysteries of faith ; nor should the mature knowledge which his experience of souls has given him be neglected by the preacher." An ideal of course ; yet it is a useful testimony to the capacity of the audience, judged by a man who knew Christendom well and was friendly with every sort and condition of men and could advise his brethren how every class of society, religious and secular, how each sex and every age, was to be addressed.

" On account of the sins of our first parents," he says when he is suggesting matter for a sermon to be preached to medical students, " the condition of the human race was worsened in three ways : (i) In the darkening of the reason and this touches

---

[1] Cf. *English Historical Literature in the Fifteenth Century,* by C. L. Kingsford, 1913 ; also his *Prejudice and Promise in Fifteenth-Century England,* 1925.

the soul. Against this were discovered the liberal arts which give light to the reason. (ii) In disease on account of the corruptible nature of man and this touches the body. Against this was discovered the art of medicine. (iii) In private ownership, for all things had been in common. Against this was discovered the science of law by which are given and preserved to each his own. Further, of these three sciences, in many ways medicine is the greatest. Because it teaches knowledge of corporeal nature. . . . Because it is a work of mercy. . . . Because it includes a spiritual healing of the soul. . . . Yet many sin in this art. For some through their ignorance do not perform operations when they should and are guilty of the death that supervenes, and this is the sin of murder. Others force their clients to buy more expensive things when simpler remedies would be as effectual, and this is a lack of professional loyalty. Others neglect what the Church has ordained for the sick, such as confession, communion and so on, and are therefore disobedient to the Church. . . . Hence in order to turn their study to good purposes, they should follow that which is useful. They should not enter on the practice of this art till their knowledge of it is sufficient" (Serm. lxvii., pp. 488-489).

This last sentence contains a sentiment in education which is frequently expressed by other mediæval writers.

Literature had perhaps least place in the education of the boy, as literature is now understood. But the thirteenth-century art, in carving and sculpture, and the songs and ballads of the time, show us a temper of mind not insensitive to the beauties of nature.[1] Says Gautier de Coinci, a monk of St Médard, near Soissons, in the thirteenth century : " Therefore will I do even as he does who seeks flowers in a meadow the which is all springlike and bedecked with flowers and who sees all round him so many divers ones, crimson and violet and yellow and dark blue, that he knows not the which to pluck first" (*Our Lady's Tumbler*, p. xix., London, 1909).

Again there are the similes of Dante, the descriptions of Chaucer, the exquisitely fragrant verse of *Pearl's* anonymous

---

[1] William P. Shephard, *Les Poésies de Jausbert de Puycibot*, 1925 ; Arthur Langfors, *Les Chansons de Guilhem de Cabestank*, 1925.

author, and countless songs and prose writings to prove how clearly all the poets and writers of that day saw and taught the beauty of the world around :

> " Wide the lime-tree to the air
> Spreads her boughs and foliage fair ;
> Thyme beneath is growing
> On the verdant meadow where
> Dancers' feet are going.

> Through the grass a little spring
> Runs with jocund murmuring,
> All the place rejoices ;
> Cooling zephyrs breathe and sing
> With their summer voices." [1]

But even Bromyard (*Summa Prædicantium*, Lyons, 1532, vol. i., fol. iv*b*), under the heading *Ab Infantia*, urges the taking of children into the fields and woods : " It were better, therefore, to take boys and girls, servants and maids, to church or to the fields rather than to games and taverns. But young folk should not be let wander without good companions. Even to be shut up at home were better than that." It is easy to see how evil in his opinion were taverns when the gloomy enclosing of young folk seemed to him grimly preferable.

Included in literature at last, but coming very slowly, would have been a study of the vulgar tongue. Dante had to defend his *dolce stil nuovo*, and the difficulty he faced was felt even more strongly elsewhere. The *Song of Roland* and the *Legend of the Cid* were great examples of what France and Spain had been able to achieve, though, like the *Divine Comedy*, they represent rather the opening of a great period than its apex. In England Chaucer considerably later cannot think of his native tongue as capable of the effects of the classical or romance languages, for he writes of Canace's beauty :

---

[1] Making allowance for the fact that Symonds' translation is more lyrical than the original, the original is still musical and descriptive. *Cf.* Symonds' *Wine, Women and Song*, London, 1907, p. 185, and the reference he gives to the *Carmina Burana*, Stuttgart, 1847.

" I dar nat undertake so heigh a thing.
Myn English eek is insufficient;
It moste been a rether excellent,
That coude his colours longing for that art,
If he sholde hir discryven every part."

(*The Squire's Tale.*)

Trevisa's translation (*d.* 1402) of Higden's *Polychronicon*
(1387) has even later much the same tale to tell:
" Also Englische men, they hadde from the bygynnunge
thre manere speche, northerne, sowtherne, and middel speche
in the myddel of the lond, as they come of thre manere peple
of Germania, notheles by comyxtioun and mellynge firste with
Danes and afterward with Normans, in meny the contray longage
is apayred, and som useth straunge wlafferynge, chiterynge,
harrynge and garrynge, grisbayting. This apayrynge of the
burthe of the tunge is bycause of tweie thinges; oon is for
children in scole agenst the usage and manere of alle othere
naciouns beeth compelled for to leue hire owne langage, and
for to construe hir lessouns and hir thynges in Frensche, and
so they haueth seth the Normans come firste into Engelond.
Also gentil men children beeth i-taugt to speke Frensch from
the tyme that they beeth i-rokked in here cradel, and kunnethe
speke and playe with a childes broche; and uplondisshe men wil
likne hym self to gentil men and fondeth with greet besynesse
for to speke Frensche, for to be i-tolde of.
" This manere was moche i-used to for firste deth, and is
siththe sumdel i-chaunged; for John Cornwaile, a maister of
grammer, chaunged the lore in grammer scole and construc-
cioun of Frensche in to Englische; and Richard Pencriche
lerned the manere techyng of hym and of othere men of
Pencrich; so that now, the yere of oure Lorde a thowsand thre
hundred and foure score and fyve, and of the secounde kyng
Richard after the conquest nyne, in alle the gramere scoles of
Engelond, children leueth Frensche and construeth and lerneth
an Englische, and haueth thereby auauntage in oon side and
disauauntage in another side; here auauntage is, that they
lerneth her gramer in lasse tyme than children were i-woned to

43

doo ; disauauntage is that now children of gramer scole conneth na more Frensche than can hir lift heele, and that is harme for hem and they schulle passe the see and trauaille in straunge landes and in many other places. Also gentil men haueth now moche i-left for to teche here children Frensche. Hit semeth a great wonder how Englische (that is the burthe tonge of Englisshe) men and her owne langage and tonge, is so dyuerse of sown in this oon ilond, and the langage of Normandie is comlynge of another londe, and hath oon manere soun among alle men that speketh hit arigt in Engelond. Nevertheles there is as many dyuers manere Frensche in the reem of Fraunce as is dyuers manere Englische in the reem of Engelond. Also of the forsaide Saxon tonge, that is i-deled athre, and is abide scarsliche with fewe uplondisshe men is greet wonder ; for men of the est with men of the west, as it were undir the same partie of heuene, accordeth more in sownynge of speche than men of the north with men of the south ; therefore it is that Mercii that beeth men of myddel Engelond, as it were parteners of the endes, understondthe bettre the side langages, northerne and southerne, than northerne and southerne understondeth either other " (Rolls Ser., vol. ii., pp. 159-165).

However, in spite of John Cornwaile and Richard Pencriche and " other men " who learnt of them, English still lagged behind. It had begun to be taught at last in the schools yet had but scant respect paid it. A visitation of the grammar school attached to the Collegiate Church of Southwell (Notts) in 1484 reports under breaches of good order and discipline that the boys do not speak Latin in school but English (*non locuntur Latinum in scola sed anglicum*) (V. C. H., *Notts*, ii., under " Schools," p. 185). The mother-tongue had not yet conquered the prejudice against it of scholarship.

> " For though many make bokes, yet unneth ye shal
> In our Englyshe tonge fynde any warkes
> Of connynge, that is regardyd by clerkes.
> The Grekes, the Romayns, with many other mo,
> In their modir tonge wrot warkes excellent
> Than yf clerkes in this realme wolde take payn so,

EDUCATION

Consyderyng that oure tonge is now suffycyent
To expound any hard sentence evydent,
They myght, yf they wolde, in Englyshe tonge
Wryte workys of gravyte sometyme amongie
For dyvers prengnaunt wyttes be in this londe
As well of noble men as of meane estate,
Whiche nothynge but Englyshe can understande."

This is the judgment of John Rastell in 1515 or thereabouts, when our period is over, but when the dawn of one of the most splendid days of English literature was just about to begin (cf. *Interlude of Four Elements*, quoted in A. W. Pollard's *English Miracle Plays*, Oxford, 1914, pp. 97-98).

But we are able to reconstruct a good deal of the education as it existed in England throughout the mediæval period thanks to researches of many scholars (especially Leach, *English Schools and the Reformation*, London, 1896; also Abram, *Social England*, 1909, London, p. 177 *et seq.*; A. W. Parry, *Education in England in the Middle Ages*, 1920). The opportunities for it, though not sufficient, were still considerable. Connected with cathedrals and monasteries were grammar schools and choir schools; with collegiate churches again song schools, and grammar schools which took boarders as well as day scholars—as we learn from the petition of Southwell (Notts) to Henry VIII. protesting against the suppression of the grammar school attached to the collegiate church — the schools attached to hospitals which fed the boys except during vacations; the guild schools, as in Deritend, or the mercers' school in London; the chantries in the fourteenth and fifteenth centuries especially, some of which provided masters and sometimes maintained schools as well whose loss, when they were swept away by the successive Acts of Henry VIII. and Edward VI., provoked protest, as at Wimborne (Dorset), where the commissioners reported of the "schole masters chauntry" founded by Margaret, Countess of Richmond and Derby, the mother of Henry VII., in the Collegiate Church of Wimborne Minster, "it is very requisite that the said school may remain still for the bringing up of young children in larnyge . . . without

45

anything paying at all as it was in time past " (Chantry Cert., Dorset 16, No. 106). There were the independent schools superintended by laymen like that at Chipping Camden in 1847. There is a notable increase in the establishment of schools in the fifteenth century, but even in the time of Becket we hear of schools in London attached to the three principal churches " by privilege and long-established worth. Most often, however, by the personal favour of someone very well known more schools are permitted there for philosophy "(*Vita S. Thomae*, in *Materials for Life of St Thomas Becket*, Rolls Ser., vol. iii., p. 4).

From 1200 to 1500 is the great period of the rise and spread of the University system throughout Christendom. When it opened six centres for General Studies, as they were called, had been established, Salerno, Bologna, Reggio, Montpellier, Paris and Oxford. Within a hundred years eight more were founded in Italy, five in Spain and Portugal, three in France, and in England, Cambridge. With the lapse of another hundred years twenty-two more were added, of which five were in Germany. By 1500 the six *Studia Generalia* had increased to eighty universities, eloquent witness both to the desire for knowledge and the patronage of learning.

Although in process of time each university acquired a number of faculties or schools, the tendency at first was for each to specialise and to attract students for some particular branch of learning. Bologna, for example, which had its school of law established in 1158, did not add its school of medicine till 1316, nor of theology till 1360. The regular faculties were four : law, medicine, theology and arts. At Paris these were established within comparatively a short time : in 1200 arts, in 1208 theology and canon law, in 1271 civil law, and in 1274 medicine.

A much-quoted Latin rhyme describes the four great schools as follows :

" In morbis sanat medici virtute Salernum
Ægros. In causis Bononia legibus armat
Nudos. Parisius dispensat in artibus illos
Panes unde cibat rubustos. Aurelianus
Educat in cunis antorum lacte tenellos."

Certainly it was arts that Paris dispensed to the world, " the famous city of arts," as Alexander IV. calls it in 1256 (Denifle, *Cartularium Universitatis Parisiensis*, 1889, Paris, i. 343). Civil law had been forbidden it in 1219 by Honorius III. (p. 92), and though canon law was allowed it, it never developed into a well-organized school. But the point to be noted in the fourteenth century is the gradual lowering in Paris, and probably elsewhere, of the standard of learning accompanied, at the same time, by the wider diffusion of knowledge. What had been gained in width had been lost in depth. The writers of the fourteenth century speak of Paris still as " *studium studiorum* " (p. vi.), yet it had already lost its old pre-eminence. Originally it alone could confer the mastership in theology, with the curious exceptions of Oxford and Cambridge ; but, down till the time of John XXII., the Roman Curia gave dispensations freely for the degree to be taken elsewhere, even, so Paris complained, " in a pigstye " (*cf*. the *Philobiblon*, cap. 9, p. 87, completed on 24th January 1345). In 1335 Benedict XII., the only Avignon Pope who did not interfere with the privileges of Paris, was " astonished to learn " that the studium at Toulouse had ventured to give a degree to a certain Franciscan, " although in the Toulouse studium the honour of the mastership had not hitherto been wont to be given in the faculty aforesaid " (p. 451).

But the Schism, which placed Paris within the territory of the anti-pope, made the Roman Pontiff anxious to foster the universities within his own obedience. Consequently everywhere else the mastership was now conferred by pontifical charter.

In the fourteenth century medicine and music greatly improved, while Latin grew very much worse, and the loss of patristic studies was especially noted (vol. iii., p. ix.). Efforts were made to establish chairs of Oriental languages, the General Council of Vienne in 1312 even imposing the study of Hebrew, Chaldaic and Arabic in the universities of Paris, Oxford, Bologna and Salamanca. In 1325 John XXII., the great foreign missionary Pope, ordered the decree of Vienne to be carried out with austere vigilance ; but in 1430 it remained still ineffective. The Paris masters then proposed that Greek, Hebrew and Chaldaic should be taught and that the university should pay for their teaching. Yet in 1434 the Council of Basle had to reimpose the old and still ineffective decree of Vienne. To what extent these languages were known is, however, extremely difficult to say with any certainty for, despite the seeming neglect of the ordinance of 1312, in the library of Tours in the thirteenth and fourteenth centuries were to be found Greek, Hebrew and Slavonic manuscripts apparently much used by the readers (Delisle, *Notes sur quelques Manuscrits de la Bibliothèque de Tours*, 1868, Paris, p. 17 *et seq.*, also *Les Ecoles d'Orléans* by the same author). At Paris also there existed in the thirteenth century a college for Oriental studies receiving letters of encouragement from Innocent IV. (1248), Alexander IV. (1258), and Honorius IV. (1285), and financed by a system of taxation imposed on various religious houses which are chiefly known to us owing to their refusal to pay (Charles Jourdain, *Un Collège Oriental à Paris au Treizième Siècle*).[1]

We can perceive that despite the degradation of learning in the fourteenth century a master of learning might still be honoured, for a bas-relief on the tomb of Cino Sinibaldi in the cathedral of Pistoia represents him lecturing to his pupils, among whom is Petrarch. Robert of Sorbonne a century earlier had denounced the " proud masters and preachers who refused to lecture or preach unless they had a crowded hall or church " (*De Conscientia*, Bigne, p. 350), and Guillaume de Perault in his turn laid down for his generation the five essential qualifications of the teacher, that he should be ingenious in mind, honest in life, humble in knowledge, eloquent in speech, and skilful in teaching, and by this last, he explained, was meant a mind clear, concise, practical, sweet and mature (*De Eruditione Principum*, Bk. V., cap. 6).

But meanwhile a new educational movement was beginning. In 1333 Petrarch discovered two orations of Cicero, in 1416 a copy of Quintillian's *Institutes of Oratory* was found in the

---

[1] For Nature science *cf.* Langlois, *La Connaissance de la nature et du monde au moyen age*, Paris, 1911.

Abbey of St Gall, giving a detailed explanation of the old Roman theory of education. By these discoveries was the new style inaugurated. The older text-books and authors—Philippe de Thaon with his computation, lapidary, and bestiary of the twelfth century, Aldobrandino of Siena with his governance of the body of 1250, Henri de Monderville of 1280 with his study of surgery, the Catholicon dictionary of John Balbi of 1286, the Huguitio of Pisa, Bishop of Ferrara, with all its derivations dating from 1210—were clean swept aside in the new curriculum.

Vittorino da Feltre (1397-1446) at Mantua and Guarino da Verona (1429-1460) at Ferrara were the new headmasters who took Quintillian as their guide. Latin was taught, with attention given to articulation and accent, and easy readings were arranged, in prose from Cicero and Quintillian, and in verse from Virgil, Lucan, Horace, Seneca, and Claudian. History and manners were taught from Livy and Plutarch. Greek was now learned from the grammar of Theodore Gaza ; after thorough grounding in this the boy passed on to Xenophon, Isocrates, Plato, and parts of Homer and Hesiod. John Wessel (d. 1489), moving farther from the old standards, threw over the whole of the mediæval tradition : " Thomas scarcely knew Latin and that was his only tongue whereas I have a fair knowledge of the three languages. Thomas saw Aristotle only as a phantom ; I have read him in Greece in his own words " (Erasmus, by P. S. Allen, 1914, Oxford, p. 30) ; Agricola, another well-known authority, with his De Formando Studio, in 1486, was even more anti-scholastic.

But the innovators were not left unchallenged. A war of pamphlets ensued, a perfect battle of books. Cardinal Giovanni Dominici (1358-1420), without fanatical opposition to the newer learning, defended the old school (cf. Kardinal Johannes Dominici, by Rösler, C.SS.R., 1894, Freiburg ; and, more important, Dominici's Lucula Noctis, edited by Père Coulon, Paris, 1908). Savonarola also entered the lists : " Even the best of these heathen poets should only be studied after a strong and healthy Christian training. Let them accordingly be kept from the eyes of the young until the latter have been first nourished on the Gospel teachings and had them firmly impressed on their tender minds. It is not a matter of slight importance to give a good direction to their first training but rather of great and the greatest importance, since the beginning is always more than half of a work. For my part, I hold it better to see Christians adorned with good morals but scanty eloquence rather than see them rendered unworthy of the name of Christ despite the brilliance of their eloquence" (*Apologeticus*, p. 55).

In such a conflict both sides were carried away and made too harsh an attack on their opponents. Almost in the year of Savonarola's death, at Easter 1498, Erasmus was taking his degree of Bachelor of Divinity in the university of Paris; it was the parting of the ways between the old education and the new. Yet the new educators could not be wholly satisfied. About 1500 Butzbach described the boys as working harder under the old system than under the new, "for virtue and industry are declining."

But there was one writer who stood half-way between the two schools, and who has left a treatise on education which is without question the most masterly production of that age. His name is perhaps entirely forgotten, except for anyone who, prying round the Church of St Agostino in Rome, comes on the little bare chapel to the left of the high altar where is preserved the body of St Monica. On the left wall is the tombstone of Mafeo Vegio of Lodi, who conceived his highest honour was to have brought from Ostia, at his own expense, the relics of the mother of Augustine. A Milanese from Lodi, he was much thought of as a poet, and on the strength of this public repute he ventured to write a Thirteenth Book to the *Æneid*. With this exception there appear to be no dark places in his history. Eugenius IV. took him as his secretary (it is only fair to the Pope's memory to state that this was done before the unlucky numbered Thirteenth Book had appeared), and after the death of that Pontiff he served successively Pope Nicholas V. and Pope Pius II. A canon of St Peter's, a liturgical scholar, no mean Latinist, he died in 1457, under Pius II., and was buried in the place where his simple tomb still stands.

His book, *De Liberorum Eruditione* (edited by Bigne, tome xxvi., pp. 634-688), stands uniquely as uniting in itself the mediæval tradition and the newer spirit. It is a leisurely conspectus of a child's life, full of advice, of careful warning, helped out with personal anecdote, with piety, and with a saving sense of humour. It may seem to be out of proportion in such a work as this to give so much place to one writer, for we are about to give an account of this immense volume. Yet every statement of it could be paralleled from other writers, without adding one real valuable note of difference. More than any other it gives a true picture of the older theories at their best and the new at their most Christian moment; it shows us the past and with a note of prophecy it foretells the future. It harmonizes the swan-song of the Middle Ages with the shrill and eager chirping of the birds before the dawn.

The book opens with praise of St Augustine and St Monica, the saintly mother and the brilliant, unstable son. It is full of quotations from the writings of St Paul, St Ambrose, St Augustine (particularly from those parts of the *Confessions* that deal with his boyhood and his schooling and university days), and the classical writers. Scholastic in form, the opening chapters deal with the responsibility of parents for their children. Obviously they have to set a good example, and greater fidelity to their duty is expected of them than of their immature children. But the duty of the parents goes back further than attending to the children after they are born. In its pre-natal state the child is subject to influences dependent upon the mother and father. The mother naturally impresses her character on the child in the months when the two lives are so closely linked, but the father's sobriety or lack of it can also be traced in the physical and moral tendencies of the child. Beautiful statues should be placed in the home, since even these material representations, provoking the imagination to fixed contemplation of noble forms, can affect the body of the child in the mother's keeping. It is interesting to notice here the influence of Plato affecting the ideals of the Christian home.

When the child is born the doctor should be consulted so that the mother may be able to nurse it herself; but sometimes this cannot be done. In this event care should be taken in selecting the nurse. She should not be morose, nor difficult, nor foolish, nor stolid. Especially she should not be unclean. " We believe this to be of most benefit to their souls and bodies that they be not too delicately reared, clad not too sumptuously nor yet too roughly, fed and clothed in a word as nature would have them, bare-footed and without a cloak " (p. 641).

" It is better for them to be accustomed to the cold : it makes them hardy. . . . Food and sleep should not of course be denied them lest they be dwarfed in their growth, but too much of either breeds laziness, stupidity, and ill-shaped bodies . . . and wine, since it abounds in heat, should as little as possible be given them. . . . Doctors say that never should it be given them under nine years of age. Some more recent theorists think it should be added to their milk to make them strong. It certainly does do that, but it also makes them quick to anger, for the body of a child is already by its nature very full of heat. Wine serves only to increase this in them " (p. 641).

You have here the mediæval doctrine of the intimate relation between food and the passions of the soul. The psychology of St Thomas, partly derived from Aristotle, partly from his own intimate experience, is based upon the unveiled intimacy and reaction of soul and body. In scholastic theories of education, therefore, naturally much importance was given to the purely material side of the child's life.

" Children should not be checked in their crying, for this is thought to develop their strength. Yet till they are five, little attempt should be made to discipline them by laborious ways. Only very gentle exercises should be permitted them. These they must have for without them they will grow up incurably lazy " (p. 642).

In spite of what he has said about refraining from giving them too much discipline he proceeds to deal with them even in their tenderest years, and always counsels, as mediæval theorists consistently do, the most manly form of upbringing : " No silly baby-talk, half-words only, should be taught them, still less unclean tales, nor should they be given baby-names, for these often cling to them for life and are unworthy of them and savour of femininity, nor should they bear barbarous names nor the names of gods. The names of great men may be allowed them, Cicero, Brutus, even Antonino, which is but Anthony made little and was borne by one great man. But not Nero, for though it be a good name in itself, signifying in the Sabine tongue 'strong and strenuous,' yet because of the great crimes of one who carried the name it is not honourable for another to have it. . . .

" No tales of monsters should be told them ; nor should they be frightened with names of terror, nor bogies, such as those with which nurses love to terrify them. Let them learn instead the great stories of long ago and all brave deeds. Divine things should be taught them and reverence for the Name of God and the virtue of truth " (p. 642).

" Even as their food is to be carefully chosen, so as carefully should be the words they hear. From the servants and from their comrades let only comely words reach them, not obscene things nor the talk of slaves. So again from public shows and indecent pictures, and whatever else might sully the delicacy and tenderness of their childish minds, let them be protected, and from the company to be found in public inns. Justice, modesty, truth should be taught them, nor should manners be forgotten, the proper ways of salutation, the urbanity of human converse, methods of address, the time to rise or remain seated, the due reverence for age, solicitude for the infirm. To the old and to the learned let them acquit themselves well in speech and courtesy and politeness " (p. 643).

It should be remembered that Mafeo Vegio is still dealing with quite little children who have not yet reached the age of reason, as we in the North would consider it ; but he is an Italian dealing with the precocious little folk of the South, fiery, hot-blooded, half-timid, wholly wild : " It is a mistake for parents to frighten their children with threats or beatings." Here Vegio is moving away from the older tradition which believed, we have seen, in threats though not in beatings, itself a movement of the thirteenth century from the sharper discipline of the Rule of St Benedict and St Bernard's reform. " Beatings may stupefy a child more than enlighten him. Boys should not be lowered to the level of beasts and horses to be so whipped, nor do their bodies benefit by such harsh treatment. They are to be considered as children, not as slaves. Whatever there is of generosity in them can be touched easily by kindness. A bullock may have to be struck before it will work properly, but a dog, a beast of nobler worth, is better managed by kindness (*Eccles.* xxiii. 25), and certainly gentleness is to be used towards boys. This must not be taken to mean lack of discipline, for in these modern days children are being spoilt by softness of education. Let example move them and the stories of the great. Sometimes, if you will, let them learn the reward of evildoing in the punishment of the wicked. To let them witness a public execution is sometimes not at all a bad thing " (p. 644).

A whole chapter is devoted to the proper kinds of punishment to be administered to children. This part of the book is wholly of the mediæval time, quoting dogs, apes, bears, lions and elephants, to prove what can be done with proper training by a man who will be patient and devote himself to the work. But there is, as the mediæval teachers like Aquinas always insisted, a careful desire to treat each case on its own merits, reverencing the individuality of each soul : " It is of the greatest necessity that one should with prudence and judgment measure the capacity of each child, so that in correcting their morals we should be able to propose a remedy for their ills as a doctor would in curing their bodies. . . . Some there are in whom the sweetness of their future virtue is early fragrant ; timid, sensitive souls, yet often on that account with exquisite and elegant taste. Others are bold and full of daring. Some you see talkative, garrulous, others who will hardly answer a word. Many are boastful, more are eager of praise, a few have no ambition at all. Some are inconstant, of unstable humour ; others are intrepid and steadfast. Some again know not how to obey, others are docile even to their inferiors ; some there are to whom ease has no attraction, and others whose natural bent is to be lazy and do nothing at all. Some are eager to show you all they have, and others secretive about things even of no importance ; some careless of food, others hardly thinking of any other pleasure ;

some gentle, others quick to anger; some to whom peace is dear, others always in disputes. How can these be helped, or developed, or cared for, or cured, without an intimate knowledge of each one's character?" (p. 645).

It is certainly a note of mediæval training to foster the individuality of each soul. Their treatises on prayer frequently suggest the advice that each must find his own way to God. Not only do mystical writers like Mother Juliana of Norwich or Richard Rolle of Hampole do this, but the professional theologians as well. Aquinas, Scotus, Bromyard all repeat the advice. It was this sense of individuality that stamped their art as well as their prayer; and it occurs over and over again in their educational treatises. Vegio is here typical of them, for De Romans and Perault take the very same line. The authority they quote is nearly always the Gospel, with its exquisite touches of personal character and the peculiarly different way each soul was dealt with by Our Lord. It is, therefore, experience and the Scriptures that confirmed them in what Aristotle had laid down in his own theory of education, the sacredness of the individual character and the need of its perfect development and the consequent watchfulness required in all helpful training.

Mafeo has a charming sentence on the next page which gives a true and valuable simile: "Let children be so treated that they are neither beaten like asses nor like kittens lured by silly soothing words. The noblest horses need the firmest hands" (p. 646).

That ends his treatise in so far as it deals with smaller children. After seven, it will be remembered, the mediæval child was supposed to be sufficiently emancipated to leave home. Mediæval biographies and records (even the records of the Inquisition) prove that this was nearly always carried out. Sometimes the child left home earlier, seldom remained longer under the care of the mother than the seventh year. St Dominic was sent from home to his uncle, the arch-priest of Gumiel d'Izan, when he was seven; the little girls of the heretics of the Midi went to their convents at three or five or seven. Even if the children did not leave their homes, they were taken from their mothers and put under tutors or masters. The phrase of

Mafeo is that they are to be treated at first rather as " spectators of life than actors in it " when they are placed under masters, and by this he seems to mean that the transition is to be as gradual as possible, so that every stage of life may lead on to the next without the child being frightened or burdened. The influence of the woman now, however, ceased in the child's life if the child were a boy, and Mafeo considered that it was a good thing for the child to be spared an intimate acquaintance with servants and " the more sordid and domestic business of the home." The implications are that the domestic side of a mediæval house was not of a nature to benefit the growing boy and presumably the openness with which human relations were carried on and the lack of privacy, due in part to the small number of rooms in a house and the consequent community of life shared by family and servants, were better avoided till the child had been trained by contact with other boys and the development of his judgment and maturity.

The masters should be chosen carefully and not too often changed. It might be possible ordinarily for an elder brother to play the part; and " in any case it is better for the boy not to be sent away because the father is the better supervisor of his child." The master is the name given to the one who at school or at home directed the work of education ; in addition there was the tutor (this is where the elder brother's services should be made use of), who was to live with the boy, share his sports, and by contact as well as by repetitionary lessons teach him what could be better taught by man than by book. The master was to be chosen for his virtue, his learning and the elegance of his language. It were better if the master had not too many pupils to attend to, for thus each would get the more individual attention, and it was always the main purpose of having a master that the boy should be guided and inspired by personal presence and skill.

If the boy were sent away from home not only was the character of the master and the standard of the learning he gave to be considered, but not less the repute of the town in which the master lived. The boy would be out a good deal and even indoors would mix with folk who came calling or visiting, he could not escape the local influences of the town, its character, its licentiousness or decent gravity, its art and political ideals (pp. 647-649).

The relationship of the parents, presumably the father really, to the school or class was particularly insisted on. It would be good for the father sometimes to attend the lectures to see whether they were really of a type that would educate the boy to be the kind of man he wished him to become: "Pliny, when superintending the education of the sons of a dead friend, used at times to sit among the boys as though to live over again his boyhood's happy years" (p. 650).

Moreover, there is much advantage gained from paying good fees to the master, and even giving him presents as well from time to time. It secures better attention to the child: " Some parents spend more on their horses and cattle than on their sons. Whatever money they do pay has to be drawn from them grudgingly, as you would draw a tooth from them or even an eye " (p. 650).

In their turn the masters are to be loyal to their agreements and to care for their pupils as they would their own sons. If they have charge of these children, and have to provide for them, they must not forget the place food has in education, tempering food to the mind in the measure of its power and digestion. The health of the boy is an advantage to his learning. He learns better and retains his learning better in his memory when he is properly—that is, judiciously—fed. Moreover, the master himself needs good food, else he will become bad-tempered, and to lose your temper is really to lose your boy.

The emotions of shame and pleasure in being praised must be reckoned with and made use of. Everyone likes being praised. Boys particularly are much helped by it, it stimulates them to do better, they consider it betrayal to fail to work after praise. There is value also in shame. " I remember well that nothing helped me more to the appreciation of letters than this method of my master. He was wont, I remember, and laugh in remembering, to divide the class into two sides, under the leadership of the cleverest boys, and this led to many contests between us. Rather than be last in such disputes, I dare not say to what lengths I went in my vigils and labours and the burden of study, imitating the more clever amongst my fellows, avoiding those who were more remiss " (p. 651). This method of inducing learning by means of rivalry was opposed by the earlier mediæval writers, who looked upon it as an evil influence in a boy's life and likely to teach him to be envious and jealous and disputatious. St Antonino is severe on it (*Theologia Moralis*, pars iii., tit. 5, cap. 1, § 2), showing therefore that it existed in his day but that it had not his approval. By approving, Mafeo here has parted company with the older school. The result was soon seen in the endless quarrels of the later Renaissance, begotten of this new rivalry already introduced in Mafeo's schooldays.

" After this master had left Milan," continues Mafeo, " my father sent me to another master, an old man in whom my memory delights. He used to teach us gradually our lessons and give higher places to those best skilled, and commit to their care the less clever whether older or younger. When any of these were ready, the master was to be informed. Then this group, as happens in the schools of law and medicine, would be questioned publicly by the others and the audience would vote on the results at the end. The master finally would himself question the successful candidate to see whether he should be promoted to a higher class. Again the more learned would be told days beforehand to prepare conclusions which they had to defend against all comers. Do you laugh at the gravity with which I tell all this? Laugh if you will but not before you have learnt to write more elegantly the battle of frogs and mice. Again, I remember how when I passed to my second master and he found that I was not ignorant (though I was not yet eleven years old) of much that he did not know I knew, he put me before all the class and praised my first master and myself, and foretold a great future for me. Certainly to his praise and kindness I owe a very great deal of my devotion to study, setting myself to read the volumes of the poets and writing verses myself without anyone to teach me " (pp. 651-652).

The practice of writing prose and verse he considered should be taught them, now one, now the other, so that they should learn how to state ideas clearly and yet to give them a cadence, for "verse certainly helps a boy the better to write good prose" (p. 652). The tendency had been noted by Antonino and applauded by him. Cardinal Dominici had even urged it, opposed though he was to many of the new ideas now coming into education. Even in the Dark Ages, when the waters of barbarism were only beginning to abate, verse had become part of the education of a child. This the thirteenth century had inherited and developed, and had devoted itself to the virtue of rhyme. The Latin songs and ballads, the liturgical hymns and proses, were frequently interspersed with rhymes. It is quite certain that snatches of song were to be heard in the streets. Men whistled and sang at their work, on their way to work. Letters are written in verse sometimes by way of jest.

Mafeo Vegio commends the learning by heart of passages of great writers. It was an early practice in mediæval time. A novice was supposed to know by heart the Psalter and the epistles of St Paul. The example of Cato is quoted by Vegio, who used to try in the evening to remember what he had read during the day and so built up a ready and retentive memory. Memory is indeed to him, "the holy interpreter of human life," "the guardian of education," "the precious treasure-house of nature," "not unjustly has it been called by poets the mother of the Muses" (p. 653).

He urged, therefore, that boys should be examined every week or fortnight in their lessons. We have already quoted from Robert of Sorbonne to show that this was the mediæval custom every Saturday, a repetition by way of examination in the week's work. Perhaps it was especially then that the two divisions of the classes had their grand contests and were awarded marks according to the vote of the whole. It seems that during the week the brilliant boys had to coach their side for this contest, and that the questioning was done partly by the boys and partly by the master, who asked questions of both sides.

The earlier form of education had encouraged particularly the ready speaker, for it was an age of disputation when dialectic had come suddenly on men almost as a new science. Abelard had produced such a school of talkers and disputants, and St Bernard was shocked at their readiness and contradictions, and had taken seriously as their mature judgments the clever paradoxes of the young Paris students. St Antonino commends this quickness of speech and thought (tit. 5, cap. 1) but to Mafeo there is a danger in it. He prefers that boys should not be taught extempore speaking, nor on the other hand be allowed much time for premeditation. The first seemed likely to produce " an inveterate habit of shameless garrulity " and the second " a foolish self-esteem based on affected wisdom. . . . Therefore, they are to be taught carefully to weigh their words, preferring sense to sound, nice in their choice of words, using their words only in the sense that the learning of antiquity has consecrated so that their speech should be graceful and exact. The first quality of speech is that it should be clear, perspicuous, needing no interpreter, careful in its distinctions, careful in its order " (p. 653).

But he points out that, while careful in using words only in the sense of learned antiquity, a boy should avoid all obsolete words. Affectation is as harmful as slipshodness, and is opposed to the prime purpose of speech—namely, the making an ideal clear to the person who is listening. Rare words should be used rarely, to express ideas that are themselves rare. The author he most praises and recommends is Cicero, on whose writings he has quite obviously modelled himself. He finds Cicero " so exquisite and tender a stylist, whose words are easily understood yet whose phrases are so flexible . . . whose movement of language is so spontaneous, yet in the highest degree quiet and sane." It is the majesty of classical literature that impresses him, yet its austerity, " like a religious matron who goes draped amply yet without giving a sense of richness." In literature and in the search for the appropriate word, " custom is to be followed, the surest leader in the art of speech." The origin of words, their exact significance, their analogies and differences, their construction, are all to be studied with diligence. But vain etymologies are to be avoided (p. 654).

" Grammar is the gate of the sciences " was a mediæval phrase, and grammar was considered indispensable to the study of speaking. Accuracy, scientific precision, is the gift of Aquinas, who reached the highest peak of mediæval exactness and even bareness in speech. There is no attempt at rhetoric in his works, though he has left us exquisite poems to show how he could have embellished his writings had he so desired. His autograph copy of the *Summa contra Gentiles* is illuminating as indicating his method of writing, not least by its showing how he corrected his text. He is writing at full speed—the script shows it—and thinking as he writes. Words are begun and then midway abandoned, arguments are altered, rewritten, and then omitted altogether as inadequate. It is possible to gather from his corrections and changes, the character of his mind. Without exception his alterations are all in favour of brevity and conciseness. Every unnecessary adjective is jettisoned. Simpler than ever as he grows older, few words, clearer sense. That is " the architectonic mind," as a mediæval critic styles him, of Aquinas ; he builds his theses one by one, without decoration or ornament, trusting for any beauty to the exact proportions and perfect lines of his structure. The success is indisputable.

Vegio, however, pushes further than Antonino the resources of sheer ornament, his school of literature has moved from the early Medici to the Middle Renaissance. Beauty is almost a purpose in itself.

" Words and style should be appropriate to the matter . . . in a picture the lights are no more to be commended than the shadows." Every beautiful thing has three qualities, it should be magnificent, graceful and restrained : " Magnificence without restraint, grace without magnificence, restraint without grace, would all fail in literature as in every other art. Let boys then be trained to eloquence but also to elocution—that is, to pronunciation, inflexion of voice, knowing where to pause, where to breathe, where to speak loudly or softly, how to pose face and hands and the whole body so that the discourse may lack both awkwardness and artificiality " (p. 655)

He returns to the subject of education, and thinks that the comic authors ought to be read later on in the course to perfect the young man's style, but not in boyhood, because the wanton

loves of the gods are unsuited to the boy's mind. The Jews
were not allowed to read the Book of Genesis, nor parts of
Ezechiel and the Canticle of Canticles, till they were over
thirty years old. Vegio thinks that at least the plays of Plautus
and Terence should be deferred till the end of the studies
when the mind is more mature and able to appreciate beauty
without passion. Latin and Greek should certainly be taught
to everyone; but after the alphabet he would put the Book of
Psalms, then the Proverbs of Solomon or the Book of Ecclesi-
asticus, then the Second Book of Maccabees. This last he
judges to be good Latin, to be pleasing to read, and useful.
After this, or at the same time, Æsop's *Fables*, so as thus to begin
to mingle sacred and profane learning; also the *Catilinarii* of
Sallust, because of its eloquence and its brevity. The tragic
poets should then be taught, then Homer, then Virgil: " The
whole *Æneid* is a *Summa* of philosophy wherein are hidden
under poetic imagery deep mysteries " (p. 657).

Virgil was always a half-Christian poet to the Middle Ages,
partly because of his so-called Messianic prophecy, partly
because his Sixth Book seemed so nearly a frescoed picture of
purgatory, partly because of the devotion to his tomb near
Naples which is to be seen in the famous lines that worked
their way into the Sequence of St Paul's Mass in the liturgy of
Naples. Vegio, therefore, is hurt that lately some " garrulous
persons have been attacking the poet because of his obscenity."
Vegio can find no obscenity, nor indeed did anyone else before
these scribblers discovered it. The significant remark is made
that Martial justified himself when rebuked for his " nauseous
epigrams " by mentioning other great names equally guilty of
coarseness under whose shadow he endeavoured to find shelter
himself, among whom was Catullus, but Virgil was not named
among them.

Before the boy comes to the classics themselves, Mafeo
would have him taught the stories of the mythologies and the
great legends of pagandom, so that the plots of the plays and
the lives of the heroes and heroines should be familiar to him
and thus make his reading less laborious. The aim of education
is to enable a boy to learn all knowledge and not be burdened

by it, to be enlivened by its grace and wit and variety, and to find the hours of schooling not wearisome (p. 658).

The principle of education to which he again returns is the development of each boy's individuality. Parents and masters must remember this : " Each is to be taught especially what he is most inclined to, ' lest anything should be done against the wish of Minerva ' as the proverb ran. Each, therefore, is to be exercised in the studies in which he is most apt, for whoever by nature is attracted to oratory or poetry or dialectics or medicine or law or any other art, if he be allowed to devote himself to it, will undoubtedly become most learned and most powerful in his own particular line. But these last two arts, medicine and law, have so many foolish and ignorant professors that we can guess it was not by any natural talent or attraction that they sought them out but only a love of gain." Even poetry has its quack professors ! " There is one in our time [is it Petrarch he can be alluding to ? Petrarch has been dead many years] who has been wearing a laurel crown." Poetry does not *receive* crowns, is his epigram, poetry *gives* crowns to athletes and musicians and gods ! No poet should ever debase himself to receive honours ; he gives honours because his art cannot find any greater than itself from which it can receive them. Then he goes back to speak of God's skill in making the world full of variety so that no one should ever despise his fellows —soldiers, sailors, husbandmen, and the rest ; no one should imagine himself to have few talents and, therefore, make lament. " We have them if we will only look for them and employ them " (p. 659).

Music, therefore, no less than the rest of the arts is not to be neglected in the training of boys, in spite of the fact that bad music, like bad songs, has a lascivious effect, particularly on the young. Of old, indeed, the prophets were all poets and singers. Painting and sculpture also should be used to train the taste (p. 660).

The place of athletics in the curriculum is duly noted, the type of game becoming more violent as a boy grows up. Games give health or confirm it. They make boys " more erect and more eager, enable them to meet sadness and depression with untroubled brow. A solemn mien in the old is to be commended, in boys to be denounced." This gospel of joyousness can be found even earlier, for Humbert de Romans had urged that there were six things required of novices : that they should be "faithful, helpful, docile to advice, humble, disciplined and joyous, for they should be loved as sons are loved by their mother" (Serm. vii., *Ad Novicios in quocunque ordine*, p. 460).

Mafeo concludes that there should be stated times for games. After puberty, he counsels riding, shooting, slinging and throwing javelins. At school, however, lesser sports should be taken up. Military drill is admirable for boys. He adds leaping, games with balls, but not dice, for these lead to covetousness, a heinous crime in a child. He recommends reading and talking, walking by streams and woods and the seashore, fishing, bird-catching (though this ceases to be a recreation when it includes birds of prey) and teaching birds to talk (pp. 661-662).

The importance of philosophy in the school *horarium* naturally appealed to the mediævalist; though the arrogance of the philosophers of Paris and Oxford had become a by-word in Florence, as St Antonino notes (tit. 5, cap. 2, § 10). He saw, however, that the modern mind was beginning to be too positive to care longer for metaphysics, the noblest of the sciences (§ 4). Mafeo adds therefore, as an alternative, farming and other trades; farming particularly this Virgilian praises, as became the author of a Thirteenth Book to the *Æneid*: "Farming is the jolliest of occupations, the most successful and most dignified." Then there were the professions to be prepared for, the army, the priesthood. Already in the fifteenth century we have arrived at vocational training—an army-class and the church-boy. Even the wealthiest should learn a trade. No one knows when it will be needed: "Fortune's wheel has many turnings. We who are life's watchers see this daily happening. We write what we know."

"Certainly youth needs care with its sudden and passing friendships, its violent loves, its zest for gambling and risk, its delights in horses and dogs and birds. Yet over all love is strongest. What fine fellows there are! Freed from the degradation of passion, scorning indecent speech and fellowship, upright, manly, how splendid such a youth can be. How has not St Augustine, from sixteen years of age upwards at the mercy of his passions, regretted the irrecoverable fragrance of boyhood! The pages of the *Confessions* are a pathetic warning of the beauties of youth, and the possibilities of their being stained, and the undying sadness if this should be" (p. 663). Mafeo remembers as a boy being sent by his master to watch the execution of a thief. The thief saw him and told him much the same thing: "boyhood's irrecoverable fragrance." He remembers still how terrified he was at this personal and public appeal by the man so near death. Certainly a boy needs discipline, but most of all gentleness and patience, if he is to escape "the ambush of young days."

Mafeo has spoken of boys throughout; but he thinks there is hardly anything that he has written that should not equally be applied to girls, after the example of St Monica (pp. 655-666).

The roots of wisdom are hard to plant, but the fruits of wisdom are full of delight. In youth they are planted, or planted never at all. Youth is the springtime of life, easily shamed, transparent, blushing so easily because it is virginal, exquisitely sensitive to the knowledge of good and evil. It should be taught early the duties that it owes to God, to its parents, to its fellow-pupils; it should be trained to reverence priests and old people, scholars, magistrates and princes, the needy and all in trouble. "There is no freedom save in the freedom of the heart, bondage to the law secures this, those who are law-abiding alone are really free. He is no slave who, with a heart high and constant, orders his affairs" (pp. 667-671).

Reverence again for women should be taught him, reverence for himself, "the secret shrine of the Muses." Particularly when he is alone he should be careful of his virtue, his one treasure, "at once a sea and a shore." The remembrance of God's presence will support him to foster always clean and gentle thoughts (p. 674).

Therefore modesty should be taught youth, modesty in gesture and outward showing; but this is not true modesty unless it is sincere. The heart must be modest if life is really to be what it should be. Eyes and lips should be carefully guarded. Plato even taught this. A greater than he is our Master, Who taught us truly what was His law. Besides modesty, it is good to practise politeness in external expression. There are things which, though not wrong in themselves, cannot be done in public without displeasing others—such as scratching the head or cleaning the ears. Further, all peculiarity of gesture should be avoided. It annoys people and distracts them. St John Chrysostom, great preacher though he was, offended or diverted people by his favourite gesture of striking the palm of his left hand with his right forefinger. It were better to correct these mannerisms and try to be as free as possible from all such tricks as irritate listeners. A boy is malleable, not yet stiffened. Let him beware of hardening into set affectations.

A boy should be trained to be reserved with friends, but not sad or gloomy. Cleanliness is urged on boys and niceness in person and in attire. Virgil's lines on Charon's unshaved chin and ill-kept clothes are quoted as a sign of what not to copy :

" Cui plurima mento canities inculta jacet
 Sordibus ex humeris nodo dependet amictus."

Indeed Vegio would allow a great deal more to the young man than the mediæval moralists considered safe. He had the spirit of the Renaissance in him. We see him in Milan with the Sforza, in Florence with Eugenius IV., in Rome also with him and with Nicholas V. and Pius II. in the very hey-day of the movement of that new birth of the spirit. The Medici have influenced Eugenius; Nicholas has the librarian's love of books ; Pius is the politician, the scholar, the wit turned into a mediæval Pontiff who bears his gout with exemplary patience and dies preaching a crusade. The young man, therefore, of Mafeo's day was one whose magnificent life he had watched and sympathized with. He had heard the complaints of anxious mothers about the unbridled freedom of their children and perceived the truth of all they said ; he consoled them by writing an office for the Feast of St Monica. His sympathy, too, went out to the Augustines. Hence he allowed them the use of many vanities, as Savonarola would have called them later and would have, therefore, burned. The mirror and the hair brush, which the friar was to reprobate, were allowed by Mafeo, and also the careful cultivating of the hair, because in this way the divine gifts are better cared for, and the world made brighter. What alone he halted at was ointment for the hair, and scent (p. 681).

As became so devout a Virgilian he ends with a chapter on the delights of country life (Bk. IV., cap. 4). It is, he thinks, the centre of all that is best in national existence, the condition necessary for the due perfection of a man's soul. It gives him the spirit of contemplation, it gives him a healthy view of the world, it heals his eyes and his lips, it restores his quiet, makes him sane. "Think," he says, appealing to boys and youth and parents, "what wonderful things have come out of the country! Soldiers for instance. You cannot match the country-born soldier, he knows the ways of the country, he can hide and he can see better than the town-bred fellow, and he is more constant and intrepid and will never run away." Strange that this scholar and poet should think of soldiers as the first gift of the land! Then he adds the delights of hunting to the gifts of the country, and then as two blessed gifts, appetite and sleep. The picture he calls up shows us not only his own mind but the minds of the schoolboys of his own generation, for he thinks evidently that they can be tempted in this way. Then the river-side and the strange pleasures of the water and the absorbing art of angling are described; nor does he forget to mention Mark Antony and Augustus Cæsar as famous fishermen of history (pp. 685-686).

He has, however, one warning to give to the country-dweller; if you want to enjoy the country, he says to the boy, you must pay no attention to weather. If you are unable to get on without sunshine and fine weather go back to your cities, and the arched street-ways, where you can walk securely without wet. If the cold irks you, and mud, and the baking heat, seek the more artificial life of the town. But if you are above those fears, and have learnt a sense of beauty and have gathered from your education a determination to see life whole, then make for the country. Do not trouble about the seasons, but trouble about fleeting time (p. 687).

And so he ends.

He is of all our period the most typical guide to education, showing us the ideals of the mid-fifteenth century when it was still hoped that the mediæval and the Renaissance theories could be made to fit in. A little earlier in point of time than Savonarola, yet his treatise contains more of the new spirit than do the sermons of the friar. It is a little later than the writings of St Antonino, yet it is as mediæval as anything he ever wrote. It looks backward and forward. It sums up the old learning and it begins the new. It is typical of the new learning in 1500, growing out of the past, not yet broken off from it, on the edge of the revolution that was suddenly to change the development of the ways of life.

Education had come out of the sanctuary into the library, it had not yet left the library for the counting-house. It had ceased merely to train the mind and will, it had not yet begun to teach men how to make a livelihood, it was still engaged in teaching them how to live.

CHAPTER III

WOMEN

THE position of women in mediæval society is not difficult to discover, for the records of that society in its treatises on womanhood are seldom ambiguous or obscure. Very much was written and much was preached. Also a great deal was done. We have letters, familiar and official, surviving still that show in practice how these theories were lived and carried out. We have the stories of human lives, wherein the romance of love, lawful or unlawful, is told us, quaintly perhaps, or movingly, but surely and with clearness. Then there are the romances or novels, especially of Italy and of France, which give us not necessarily indeed definite instances of what actually occurred but at least glimpses of what was thought possible of occurrence.

Undoubtedly the most obvious thing to be said of the position of woman in that age was that it was one of subjection to man. The argument used by mediæval writers to describe woman's place in the world is consistent and unchanging. It is found everywhere. But when we try to reconstruct the conditions affecting a woman's life in the Middle Ages, and to discover from their writings how womanhood was regarded by man, we find it needful to distinguish many classes of literature which treat of women and to consider each precisely in regard to the public it was meant to serve.

For example, monastic writers, who were writing for a monastic audience, quite naturally were concerned chiefly with the relation of monks to women, so that, since chastity and virginity were essential to religious life, it was woman as a danger to their vocations who was most frequently described. It would be grossly unscientific to take these monastic writers in their monastic treatises as representative of mediæval thought on womanhood, for they are not intending to write primarily on women as women, their greatness or their littleness, but solely on women as dangers to monastic observance. No monk was unmindful of the mother that bore him; but he recognized that honour to his vow implied a careful reserve towards those who might endanger his keeping of it. There were scandals enough in mediæval monastic history to make this not unnecessary. Literary criticism would, then, be false to itself if it fastened upon these sayings without considering precisely to whom they were addressed.

Again, it is not to be supposed that an age which was hardy, and physically inured to much that would try severely more delicately nurtured frames, would look upon bodily violence with great repugnance. The Inquisition was itself not cruel enough to scandalize public opinion, for public opinion on such a matter as physical suffering varies considerably with the customs of the time.[1] Each age has its own conventions and its own nervous sensibilities, as has also each class of society. Wife-beating, for example, was commoner no doubt than it would be to-day in the higher classes of society; but that was only because there was nothing like the same sensitiveness to pain that later ages have developed. An angry husband would beat a disobedient wife,[2] in the same way as an angry client would beat the statue of a saint who had not answered his petitions; and all without loss of respect for one or the other. These things are the commonplaces of divergence between one period of history and another. Morals remain largely stationary in Christendom; it is manners only that change. Mediæval chivalry was not so shocked at physical violence to women as we should be.

Basing the argumentation on the Scriptures, the mediæval theologian or moralist made the man the head of the woman. St Thomas, for example, writes thus : " The image of God in its principal signification—namely, the intellectual nature—is found both in man and in woman. . . . But in a secondary sense the image of God is found in man and not in woman : for man is the beginning and end of woman, as God is the beginning and end of every creature. So when the Apostle had said that

---

[1] Moneta (*Adversus Catharos et Valdenses*, Rome, 1743) asserted (p. 508) that the Cathari defended persecution; he had been a Waldensian himself and became a Dominican, 1218; died, 1250.

[2] Cf. *The Pastons and their England*, H. S. Bennett, Cambridge, 1922, p. 80.

man is the *image and glory of God but woman is the glory of man*
(1 Cor. xi. 7) he adds his reason for saying this : *for man is
not of woman but woman of man; and man was not created for
woman but woman for man* " (*Summa Theologica*, i. 93, 4, ad 1 m,
p. 289). It should be remembered that the philosophy of
Aquinas is essentially teleological. Its purpose is always to him
the dominant characteristic of a thing, and its value corresponds
precisely to that purpose. For Aquinas, therefore, the Biblical
account of man's creation is the divine expression of a social
truth, that woman was created to be man's helpmate. According
to the Bible in point of fact she was made for him and in point
of fact he was not made for her. He was already there before
her. Humbert de Romans, who ruled the Dominican Order
as Master-General during the middle period of St Thomas's
life, has left us a sermon which was intended to form a model
for other friars when preaching to women, and to furnish ideas
to be adapted by them to the circumstances of their audience.
In it we have this characteristic passage : " Note that God gave
women many prerogatives, not only over other living things
but even over man himself, and this (i) by nature ; (ii) by grace ;
and (iii) by glory. (i) In the world of nature she excelled man
by her origin, for man He made of the vile earth, but woman
He made in Paradise. Man he formed of the slime, but woman
of man's rib. She was not made of a lower limb of man—as for
example of his foot—lest man should esteem her his servant,
but from his midmost part, that he should hold her to be
his fellow, as Adam himself said : ' The woman Whom Thou
gavest as my helpmate.' (ii) In the world of grace she excelled
man, for God, Who could have taken flesh of a man, did not do
so, but took flesh of a woman. Again, we do not read of any
man trying to prevent the Passion of Our Lord, but we do read
of a woman who tried—namely, Pilate's wife, who tried to
dissuade her husband from so great a crime because she had
suffered much in a dream because of Christ. Again, at His
Resurrection, it was to a woman He first appeared—namely,
to Mary Magdalen. (iii) In the world of glory, for the king in
that country is no mere man but a mere woman is its queen.
It is not a mere man who is set above the angels and all the

rest of the heavenly court, but a mere woman is; nor is anyone who is merely man as powerful there as is a mere woman. Thus is woman's nature in Our Lady raised above man's in worth, and dignity, and power : and this should lead women to love God and to hate evil" (Serm. xciv., *Ad omnes mulieres*, p. 503).

It is quite evident that this sermon of Master Humbert was extensively used. The ideas in it are commonly to be found in many mediæval sermons. James of Voragine repeats them ; so does Bromyard ; so one after another do the rest whose sermons have survived. Woman was meant as the helpmate for man, and despite her prerogatives and her own essential excellencies, which surpass man's, she has to remain in subjection to man for whom she was made. To the mediæval moralist the question never poses itself simply : Is man better than woman ? That is a form of question he could only have answered with many distinctions. But he was content to have found in his scripture that the woman was to be subject to man.

" But subjection is twofold. One is servile, by virtue of which a superior makes use of a subject for his own benefit ; and this kind of subjection began after sin. There is another kind of subjection, which is called economic or civil, whereby the superior makes use of his subjects for their own benefit or good ; and this kind of subjection existed before sin. For good order would have been wanting in the human family if some were not governed by others wiser than themselves. So by such a kind of subjection woman is naturally (*i.e.* by nature) subject to man, because in man the discretion of reason predominates " (*Summa Theologica*, i. 92, 1, ad 2 m, p. 276). Here, again, we have the constant thought of the Middle Ages. In the *Supplement* to the Tertia Pars of the *Summa* St Thomas cuts down the argument very briefly : " Now a woman is subject by her nature whereas a slave is not " (*Supp.*, 39, 3, p. 57) ; " Woman is subject to man on account of the frailty of nature as regards both vigour of soul and strength of body " (*Supp.*, 81, 3, ad 2 m., p. 191) ; " Since it is not possible in the female sex to signify eminence of degree, for a woman is in a state of subjection, it follows that she cannot receive the sacrament of orders " (*Supp.*, 39, 1, p. 52); " Since in matters pertaining to the soul woman does not differ from man as to the thing (for sometimes a woman is found to be better than many men as regards the soul) it follows that she can receive the gift of prophecy and the like, but not the sacrament of orders " (*Supp.*, 39, 1, ad. 1 m, p. 53).

For the mediævalist, therefore, the position of a woman was governed exclusively by her purpose in the mind of the Creator as the Bible had expressed it. There was no possibility or desire of assigning to woman an inferior place because of her lesser capacity for goodness or divine love, for no one would have admitted this to be true or even possible. As human souls men and woman were equal, as saints a woman might be a better lover of God than a man.

The social theorist who considered the position of women primarily concerned himself with the family in the abstract as he found it, proving the family to be in his theories the unit of society. He no longer gave to the father of the family that absolute mastery over women and children that the Roman law had given him ; he gave the father a directive power, purely " civil or economic," natural and not conventional— that is to say, it was not a legal ownership established by capture, or the rights of war, or the enslavement of a people ; it was a purely natural subjection required for the ordered well-being of social life and for the development of the family, and determined by Divine law as taught by the revealed dogmas of the Faith.

The concept is purely abstract and deals with the place of woman as woman in the family life. " A man," says an Italian writer of the fourteenth century, " is obliged to attend to his business without doors, that so he may provide for the things of the house, and it is the woman's duty to attend to the affairs of the family and the house " (Del Lungo, *Women of Florence*, London, 1907, p. 107).

The same abstract and ordered view of family life is met with in another connection, which also has some bearing on the part played by women in the family. In mediæval books the curious question was asked as to whether a child were obliged to love better father or mother. St Thomas (*Summa Theol.*, II. ii. 26, 10, p. 349) answered at once as we would have expected him to answer: " In making such comparisons as this we must take the answer in the strict sense, so that the present question is whether the father as father ought to be loved more than the mother as mother. The reason is that virtue and vice may make such a difference in such-like matters that friendship may be diminished or destroyed, as the Philosopher remarks (*Ethics*, viii.). Hence Ambrose [Chrysostom] says : ' Good servants should be preferred to wicked children.' Strictly speaking, however, the father should be loved more than the mother. For father and mother are loved as principles of our natural origin. Now the father is principle in a more excellent way than the mother because he is the active principle, whereas the mother (physiologically) is a passive and material principle. Consequently, strictly speaking, the father is to be loved more."

It is necessary to note how careful St Thomas always is to guard against misunderstanding; but he is evidently afraid that he will be misquoted, for he reaffirms again in an answer to an objection what he had already insisted upon in the body of the article: " The friendship we are speaking of here is that which a man owes his father and mother through being begotten of them " (ad 2 m, p. 350). If friendship be understood as a sense of duty or obligation, and if father and mother be merely looked upon as the origins of our being, then logically, so runs the argument, you should have a greater sense of duty and obligation to your father than to your mother, since physiologically your father contributed more actively to your conception than did your mother. The type of argument is profoundly illustrative of the curiously scientific nature of speculation common then, and becoming later repulsive and unhelpful.

" Now it is evident," again writes Aquinas (II. ii. 154, 2, p. 135), " that the upbringing of a human child requires not only the mother's care for his nourishment, but much more the care of his father as guide and guardian under whom he progresses in goods both internal and external." Reference has been made already in the previous chapter to the place taken by father and mother in the child's life. It will be seen how this position of the father and mother was always judged in the abstract and independently of what either were like. So again is it here when the place of woman in society is considered; attention is paid almost exclusively to her purpose, her origin and her contribution to the child's conception. Indeed we might note in passing as most characteristic of the Middle Ages that in this question it is the father's active participation in the conception of the child, and not the mother's travail in the birth of the child, that enters into the horizon of the social theorist. It was his concept of the physiology of the child's birth, and not the personal cost of it, which was envisaged. The pre-occupation of the mediæval moralist was to judge the place of woman in life by the origin of species. He would have agreed in basing social theories on the biological sciences, if only he could have been got to accept the biological sciences. He appears to us now to have been intensely cold-blooded, knowing emotions but not sentiment.

Nor must we imagine that the subjection of the wife to the man was merely theoretic. It most certainly was carried out in practice to judge from the advice freely handed out to wives throughout the mediæval period. The fourteenth-century writer, whom we have already quoted, from Italy, wastes no circumlocutions in getting his idea home: " The seventh commandment is that thou shalt not do any great thing of thine own accord without the consent of thy husband, however good reason there seem to be unto thee for doing it : and take care thou dost on no account say to him, ' My advice is better than thine,' even though truly it were better, for by so doing thou couldst easily drive him into great anger against thee and great hatred " (Del Lungo, p. 106) ; and this also : " Cheerfully do greater honour unto his kindred than unto thine own, for so will he do unto thine " (p. 109).

In more beautiful language the same thing is said in the famous letter of St Louis IX. of France to his daughter Isabella, Queen of Navarre, in which he shows her how she should truly live : " Dear daughter, because I think you hearken more to my words than anyone, for the love you bear me, I purpose to give you some advice. . . . Accustom yourself to confess frequently and select always confessors of holy life and good education. . . . Obey your husband humbly and your father and mother also in all that is pleasing to God. You must give to each of them your due for the love that you have for them and still more you should do it for the love of Our Lord" (*Acta S.S. Bollandists*, 5th August, p. 588).

Marriage itself was a state blessed by God and invested by Christ with the honour and dignity of a sacrament. Virginity, indeed, was generally looked upon as higher in itself, for this had been the unanimous teaching of the Fathers of the Church, and seemed to be derived from the Gospel itself. The Epistles of St Paul were clear and convincing on that point and no writer in the mediæval period seems to have questioned it. The abstract proposition that virginity was nobler than marriage, among heretics as well as among the orthodox in Christendom, received universal assent.

That curious tract of the early fourteenth century, *De Eruditione Principum*, from which we have already quoted as by Vincent de Beauvais, though it figures in the Parma edition among the spurious works of Aquinas and may be by Guillaume de Perault, insists on this preferment of virginity above marriage (Bk. V., cap. 27, p. 62), yet at the same time commends marriage highly for a reason that is curious enough to our way of thinking. " Other orders of life," says he, " had saints for their founders, one Augustine, and another Benedict, but this Order, the Holy Order of Wedlock, is greater since its Founder was God" (Bk. V., cap. 26). The conclusion as to the supereminence of virginity seems, with such a beginning, hardly logical. Nevertheless it is made. On the other hand our author states that married life is a blessed state and that the marriage-act is not in itself sinful. It can be sinful and it can be without sin, mortal or venial (cap. 27). It was necessary for him to state this because it was the universal teaching of theologians that the marriage-act was of general obligation in married life; virginal life in marriage might be a distinct call from God, yet it would remain an exceptional call. On the rest this obligation remained. The marriage-act was lawful of course, since it was necessary, but it was not to be sought for merely for its own sake. This is another instance of the teleological nature of mediæval thought. Marriage had a purpose; it was justified by that purpose; the absence of that purpose might easily make sinful an act otherwise justifiable and praise-worthy.

In his *Commentary on the Proverbs of Solomon* (lect. lxxii., fol. lxxxix.*b*, in the edition printed in Paris, 1515), Robert Holcot of the Dominicans argues from the Master of the Sentences, and following up his line of thought, that a man whose motive in such an act is merely coarse and carnal has spoilt the perfection of it and has imported into it the taint of sin: " The man has lost," such is the delicate expression of this exquisite writer, " all sense of the personality of his wife." He might as well be a mere animal and miss the meaning of human love. Holcot has some delicious pages wherein he speaks of the ideals of married life, the freshness, the restraint of them, the frail nature of this human love, its perfume so easily lost, its chaste bloom so quickly spoiled. Particularly he laments the decay of these ideals in the England of his day. It is almost the mysticism of human love that he speaks of, in crisp sentences too narrow for their lyrical ideas, of marriage as a perfect act in the choice of a true partner, and the endurance of mutual reverence and respect. Before becoming a friar he had been a judge in the King's Court, and perhaps had seen the sordid side of married life very much in evidence. He was old when he was writing his commentary, and he seems to be shaking his head over the new generation: " Amongst us," he says (lect. lxxii., fol. xc.), " whether girls be fair or ugly is of no consequence, for the first consideration nowadays is always what their dowry may be.[1] Whence Marcia, the younger daughter of Cato, when she was asked why she had not married again, made answer: ' I have not found,' quoth she, ' a man who loved more what I was than what I had.' Best, then, and most healthy, is the wedding which avarice has not motived nor

---

[1] For examples of this *cf.* Abram, *Social England in the Fifteenth Century*, London, 1909, p. 172, etc.

lust inflamed, but the hope of children lured, for else it cannot last long without distress."

" Choose a good woman," says the author of *De Eruditione Principum*, " not the daughter of a usurer, and let her be your equal in age and in good looks " (Bk. V., cap. 27). Her consent of course is necessary (*ibid.*, p. 60) for the marriage to be valid. There still survives in the Vatican a series of sonnets labelled the *Accomplished Damsel of Florence*, the lament of a girl constrained to marry against her will. This pathetic protest shows us the exceptional nature of her condition, for it was this precisely that moved her to her tears :

> " Delivered I am to fear and only grief,
> Whiles every other maid in joyance dwells,
> For as my father is with me displeased,
> In durance sore he maketh me to bide,
> Having nor will nor wish so to be eased
> Who fain would give me, an unwilling bride ·
> So of all pleasure is my life disseized,
> And e'en of flower and leaf delight denied."
>
> (Del Lungo, *Women of Florence*, p. 26.)

The lives of some of the unmarried women of the period show that sometimes, at any rate, the happiness, or at least content, of a woman's life could be achieved even in the single state. From Messer Donato Velluti's autobiographical manuscript of the fourteenth century we can gather, in its delightful and gossiping pageant of Florentine worthies, the story of two such lives : " Cilia and Gherardina never married. For a great while they remained maids in the world hoping to have husbands, but when they lost all hope they became sisters of San Spirito. They earned much money, more indeed than sufficed for their support, by winding wool, and their brothers did never need to keep a servant. They were exceedingly kind of heart and great talkers. They died in that same pestilence of 1348, being both forty years of age or more." It is a peaceful, quiet picture, the long wait (not so long if they died only in their forties), the half-conventual life, the kindness, the chatter, the home attended to, the equal end.

But peacefulness cannot be said to be the dominant note of women's lives as we find them in the Middle Ages. The sweep of war, of business, of arts and crafts,[1] of home economies, drove women as much as men into the full stream of activity. Abbesses are summoned to send and even lead their troops, to attend Parliament, to vote taxes to the king—though it does not appear that the summons was ever obeyed in person. Chaucer's Prioress, for all her tenderness of heart, could hardly be called a recluse. The *Ancren Riwle* does not give us the impression of absolute isolation; the convent as much as mart or smithy was the centre of local gossip; news somehow penetrated to the cloister and thence spread over the country-side.

Even the proverb " man proposes, woman disposes," quoted by Francho Sacchetti as already old in his day (1335-1408—he was thrice married), is not altogether a sign of quietness (Del Lungo, p. 52). It betrays that the woman was not regarded as a mere cipher in the home. Despite the doctrine of St Thomas of woman's subjection we find that actually she exercised considerable power in the conduct of the home in her husband's absence, and even traded on her own account (Abram, *Social England*, pp. 131-146). Domestic records that have survived —the Paston and Stonor Letters in England, the Florentine Letters, which Del Lungo has given at considerable length— show the wife to have been a joint ruler with her husband of the goods of the home. A protest may reach us occasionally, as in the famous three sonnets of the Vatican Codex, deploring the sacrifice of female life to the tyrannies of the home, but there are no less frequently in comic mediæval literature the jests of writers protesting humorously against the petticoat government of the world. It is not easy to feel sure which represents in fact the ways of the mediæval world.

That women could assert themselves on occasion despite their theoretic subjection appears even in ecclesiastical records.

---

[1] *Cf.* Abram, *loc. cit.* ; Cutts, *Scenes and Characters of the Middle Ages*, London, 1922, p. 419; *Archæologia*, xxix., pp. 348-361; E. G. Roper, *Select Passages illustrating Florentine Life in the Thirteenth and Fourteenth Centuries* (1920), and *Select Extracts illustrating Florentine Life in the Fifteenth Century* (1920).

The Memoranda Rolls of Bishop Dalderby of Lincoln, in 1311, record an injunction to the rural dean to make inquiry into a dispute disturbing the peace of the parish of Grayingham, in the county of Lincoln, the origin of which appears to have been a habit of the women of the parish of changing their seats in the course of divine worship, and, " the reins of their modesty being relaxed," seating themselves among the men in a higher part of the church (*Notes on Deanery of Corringham*, by Rev. C. Moor, 1897). Again the comic writings of the time, like all comic writings, make great sport of the wife's dominance. The henpecked husband is a perennial feature in farce, however ancient and however modern. The English miracle plays, for example, can be quoted as representing at least one popular view of contemporary life. It is not fair to build a theory on a joke, yet even a joke must be recognizable to be a joke at all. The Noah in the Chester Plays (*English Miracle Plays*, ed. A. W. Pollard, Oxford, 1914) gives ample rein to the comic representation of woman's place in the home in the bandying of wits between the patriarch and his wife over the threatening prophecy of the Deluge and the importance of building the Ark. There is very little suggestion of any subjection on her part, and her criticisms of his work, its futility, and the vain dread of the coming flood, are couched in language as full of the equality of their status as might be found in the most emancipated age of women's rights. Her gossips join with her in jeering at the builders, her unbelief is shared and mightily expressed by them. The wives of Noah's three sons are little less in evidence, though not quite so outspoken as their mother-in-law. Even when the Deluge comes she will not believe in its reality, and when the waters are submerging all her world she is still too self-opinionated, and too faithful to her gossips and her own way, to want to desert either one or other even to save her life. Noah, however, at last loses patience, and sends one of the sons to carry the mother struggling and screaming into the Ark—no doubt to the vast amusement of the English crowd, which must always have been entertained by this broad humour of the popular farce. Noah's comment on the situation is characteristic :

" Lorde, that wemen be crabbed aye,
And none are meke, I dare well saye,
This is well seene by me to-daye,
    In witnesse of you ichone.
Goodwiffe, lett be all this beare,
That thou maiste in this place heare ;
For all the wene that thou arte maister,
And so thou arte, by Sante John."

That is fifteenth-century judgment of woman's position in the home on the lips of a man in a coarse farce. In the thirteenth century a friar spoke more politely, and perhaps more accurately, when he described the home-coming of the bride after marriage : " And afterward, when all this is done, he bringeth her to the privities of his chamber, and maketh her fellow at bed and at board. And then he maketh her lady of his money, and of his house, and meinie [household]. And then he is no less diligent and careful for her than he is for himself : and specially lovingly he adviseth her if she do amiss, and taketh good heed to keep her well, and taketh heed of her bearing and going, of her speaking and looking, of her passing and ayencoming, out and home " (Bartholomaeus Anglicus,[1] *Mediæval Lore* (The King's Classics), p. 57).

Of course the character of women was impugned in the Middle Ages, as it always has been. The same thirteenth-century friar, for example, speaks thus of her : " And for a woman is more meeker than a man, she weepeth sooner. And is more envious, and more laughing, and loving, and the malice of the soul is more in a woman than in a man. And she is of feeble kind, and she maketh more lesings, and is more shamefast, and more slow in working and in moving than is a man " (p. 52).

Humbert de Romans, fifty years later, speaks of the mixture of heroism and frailty in women, their combination, above men so he thought, of sensuality and spirituality : " Some," he adds, " are of such silly simplicity that they are easily moved by

---

[1] Bartholomaeus Anglicus, a Franciscan friar, flourished about 1230 to 1250.

Goliards and Truands and other beggars to give so generously as to destroy their homes to the hurt of husband and children : whereas had they prudence they would devote themselves in preference to the comfort of the home." Others he found so quarrelsome as to disturb sometimes their husband, sometimes their children or their neighbours or the parish priest or strangers ; others, so indevout in church that while the sermon was being preached they talked or said their prayers out loud or genuflected to the shrines round the church or sprinkled themselves with holy water, " indeed every kind of piety would they indulge in except the more immediate one of going towards the pulpit to listen to the sermon " (Serm. xcix., *Ad mulieres pauperes in villulis*, p. 505).[1] He speaks too of enclosed and cloistered women of all sorts as being inclined to grow melancholy, so that they disturb and distress their companions and superiors and the officials of the house : " grown irritable like dogs who are chained up too much." Impatience, curiosity and sloth he considered to be their chief failings (Serm. xliv., *Ad mulieres religiosus quascunque*, p. 479 : *De modo prompte audiendi sermones*, Bk. II.). In the middle of the fourteenth century, Chaucer's Prioress is something of the type of woman thus described — sensitive, generous, impatient, an eager organizer :

> " She was so charitable and so piteous,
> She wolde wepe, if that she sawe a mous
> Caught in a trappe, if it were deed or bledde.
> Of smale houndes had she, that she fedde
> With rosted flesh, or milk and wastel brede.
> But sore weep she if oon of hem were deed,
> Of if men smoot it with a yerde smerte :
> And al was conscience and tendre herte."

At the end of the fourteenth century, Franco Sacchetti has the same tale : " What can we say now of the subtlety of feminine malice ? Their intelligence is more keen and more

---

[1] One curious fact of antiquarianism is that the few instances known in mediæval England of the payment of seat-rents or pew-dues are always by women.

quick than that of men, and they more often do and speak that which is evil." Then of course comes the contrast (essential to all novel-writers whose business it is to point the moral to the manners of the day) between the last generation and the new: " In other times they would have restrained their husbands but in these days they encourage them to fight for their factions and for this reason have they brought much evil into the world."

Is he thinking of the mother of Cacciaguida in the *Paradiso* of Dante? (Canto xv.) or of Picarda? (Canto iii.). Yet almost of that same generation Lorenzo dei Medici (1448-1492) could speak in terms of praise when he exclaimed on the death of his mother: " I have lost not only my mother but my one refuge from many of my troubles, a comfort in my labours, and one who saved me from many of those labours" (Del Lungo, p. 231); and later (1504-1641) Galileo's pathetic cry at the very end of his life thinking of his love-child Sister Celeste, who turned nun and died before him, shows the tenderness that is to be found late as well as early in the mediæval days: " Now hear I my beloved daughter calling continually to me " (p. 242).

It is as touching as that wonderful poem *Pearl*,[1] with its delicate family affection, its exquisite appreciation of childhood, its recognition of the power of girlhood to civilize and spiritualize and make virginal the dreams of men.

Women felt undoubtedly that in the society of those ages they were sometimes forgotten and pushed aside. There survives the piteous letter of a nun to Savonarola, speaking on behalf of the girls of Florence: " It seemeth unto them [maidens] that ye mostly urge that the men and boys should begin to reform and that ye give no care unto the women " (p. 237). It was only partly true, for Savonarola's letters to the Countess of Mirandola on prayer and the spiritual life are amongst his most charming and most human writings.

Truly ecclesiastics and poets do not usually, when they speak about women, have pleasant things to say. In the ironical

---

[1] Edited by G. G. Coulton, London, 1921.

ballad on the duplicity of women, verses of this type are the stock-in-trade:

> " That trust is none, as ye may seen,
> In nothing, nor no steadfastness
> Except in women, thus I mean,
> Yet aye beware of doubleness."

Again this forensic and judicial curiosity of Holcot (*In Proverbia Salamonis*, lect. 5, fol. lxi.) displays the same spirit of seeing only a woman's evil, not her good : " This is the whole end and apparatus of womanhood, that it should be garrulous and wandering, impatient of quiet, not wishing to stay at home. The Gloss says that it is a matter of astonishment that women, who have fewer teeth than men (and teeth are needed for talk), should yet have, not less to say than men, but a great deal more. But the reason of this may well be because women have much more superfluous humidity than men, for it is of the nature of the tongue, or of anything indeed that moves at all, that it should move the easier and the quicker in humid than in dry surroundings : the confirmation of this is to be found in the fish's tail, which moves considerably quicker in water than in dry air."

" Woman," it is the measured judgment of Aquinas, " was created as a helpmate for man, not indeed as a helpmate in other works, as some maintain, since man can be more efficiently helped by other men in other works, but as a helpmate in generation " (*Summa Theologica*, i. 92, 1).

Against all this was raised a famous protest : " I reflected why men are so unanimous in attributing wickedness to women. I examined my own life and those of other women to learn why we should be worse than men, since we also were created by God. I was sitting ashamed with bowed head and eyes blinded with tears, resting my chin on my hands in my elbow-chair, when a dazzling beam of light flashed before me which came not from the sun, for it was late in the evening. I glanced up and saw standing before me three female figures, wearing crowns of gold and with radiant countenances. I crossed myself. Whereupon one of the three addressed me : ' Fear not, dear daughter, for we will counsel and help thee. The aphorisms of philosophers are not articles of faith but simply the mists of error and self-deception.' " Fame, Prudence and Justice were the three in golden crowns, and they ordered the writer to build a city, under the supervision of Reason, the noblest and best gift of God to men. Then are given one by one the names of women who have excelled in various arts and aims, and have merited well of the human race : Queen Ceres, who taught to men the art of agriculture ; Isis, who taught the cultivation of plants ; Arachne, whose gifts to men included the crafts of dyeing, weaving and spinning. From Damphule came the knowledge and care and breeding of silkworms. Then are led before us a vision of Fair Women who have been great : Dame Sarah, the wife of Abraham ; Penelope and Ruth ; and Saints Catharine, Margaret, Lucia and Dorothea ; and so the apologia for mediæval womanhood proceeds.

But the greatest apologia is not this book, but the author of it, not *Le Trésor de la Cité des Dames*, but Christina de Pisan herself (1364-1430).[1] She was the daughter of a distinguished Venetian, Thomas, who came to Paris as astrologer to the King of France. At the age of fifteen she was married to Etienne Castel of Picardy ; then came on her a series of misfortunes. The King, Charles the Wise, died, and her father at once was removed from his position at Court, and finding no other patron, and growing despondent and bitter, became sick and querulous, and died in much distress. Then Etienne died, leaving her, at the age of twenty-six, a widow with two children, and a third soon came to add to her difficulties, and yet to afford some consolation to her. Driven by her poverty to look for a means of livelihood she took to writing books, which soon became popular in the royal circle and beyond it. Charles VI. allowed her a pension and made her a guest at his Court ; for his queen, Isabella of Bavaria, Christina wrote some of her best-known works. Philip of Burgundy was also a patron of hers. Her chief works are *Les Cent Histoires de Troye*, *Le Chemin de Long Estude*, *La Mutacion de Fortune*, and the book from the introduction

---

[1] Or 1363-1428 : *cf.* Lanson, *Histoire de la littérature française*, Paris, 1903, pp. 162-164.

of which we have already quoted—*Le Trésor de la Cité des Dames*. She disallows the claim of the *Romance of the Rose* to give a fair or just treatment to her sex; and attacks as untrue the anti-feminist clerks, led by John de Meung[1] who left no woman's name pure in his romance. In the pages of the *Trésor* she both recalls the past glories of her sex and salutes as already famous the coming glory of Joan of Arc.

Much earlier than Christina was Marie de France, knowing not only Latin and French (as did Christina, who also from her father had learned Italian) but English (*E.H.R.*, xxv., p. 303; xxvi., p. 317). From her we have, amongst other writings, the legend of *Guigemar*, the young knight who scorns love and chases the white doe, which turns on him at the end of the long pursuit and strikes and wounds him; and on whom the fairy spell was cast: "Vassal, none shall heal thee till thou canst meet a woman willing to suffer for thee, and for whom even worse things than she for thee shalt thou suffer." The legend tells of the many adventures of the youthful knight, and at last of his meeting with this devoted lover, who suffers for him and for whom in turn he suffers (Bedier, *Histoire de la littérature française*, 1923, p. 23, etc.). There is a tone of high and unselfish love in this, different from and superior to the very much later and more passionate romances, that became in the end emptied of all beauty and delicacy, turning coarse and grossly sensual. But this romance of youthful manhood sung by a woman just at the beginning—or even before the beginning—of the thirteenth century shows us the daintiness of women's minds under the influence of the literary movement of Eleanor of Aquitaine, whose queenly patronage of letters surpassed the three great queens of English literary history at least in this, that better than they she herself appreciated the charm of literature. Even the courtly poems that followed on her patronage sang of love disciplined and chastened, " not drunk with the cup which had poisoned Tristan." It is usually

---

[1] *Romance of the Rose*, F. S. Ellis, 1900. Compare *The Myroure of Oure Ladye*, E.E.T.S., 1873; *The Garmond of Gude Ladies*, Medieval Scottish Poetry, 1891; particularly *De la littérature didactique du moyen âge s'addressant spécialement aux femmes*, by Alice Heutsch, Cahors, 1903.

round a girl that the love story turns, not the illegitimate passion of the later fourteenth-century's praise, but the "delicate, secret and subtil" love of a maiden.

Again in the thirteenth century, besides the *Romance of the Countess of Vergi*, by the Duchess of Lorraine, there were a number of literary women who wrote what seemed to their generation masterpieces, and which were generously praised. It is difficult to find any trace of literary jealousy of men against women; or any astonishment that women should take to letters; or any pulpit attacks on learned womanhood as a disgrace to sex.

It is, on the contrary, easy to prove the opposite, the very urging of education on women.[1] Let us quote from a sermon of Humbert de Romans to show how a friar felt towards this movement of literary womanhood, remembering that the composition was intended not so much as a sermon as an attempt to set before his preaching brethren such material concerning the audience as might help them to know what to say. He left them to find the precise lessons and exhortations to suit the occasion, being bent not so much on giving a plan as a preliminary reading from which their own plans might be evolved by themselves. The sermon is labelled: *For Girls or Maidens who are in the World* (Serm. xcvii., p. 504):

"Just as it is praiseworthy in Christ to preach to boys, so is it also an act of charity to instruct girls in the faith when the opportunity occurs, either in their schools or at their homes or wherever else they be. Note that these girls, especially if they be the daughters of the rich, ought especially to devote themselves to study, for to this purpose their parents have intended them. Hence they ought opportunely to know the Psalter or Hours of Our Lady or the Office of the Dead, or other prayers to God, and so be more fitted for religious life should they wish to join it later, or more fitted for the study of Sacred Scripture, like Paula and Eustachia and others who remained unwedded, and who because of their devotion to books became deeply versed in sacred letters. Of this knowledge you have an example

---

[1] As an example of the ideal woman of Norman times in England *cf.* R. B. Morgan, *Readings in English Social History*, 1923, p. 109.

in Blessed Agnes, who went to school, in Blessed Cecilia, Catharine, Lucy, Agatha, who were all learned, as their legends bear witness. Let them, therefore, not be solicitous about their clothes . . . let them beware of levity in dance or song or game . . . let them fear men. Let them take some good spiritual man to be their father whose counsel and teaching shall rule them. . . . Let them be at home with their parents and grandparents, not wander astray from their homes."

The author of the *De Eruditione Principum* has the same counsel to give (caps. 50-52). He too urges that the girls, particularly of noble families, whilst under charge of others by reason of their tender age, should be made to study letters and occupied always with some work. Humility, piety and meekness were to be instilled into them, as well as a love of silence, and chastity : " Chastity indeed is noble and its lack most vile." A comparison may fruitfully be made, thinks the author, when we watch the painter at work, who, busy on giving us the human flesh reproduced to life, first places white on the vellum and then over the white the other colours, for chastity is even so, the pure and radiant groundwork : only over it can the other virtues be laid to give us true to life the perfections of humanity. Superfluous food then is to be avoided and strong drink ; very salt dishes should equally be left alone, indeed anything that has been found to inflame the passions materially and so to place girls in a condition to surrender themselves to a straying thought of uncleanness or a desire begotten of the eyes. Unnecessary baths he classes among these dangerous troubles for womanhood. But the public hot bath, we know from a famous inquisition of Paris for taxation purposes, was indeed a common feature in mediæval life, though possibly almost as dangerous to morality as St Augustine found the baths of the Roman cities of his own day. In 1292 there were twenty-six public hot baths in Paris, constituting a very high proportion for the little high-walled Paris of that date.

Thus the picture we get of the woman in mediæval times shows us much the same type of woman as any age would give, were we to see it through the medium of sermons, novels

and poems. She took her place amongst her menfolk mainly
on her personal merits and her personal achievement. She was
inconstant, they said of her, in some degree full of coquetry,
susceptible to compliment, even clamorous of it, courting and
needing sympathy, imaginative, a prey to diseases which her
too vivid imagination conjured up for her, which were fed by
her idleness and her indulgence, and were only subterfuges to
solicit comfort that else might never have come :

> " And here we have a fault
> Especially to be found
> In these young maidens fair
> Which, if I could, I gladly would undo.
> Many there are who to divert themselves
> Or sometimes just for foolishness
> Have a desire to see
> How much they are beloved.
> And sometimes for disdain
> Of some slight passing word
> They heard and were displeased ;
> Sometimes because they would be left
> To do as pleaseth them :
> Feign that their sides do hurt,
> Or else their teeth,
> Or else their heads,
> Or else they nonsense talk.
> And some begin this play
> Intending soon to cease this foolish thing
> But having once begun
> Find that they must go on,
> Lest, if they cease, others may say,
> ' Behold she did but feign.' "

And so on. This was the satirical description given by Francesco
da Barberino [1] (and he comes almost at the beginning of our
period, 1264-1348), who shows us the Florentine girl, whom
Dante knew as Beatrice and Petrarch perhaps saw as Laura, and

---

[1] *Del reggimento e de costumi delle donne*, Rome, 1815.

who complained to Savonarola that he never enough denounced her and her sins.

But if Savonarola kept silent, everyone else cried out. There are denunciations in all mediæval literature of the evil effects of women upon mankind, of the unhappy snares they spread for the destruction of poor innocent men. The foolishness of the ugly ones who tried to be beautiful and of the beautiful ones who tried to enhance their beauty was cried out from many an altar step, the vagaries of fashion that changed hair from black to white and from white to gold and from gold to black again were described in almost every book of sermons that appeared during our period; it is hard to find a theologian, or a scriptural commentator, or a preacher, or a poet, who did not denounce these and similar practices, and describe instead the charm of natural beauty and " the untouched complexion and fragrance of the rose " (*De Eruditione Principum*, cap. 54). Nor was it only in moral treatises that the matter came up, for the sumptuary laws of all Christendom refer in legal form and under legal penalty to this wantonness of female fashion.

Yet against this picture of women vainly running in search of idle pleasure it is equally possible to find references at every turn which describe with equal bitterness the over-occupation of the woman with her home: " Note," says Humbert de Romans, " how some consent too much to usury, when such is their husband's trade, and are partners therefore in his guilt; and some take too much care of their children, loving them only carnally; and some are so occupied in the affairs of the home and other secular matters that they have little time for God. Unless it is under stress of poverty that they are driven to this labour, they commit sin when they do not find time for divine as well as human things " (Serm. xcvi., *Ad mulieres burgenses*, p. 504). This type of exhortation is almost as frequently to be met with, in the thirteenth, fourteenth and fifteenth centuries, as the other that seemed to make women out to be hardly doing anything else than waste their husbands' goods.

Now it is evident that we must take into consideration all

this material when we try to understand what was meant by the subjection of woman to man. The mediævalist was above all else a philosopher, a scientific and formal philosopher. For him the main deduction to be made by a Christian from the facts of revelation was that woman was created for man as his helpmate, particularly in generation and the building up of the home. It seemed to him that this was the intention of the Creator as it was expressed in the sacred books, and that man could not do otherwise than accept it. Woman, therefore, was made for man. Yet she had also her own soul to save, was an independent being, with her own rights and obligations, a perfect moral personality equally with a man. They were both working for a single purpose; from some points of view they could even be regarded as a single unit, since Christ had said they were " one flesh," and since the family was held to be the unit of the city, as Aquinas repeated from Aristotle, till it became a platitude in the schools.

Since a divine purpose, therefore, was made effective by the junction of man and woman there could be nothing evil in the marriage-act in itself; it would have taken place had sin never entered into the world. Yet once sin had entered, everything became spoilt by it, so that there was no act, however simple and legitimate, that might not easily develop into evil unless care were taken to avoid any other intention entering into the mind of the doer of it than the intention proper to the act. Since this particular action of husband and wife also appealed to man's lower nature and was pleasurable to it by a divine providential design, it required especial care to see that it was kept wholly free from sin. Perhaps not a few mediæval theologians ventured to think, to hold and to teach that it was almost impossible for the actors in this divinely appointed ceremony not in some measure to fail, yet since the heresy of Manicheism, which the Church was combating in Christendom up to the end of the fourteenth century, roundly asserted that the act was directly sinful in itself, theologians were very careful to state that this teaching of the Manicheans was unorthodox and untrue. The sacrament of marriage was everywhere affirmed to have been instituted by Christ, and therefore by God. This carried with it logically a divine approval of its necessary consequences.

Again, the subject of the " Espousals of the Virgin " is not infrequently met with in mediæval art, even in the early thirteenth century ; it increased in popularity, however, as the fourteenth and fifteenth centuries moved on. The position of her in the public cultus of the Church, though not so developed in the West as in the East, undoubtedly affected considerably the position of women in public estimation. The gap separating the attitude of paganism and Christianity to womanhood is too great for that to be ignored. Nor was it ignored. The mediæval writers themselves insisted on the point. When Chaucer speaks of her as " Thou glory of womanhood " he knew exactly what he meant by that ; so did the preachers when, in their sermons and anecdotes, they made allusion to her high place in the scheme of redemption as affecting the sex to which she belonged. The devotion of the Cistercians and of the North to " Our Lady " placed her at the apex of the chivalry of the twelfth and thirteenth centuries, and perhaps alone prevented the passionate and sentimental romanticism of the fourteenth and fifteenth centuries from growing worse than it did. It is indeed difficult not to exaggerate the importance of this devotion, rising to its height as it did in the midst of the boisterous and rude awakening to beauty which the eleventh and twelfth centuries developed and made sensitive. It is only necessary to look at the art of the whole of our period to see how what might so easily have been a terribly destructive force became sublimated into a power for good.

It would be impossible to leave the subject without alluding to one author whose treatise on the position of women is without parallel throughout this period : Pierre du Bois and his *De Recuperatione Sancte Terre*.[1] It is now too famous and original a treatise to require detailed exposition, for presumably no one interested in mediæval theories, social, economic, artistic or political, can have omitted to read it. It is difficult to say what effect it had, or whether it had any at all. Its ideas seem to have sprung out of a man's brain and to have died with him, to have

[1] Paris, 1891. Written about 1306.

been the single effort of an independent thinker without literary affinities or descendants. Not that du Bois is purely abstract and unrelated to his times. He was a man of consequence. He equally appreciated other writers; he speaks of hearing Brother Thomas of Aquino preach and calls him "most wise."[1] But his daring plea for the secularization of convents and their conversion into large girls' schools was almost unique in the Middle Ages.[2] A believer in education and in the widespread development of international thought, and in the power latent in womanhood to influence and reconstruct society, he wished to place the brutal world of his day, with its crusades in little or in great, with its huge dreams and violences, with its already dowdy chivalry and knightly graces, in a new atmosphere of polite and gracious learning.[3] He appreciated the Renaissance thus early in its thirteenth-century freshness, without as yet the splendours of the great names in art, while Chartres was still the summit of its aim, while the friars were in their first fervour, while Aristotle was still new enough to be criticized freely; and he wanted that delicate renaissance in its full blossom to be a popular feature of the world. Education alone was the means to effect such a transformation of the world, and not least the education of women. But his treatise must be read to be appreciated. It might almost be said that the book was born out of due season; that it could hardly have been understood when it was written. But there can be no question of its power, its sprightliness and its interest.

---

[1] P. 53. [2] Pp. 51-70. [3] Pp. 47, 58-68.

CHAPTER IV

SLAVERY

We have described the reign of law as the ideal social concept of the mediæval age. The social virtue most highly extolled was the virtue of justice. In the treatises and tracts on government the foremost place is given to it. It is also the excuse put forward for every rebellion, or act of tyranny, or public crime, by the perpetrators of them—whenever they did put forward an excuse. It is nearly always some injustice, real or feigned, that is referred to as provoking the deed of violence that followed.

Even liberty itself was then defended only in terms of justice. Liberty does not seem to have been sought after as an ideal in itself. Its mere name was then hardly a trumpet-call challenging the oppressor and rousing the oppressed; freedom did not of itself flame the imagination, or stir the blood. It was fought for, but not so much in its own name as in the name of the charter that guaranteed it. Men rallied to a charter always, more readily than to a demand for freedom. It is true that each charter was concerned with some gift of freedom; but the charter was always more sacred to the mediæval mind than the freedom it gave: for the charter was a contract, and its infringement an act of injustice.

The plain block of stone that covers the bones of the first Edward, to the left of the steps leading to the tomb of the Confessor in Westminster Abbey, in the western bay, north of the shrine, carries as his people's proudest tribute to his greatness (as the sixteenth century viewed it) the legend KEEP TROTH (*Pactum Serva*). Edward himself was not always careful to keep his own sworn promises. More than once he flagrantly broke his oath to his people. Yet he was a legalist. He did recognize in the society emerging from barbarism the need of law, and he was careful to apply to the Pope for a dispensation from his oaths, and did not merely ignore them or rely on his power in order to repudiate them. He stands then as an example of one of the finest types of that age, which knew not how to value freedom, but to whom law was sacred and could only be overridden by law, to whom justice was the sole ideal of social order, and for whom only out of justice could spring either liberty or equality. Not, however, that it would be right to suppose that freedom meant nothing to those minds : but it was not an end in itself for them. No one was urged to strive for freedom for the mere purpose of being free, but for the purpose of fulfilling a law. Even oppressed nations (in that age when nations were beginning to discover themselves to have independent life outside the womb of their legendary imperial mother) revolted on the plea of legality ; sought enfranchisement in virtue of an earlier positive law ; based their claims not on indefeasible natural rights but on a dated charter.

After the unrest of the dark ages, grants and decretals, forged or authentic, were considered essential to peace, truth and freedom. Without such a covering document there was no law in whose name a nation might stir, and, without a law, stir it would not. In the history of England, Magna Charta is a very simple example of this, particularly because it was only one of a series of charters of liberty wrested from the royal authority in its moments of military weakness. Perhaps it would be accurate and illuminating to speak of these rather as charters of liberties than of charters of liberty. It was for liberties rather than liberty that men would die.

In their demands on the king the baronage, headed by Cardinal Langton, were not moved by the doctrine of liberty that later ages attributed to them ; they had, however, a very determined doctrine about certain " liberties " which they were bent on securing for themselves. They were not interested in building a constitution but in bridling a king.

At the beginning of the charter it was expressly stated that " to all the freemen of our kingdom " were granted " all the liberties herein contained " : and the liberties contained in the charter were carefully circumscribed by the barons, as much against their lesser men as against the king.[1] They were thus

---

[1] McKechnie, *Magna Carta*, 1914; *cf.* in *Independent Review*, November 1904, Jenks, " The Myth of Magna Carta "—an extreme view, but interesting —and *Magna Carta Commemorative Essays*, edited by H. L. Malden, 1917.

careful to state at the outset that the charter meant no more than it said. History in England is a record of the ignoring of this provision. It was misunderstood and men became free : or perhaps it may be more fairly stated that the charter was greater than the men who framed it had intended it to be. They were looking for remedies and they found principles. Chiefly a manifesto of the baronial claims and a determination to destroy what irritated them, it was subsequently discovered to imply those vague aspirations moving through the minds of contemporary thinkers, whence eventually were to be unfolded the notions of nationality, of patriotism, of equality before the law, and of the rights of men as men, that destroyed in the end the feudalism of the baronage. Its reactionary clauses were forgotten ; its revolt against the centralized justice of Henry II. in the release of the barons from being tried by any others than their peers had but a passing success ; its faltering and uncertain recognition of the rights of under-tenants, of merchants and traders and villeins, was in the end most remembered, and prevailed. It was, however, undoubtedly a feudal document in intent, drawn up by the northern barons, placing the king under restraint set out in terms of feudal principle ; it was an elaboration of his coronation oath forced on a king who had broken it. It tied the king down ; yet it set the people free. Its social effects were immense. It was really a symptom of the beginning of the end of slavery.

We have made particular reference to Magna Charta because it illustrates in so clear a manner the almost entire absence of any general principle in favour of freedom in mediæval writings. There are hardly any protests raised by any writer of that period against the drudgery of the villein life, or the hardness of the unfree life. Not freedom, we repeat, but justice, not liberty but law, is the social ideal of that age.

"That city," writes Tolomeo de Lucca in the Second Book of *De Regimino Principum*, "is wont to be the most peaceful whose citizens most rarely meet and least remain within their walls, for by frequently meeting each other opportunities are furnished them for disputes and, in consequence, matter for sedition. Hence, according to the theory of Aristotle, it is better that the citizens should be kept busy outside their city than that they should for long at a time dwell within it " (Bk. II., chap. iii). How clearly here can we see that it was peaceful living rather than civic independence that was insisted on as the basis of communal happiness.

It is true that so far we have been considering political freedom rather than social freedom as the subject of these ideal hopes of the mediæval writers ; but the same principles are invoked when they speak of what we should call social slavery and social liberty. The same ideals of justice move before them. Freedom was indeed accepted as an essential condition for the will and it was never put in question that man should have freedom of the will in his power of choice : nor was that freedom merely admitted, it was praised. It was freedom that in the consideration of that time lifted man above the beast. Man was free because he had reason ; reason was a necessary condition for freedom. Choice was only possible because it had been preceded by ratiocination, or at least by an act of the intellect understanding what it was doing. To surrender this freedom of the will would be to surrender one's manhood. It must be preserved at all hazard. Even the omnipotence of God did not constrain the will. Indeed that was the marvellous power of God that He could move the will from within so delicately and yet so absolutely as to move it to act and yet not spoil the freedom of that action. Sin was admitted on all hands to fetter freedom. The Gospel asserted it. Life proved it. " By sinning," said Aquinas in his *Summa Theologica*, " man departs from the order of reason and consequently falls away from the dignity of his manhood, in so far as he is naturally free and exists for himself, and he falls into the slavish state of the beasts, by being disposed of according as he is useful to others " (II. ii. 64, 2, ad 3 m).

Not only was the Gospel teaching accepted, therefore, that all sin was slavery, but it was even asserted that all slavery was due to sin, that the institution of slavery was justifiable because of the entrance of sin into the world, that the necessity for slavery had its origin in the fall of man. To the mediæval theologian, the social concepts of the early Church, which had

been stated in terms of Stoic philosophy, were received as the
oracles of faith, and therefore accepted as final truths. According to that early teaching, in the primitive innocence of man,
fresh from God's hands, the exercise of reason would have
sufficed to enable each to do what was wise; sin disturbed
this due exercise of reason, drove man out of his paradise, and
obscured his prudence of judgment. Some, however, of the
children of men were to be found less affected by sin than
others in the prudence of their judgment; to these, it seemed,
the race of man had turned in all ages for its governance and
its rule.

Further, it was argued that man was by nature destined for
life in community. His birth found him defenceless against
cold and hunger. He could not fend for himself. Unattended
he would die. His instincts, it was then thought, owed their
lack of swiftness and sureness to the frailty of his own nature
which did not provide him with the same unerring instinct
as to what was for his good as had been given to the beast;
Nature herself (or God as the Creator and Providence) did not
make man so clever and so unerring, because she never intended
him to be obliged to depend on his own instincts. She meant
him to live with others, and to learn and be directed by their
experience. His very power of speech, native and primitive,
showed again how Nature, while denying him instincts that his
social surroundings would render unnecessary, had endowed
him with gifts that these same social surroundings would
require.

But social life in a sinful world cried out for a ruler. Man
must live with his fellows, but in his commerce with his fellows
there must be perpetual and nice adjustment between him and
them if peace was to be established and to endure. Perfect right
reason could have ensured this, guiding each in his choice of
what to do or to leave undone, but perfect right reason had
been overthrown by sin's entry and " all our woe." Man, therefore, could not be restrained by himself—man in the mass, most
men : he needed restraint from outside ; he needed a king. Sin
begat government and put an end to general freedom.

Of course the better men are, the more freedom can you

give them, but it would be foolish to suppose that all men are capable of freedom. In *De Regimine Principum*—attributed in part to Aquinas and in part to Tolomeo de Lucca—it is noted (Bk. I., cap. 4) from Sallust, that after the expulsion of the Tarquins " it is incredible to remember how quickly, once it had obtained its freedom, the Roman city grew to greatness." But history shows, continues the author, how short a time this freedom lasted or its glory, indeed how short a time it could last. Gradually the republic degenerated till it begot tyrants again, for " most often the rule of many leads to tyranny." That was the sad part of all human government—it failed. Whatever form of it you chose to set up, you were bound to have to alter ; yet to do away with it altogether was to produce far worse evils. If you decided to have a single ruler, you would find him assuredly coveting the properties of his subjects ; if you decided to have the rule of many, you would find that you had opened wide the door to dissensions, and had destroyed peace (cap. 5). This argument seems at first as though it might lead to cynicism : not at all, it leads to optimism, for the mediæval mind loved or longed for peace. Kings will rob you, but republics will disturb you with never-ending sedition, and since you value peace more than property you will put up with robbery as the price of peace.

Is social life then so hopeless, that you can set up no remedy to restrain the rapacity of kings? But yes, means can be found to diminish that rapacity, not, however, to prevent it. Should it prove too hard even to restrain, then as the price of peace tyranny should be borne with patience. Tyrannicide failed to find support, says the author of *De Regimine Principum*, in the New Testament, though the Old Testament seemed to allow it. No, government is a sad necessity introduced by sin, as such it cannot be avoided.

But the mediæval theorist did not disdain liberty as a political ideal ; he was merely uncertain as to where it could be realized. He was often almost a materialist in his interpretation of the capacity of certain races for freedom, and in his attribution of this capacity to climate or blood. In the Second Book of the *De Regimine Principum*, where the various causes of slavery are put forward, we are told of some countries which have never had capacity for self-government : " The size of their territory and its position under the stars so mould the people of a region that we see some provinces fit for freedom and some fit for slavery; hence J. Celsus and Amonius, who have written the *Gesta Francorum et Germanorum*, ascribe to these peoples the very ways and manners that we see them still to possess " (Bk. II., cap. 9).

This was, of course, more true of individuals than of nations. Without falling into the mistake of Aristotle—who seemed to make the soul of the slave of another kind than the soul of the freeman—the mediæval theorists, from first to last, insisted on the so-evident experience of mankind that some men " cannot follow reason and are fitly slaves, and this is called a slavery by natural right " (cap. 10); "others are slaves by the fortunes of war, and this is called slavery by a legal right, for though they may have fine intelligences yet the chance of war has made them slaves, hence the phrase ' legal right ' is used of their slavery."

In his *Commentary on the Politics*, St Thomas quotes the arguments of Aristotle in favour of slavery, or at least in justification of slavery, without a protest. For example note this : " In some cases the distinction between freedom and slavery is not based on nature but on law; but in others it is based on nature, and for these people slavery is of advantage both to the one who serves and to the one who rules, and it is also just " (*Politics*, Bk. I., lect. iv., p. 380 ; Parma, 1866, vol. iv.). Albertus Magnus also passes these arguments without criticism; nor had any mediævalist, late or early, any desire to deny that slavery was part of human conditions and was required for the steady life of mankind. It was as much a feature of social life as the machinery of government was a feature of political life. A master was as necessary to society as a king.

" If we refer lordship to the state of primitive innocence, it was then not despotic but politic, for then lordship did not rest on servitude but on pre-eminence, and on the free submission of each to be governed and disposed of according to his capacity, influencing and being influenced according to the nature of each. Hence amongst the wise and great—as, for example, amongst the Romans—a politic government after Nature's fashion was found to work best; yet, since 'the perverse are hard to be corrected and the number of fools is infinite' (*Eccles*. i. 15), in corrupt nature the rule of kings is most fruitful" (*De Reg. Princip.*, Bk. II., cap. 9).

That slavery really meant slavery in all essentials, and not mere subordination of a worker to his master, seems clear enough from other passages of St Thomas' writings: " A power is called despotic whereby a man rules his slaves who have not the right to resist in any way the orders of the one who commands them, since they have nothing of their own. But that power is called politic and royal by which a man rules over free subjects who, though indeed subject to the government of the ruler, have nevertheless something of their own, by reason of which they can resist the orders of him who commands " (*Summa Theologica*, i. 81, 3, ad 1 m; English translation, p. 133).

Again we find in the *De Regimine Principum*, in the *Commentary on the Politics*, and in other of Aquinas' writings, a definite understanding of the slave as someone who is not wholly his own. Morally, religiously, it is undoubted that no mediæval theorist ever allowed the slave to lie absolutely under his lord's command, but economically there seemed in theory to be no way in which he was free. The free man is defined as *sui causa*, the slave as *id quod est alterius* (cf. *Reg. Princ.*, Bk. I., cap. 1): " Hence, if the multitude of free men are directed by their ruler to the common good of the multitude, it will be a good and just rule such as becomes freemen."

On the one hand, throughout the early Middle Ages there is the conception of a monarch who rules absolutely: " There is a difference between the lesser officials and the princes, for the rulers of a democracy are obliged by the law, nor can they exceed the law in the prosecution of justice; this is not true of kings and other princely monarchs, for in their bosoms are the laws to be found to suit each case; for the law is held to be the will of the prince, as the right of nations lays down. But of the rulers of a polity this is not so admitted, for they do not dare to introduce anything beyond the written law " (*De Reg.*

Princ., Bk. IV., cap. 1); and similarly the existence of the slave in domestic life is defended on the ground that he is required for the good of society : " The distinction of possessions and slavery were not introduced by nature but devised by human reason for the benefit of human life" (*Summa Theologica*, I. ii. 94, 5, ad 3 m).

On the other hand a great deal is to be found in favour of the elective system and of equality as general principles of social life. In his *Chronicle*, under date of 1199, Matthew Paris gives a reported conversation of Archbishop Hubert explaining why he had proposed John as king to the barons and people assembled for his coronation, and why he had preceded his proposal by saying : " None hath succession to this kingdom, unless, after invoking the grace of the Holy Spirit, he be unanimously elected by the whole of the kingdom " (*universitas regni*—a phrase and idea typical of that time). The Archbishop said afterwards " that instinctively he felt evils were about to come on them and lest a free rein should be given the king he had publicly notified to him that he succeeded to the crown not by hereditary succession but by election " (*Chron. Majora*, Rolls. Ser., ii., p. 455).

Similarly the author of the later part of the *De Regimine Principum*, at the end of the next century, approves of St Augustine's praise of the Roman Patricians " who had advised the state with unpaid counsel, setting aside avarice through which, either for the sake of rule or lust or crime, states came to ruin " (Bk. III., cap. 5) : he commends the " civil gentleness " of the Romans who " extended their rule not by calling themselves masters but friends and allies " (cap. 7) ; he is in favour of voting for the city's rulers " as is to-day the custom in the democracy of Tuscany " (Bk. IV., cap. 13), and is against hereditary princedoms " though now observed in every part of Italy." These points had also, he notes, been approved by Hyppodamus, the criticisms of whom, by Aristotle, he did not accept. Indeed, in chapter fifteen he lays down the proposition that " in every business of the state an equality should be observed in regard to every citizen in his burdens and in his honours." However, no one who is unwillingly poor should be elected judge or mayor, for, since nature abhors a vacuum, and since man's nature craves for wealth, and since none of nature's cravings are without purpose, " he will seek wealth and become corrupted." Only those poor should be elected to places of honour whose poverty, " like that of Fabricius or of Christ," was tranquil and deliberate.

So a double tendency is noted as appearing already in the thirteenth century : to accept slavery as an essential condition of social life, and yet at the same time to exalt the power of election, to insist upon the essential equality of all men, and even to bless those who set free their slaves. The formularies for the manumission of slaves given by Marculfus [1] and others do not, however, as we should perhaps expect, make any reference to the freeing of them as pleasing to God, or as beneficial to the soul of him who set his slaves free.

One point there is that must be noted in speaking of slaves and their manumission, and that is the ambiguous use of the word *servus* in Latin. Can it always be translated *slave?* At the end of the fourteenth century and the beginning of the fifteenth century St Antonino, the famous archbishop of Florence, refers to this ambiguity in his *Summa Moralis* (Verona, 1740, pars iii., tit. 3, p. 197) : " The word *servus* is used chiefly in three ways : first, in a large sense of one who is in subjection in any way to some lordship or soke. . . . Secondly, one is said to be a *servus* on account of some special obligation to serve another in something. Thirdly, one is called *servus* properly and strictly who is not of his own, but is of a servile condition. It is of this servitude that we now speak." The next pages of the *Summa Moralis* are thereupon occupied with long and extremely detailed discussion as to the rights of masters over those under them who are of servile condition : their rights of marriage, of child-bearing, the lord's right to separate husband and wife, and so forth.

At the beginning of our period each country in Christendom was covered with a network of social classes or conditions associated with land-tenure of an intensely complicated and

---

[1] *Formularum Libri Duo*, Migne, *P.L.*, tom. lxxxvii. pp. 698-954. Compare with this Morgan's *Readings in English Social History*, p. 118.

exceedingly varied nature. In Anglo-Saxon law, in Norman law, we read of all sorts of serfdom or degrees of unfree status: again in France, in the great dukedoms that were held of the French king or the Emperor, in the principalities and free cities of Italy and the Germanies, in the kingdoms of Spain and the Two Sicilies, there were still other modes of tenure, grades, classes and castes. The meaning of the word *servus*, covering so many of these, was, therefore, indeed ambiguous. But, since law tends to extend ever wider its organization, and to compress under a single denominator every variety of condition and status, the process of law-making, characteristic of the twelfth and thirteenth centuries under princes such as Henry II. and Edward I. of England, Louis IX. of France, Alphonse of Castile, and later still the Emperor Charles IV., gradually abolished these complicated gradations of tenure and reduced serfdom everywhere, as far as possible, to a uniform servile condition.

Out of this welter then of unfreedom of every description was therefore drastically evolved one servile state, the simple *servus*, the *villein* as he was termed in England. In the famous *Coutumes de Beauvaisis*, redacted at the end of the thirteenth century by Philippe de Beaumanoir, we find but one class of serfs referred to. In Germany, the unfree in the towns seem in the thirteenth century to have grouped themselves into the *Einungen* or *Inungen*, and to have attempted to capture the municipal government. To many groups included under the generic term this levelling came as a great boon ; the excessive abuse of servitude had now become obsolete, the older tyrannies and petty exactions were being surrendered or becoming reduced. But this levelling process which reduced all to one uniform grade resulted in those who, in the passage of time, had all but acquired their freedom, or had advanced so close to the border-line as to be at times even classed among the free, finding themselves pushed back into the ranks from which they were about to escape and herded again among those from whom, by usage, they had come to consider themselves wholly apart.

The abolition of the varieties of unfreedom, while it raised the lower ranks to a higher standard, called attention to those who were imperceptibly escaping from servitude altogether. Legally villeins were now all of one class; but simultaneously each lord began suddenly to discover an immense importance in ascertaining who exactly of his tenants were free and who were unfree. His records became of great value to him, for they held the proof of the nature of each man's tenure. They began everywhere to be carefully scrutinized by the lords, and everywhere to be burned by the peasants.

With the improvement in the conditions of the unfree, the number of manumissions decrease. The worse the conditions of slavery the more will humane people be impelled to liberate the slave, the better the conditions the more easily will humane people tolerate the continued existence of the institution. That, speaking broadly, is the history of freedom in Christendom in the fourteenth and fifteenth centuries.

Certainly, in many respects the life of the serf was hard. At the opening of our period, we may take from *Aucassin and Nicolete*—that charming story so fragrant and so unwise—the complaint of the runaway slave as not unfairly describing the misfortunes of his lot: "I was hireling to a rich villein and drove his plough; for oxen had he. But three days since came on me great misadventure, whereby I lost the best of mine oxen—Roger—the best of my team. Him go I seeking, and have neither eaten nor drunken these three days, nor may I go to the town, lest they cast me into prison, seeing that I have not wherewithal to pay. Out of all the wealth of the world have I no more than you see on my body. A poor mother bare me, that had no more but one wretched bed; this have they taken from under her, and she lies in the very straw. This ails me more than my own case, for wealth comes and goes; if now I have lost, another tide will I gain, and will pay for mine ox whenas I may, never for that will I weep" (ed. by Andrew Lang, London, 1905, p. 56).

Again, even more decisively is the same view of the poverty and hardships of the life expressed in the *Mediæval Lore of Bartholomew the Englishman* (The King's Classics, 1905), written about 1250. This Franciscan author defines for us the conditions of the serf; and we cannot but note how little moved he is by his own recital to any sympathy for the slave. He makes no complaints against the slave's lot: "Some servants," he writes (p. 59), "be bond and born in bondage, and such have many pains by law, for they may not sell nor give away their own good and cattle, nother make contracts, nother take office of dignity, nother bear witness without leave of their lords. Wherefore though they be not in childhood, they be oft punished with pains of childhood. Other servants there be, the which being taken with strangers and aliens and with enemies be bought and sold, and held low under the yoke of thraldom. The third manner of servants be bound freely by their own good will, and serve for reward and for hire. And these commonly be called Famuli."

Just before this (p. 54) he had written: "A servant woman is ordained to learn the wife's rule, and is put to office and work of travail, toiling and slubbering. And is fed with gross meat and simple, and is clothed with clothes, and kept low under the yoke of thraldom and serfage; and if she conceive a child, it is thrall or it be born, and is taken from the mother's womb to serfage. Also if a serving woman be of bond condition, she is not suffered to take a husband at her own will; and he that weddeth her, if he be free afore, he is made bond after the contract. A bond servant woman is bought and sold like a beast. And if a bond servant man or woman be made free, and afterwards be unkind (ungrateful), he shall be called and brought again into charge of bondage and of thraldom. Also a bond servant suffereth many wrongs, and is beat with rods, and constrained and held low with diverse and contrary charges and travails among wretchedness and woe. Unneth he is suffered to rest or to take breath. And therefore among all wretchedness and woe the condition of bondage and thraldom is most wretched. It is one property of bond serving women, and of them that be of bond condition, to grudge and to be rebel and unbuxom to their lords and ladies, as saith Rabanus. And when they be not held low with dread, their hearts swell, and wax stout and proud, against the commandments of their sovereigns. Dread maketh bond men and women meek and low, and goodly love maketh them proud and stout and despiteful."

In the fourteenth century quotations could be paralleled from the mass of literature that surrounds the rising of the people which was universal throughout Western Europe. The horrors of the Jacquerie in France (1358), of the Ciompi in Florence (1378), and the Peasant Revolt in England (1381), are symptoms of that common distress which embittered the hearts of the poorer sort and drove them to desperation. Nor did their troubles end with the improved conditions that followed.

From St Antonino to St Thomas, in the pages of every writer who mentions contemporary social conditions, we may read of the hardships and the lack of freedom of the lowest classes of the nation. In *The Shepherds' Play* (*The Towneley Plays*, ed. by A. W. Pollard, E.E.T.S., 1897) is put into the mouth of the shepherds themselves the story of the "wretchedness and woe of the bond life," particularly the lack of economic freedom :

Shepherd 2—

    Bot we sely shepardes/that walkeys on the moore,
    In fayth we are nere handys/outt of the doore ;
    No wonder as it standys/if we be poore,
    For the tylthe of our landys/lyys fallow as the floore,
        As ye ken
    We ar so hamyd,
    For-taxed and ramyd,
    We ar mayde hand tamyd,
        With thyse gentlery men.

Shepherd 3—

    Thus they refe us oure rest/oure lady theym wary !
    These men that are lord fest/they cause the ploghe tary.
    That men say is for the best/we fynde it contrary ;
    Thus ar husbandys opprest/in pointe to myscary,
        On lyfe.

Thus hold thay us hunder
Thus thay bryng us in blonder ;
It were greate wonder
    And ever shuld we thryfe.

Shepherd 4—

For may he gett a paynt slefe/or a broche now on dayes,
Wo is hym that hym grefe/or onys agane says !
Dar noman hym reprefe/what mastry he mays
And yit may noman life/oone word that he says,
    No letter.
He can make purveance,
With boste and bragance,
And alle is thrugh mantenance
    Of men that are gretter.

Shepherd 5—

Ther shall come a swane/as prowde as a po,
He must borow my wane/my ploghe also,
Then I am full fane/to graunt or he go.
This lyf we in payne/Anger and wo,
    By nyght and day ;
He must have if he langyd,
If I shuld forgang it,
I were better be hangyd
    Then oones say hym nay.

And so it runs on, the long tale of bitter complaint. It is perhaps to be noted, however, that it was one of the wealthier guilds that staged the play with its lamenting cry, and this may show in the part of the town worker, even of the more prosperous sort, some sense of compassion for, or, at least, interest in, the lot of the agricultural worker in his unfree condition. Indeed, it cannot be too often emphasized that the moral writers of the mediæval period never cease to insist on the basic equality of every human soul. However much practice might fail to rise to the level of theory, the theory was plain enough. The *De Eruditione Principum* remarks that " before the poor man does homage to knight or prince he is to be remembered as his Christian brother; nor does homage destroy this brotherhood, but rather draws tighter the bond. The relationship between lord and subject should be one of faithfulness " (chap. iii., *cf*. chap. iv.).

The extreme view of the position of the serf or villein can be read in the quaint *Dialogues de Scaccario*, dating from the twenty-third year of Henry II., where serfs are described as " those who are not free to leave the condition of their state against the will of their lords " (Stubbs, *Select Charters*, p. 202), and this is expressly declared to be the legal theory of their condition : " they may not only be transferred from one place to another by their lords but can also be lawfully sold and alienated from their holding [*distrahuntur*]" (*ibid.*, pp. 203-204). Though the villein had the protection of the criminal law, and of the civil law—except against his lord—he was not accepted as a recognitor (*ibid.*, p. 106), nor eligible for the Assize-of-Arms (*ibid.*, p. 156), he could not become a cleric or a monk (*ibid.*, p. 145).[1] It may at first sight seem strange to find the clergy themselves, as well as the civil law, forbidding the serf to be tonsured, or to be received into the cloister, without the express sanction of his master, and this has been attributed to the wish of ecclesiastics to stand well with the secular authority, or to their anxiety not to lose their own serfs, for ecclesiastical estates were worked by villein labour in the same manner as the estates of secular lords. However, it would appear more in accordance with fact to look on these injunctions as springing from the desire of the Church to raise the status of the priest and monk. The clerical profession was always in danger of being despised by the feudal body that surrounded it. Were it to receive villeins into its ranks it would still further lose prestige, and the eclipse of the dignity of the priesthood would have boded ill for the civilization of the Dark Ages. Going back behind the Dark Ages these prohibitions continued to figure even under the Cluniac Reform and into the full light of the Mediæval Age, not dictated by mercenary motives lest their own slaves should desert them nor by a desire to ingratiate

---

[1] *Cf*. St Antonino, *Summa Moralis*, pars iii, tit. 3, cap. 6, § 7.

themselves with the nobility, but by the conviction of ecclesiastical authority that the priesthood should consist only of free men in order that it might retain the spiritual and intellectual leadership of Christendom. The local lord might be more tempted to treat the priest as his servant if he had once in reality been his servant, more likely to enslave the priest if the priest had once been his slave. To remain free the Church must be recruited from free men.

Yet, as has often been pointed out, there were various influences at work in mediæval social life which not only modified the system of serfdom and robbed it of some of its harsher features, but in time modified also the very theory of serfdom itself. The manor itself to which the villeins were attached was a social and political organization perpetually in process of change and development arising from the struggle between certain free elements and certain elements tending to despotism. Feudalism, of which the manor was the outward and visible sign, was the outcome of the amalgamation of Roman and barbaric ideals and customs whose balance was never still, each element in turn prevailing. In this swing of the balance villeinage, like other parts of the system, was affected sometimes by its tradition of beneficent absolutism, and sometimes by its tradition of free and independent co-partnership. Again the tendency of the law courts was on the whole in favour of freedom. They "leaned to liberty."

Moreover the practice of money-commutation for unfree service spread considerably, and perhaps more than anything else contributed to the improvement in the lot of the labouring classes. Wider research and investigation of agrarian records has justified the conclusion that this system of substituting money for villein service had by the fourteenth century been in vogue for many generations, and that it accompanied the rise of a large class of free labourers whose services were available on the manor at special seasons of the year and for the rest were freely hired out to whomsoever required them. It was a convenient arrangement both for the lord and for the worker. Nor side by side with the increase of prosperity is evidence lacking of the influence of that other and more liberal interpretation of the servile condition. As early as the twelfth century we find in the *De Legibus Angliæ*, which, dating from the reign of Henry II., was the work of Glanvill or Hubert Walter, the villein's right to leave his lord's land admitted on condition that compensation was paid to the lord he was quitting by the lord to whose service he was to be transferred. Another lord could therefore buy a villein's freedom. Yet it was sometimes held that a lord could free his villein only as regarded himself and his heirs, not as regarded others, who could thus always set aside a plea of emancipation on the ground of villein birth. This, however, has been denied by Professor Vinogradoff (*The Growth of the Manor*, pp. 87-88).

The Constitutions of Clarendon, again, on the eve of our period, allowed the villein, with the consent of his birth lord, to become a cleric (Stubbs, *Select Charters*, p. 140), and again, if he could make his escape to a privileged town and remain there without being captured a year and a day he was then to be regarded as a free man (*ibid*, p. 102). Under Richard I. the villein represented the village in the Hundred Court and the Shire Court as one of the land jury (*ibid.*, p. 46), and the writ seems to imply more than this. The steady improvement in the position of the unfree is reflected in Magna Charta, which, in the famous fortieth clause, promises justice to all without restriction, whether bond, therefore, or free (*ibid.*, p. 301). The importance of the villein and of his position in the social framework of the community had become generally recognized by the beginning of our century. He was accepted as the chief representative of a class on whom the welfare of his country depended; he had his equipment, and in two several writs—namely, of 1225 and 1242 (*ibid.*, pp. 356, 366)—was entered in the list of those charged with duties of watch and ward.

These may be taken as signs of the position to which he had advanced in social theory, or, at least, of the extent we should expect to find his progress reflected in current theory. Indeed his position, both personal and official, was now so fully recognized that the scheme of representative assembly had to find a place for him as an essential element of the nation. Can the serf be any longer a serf when he has been allotted a place in an elective parliament? Can his social position as an unfree member of the community remain untouched when he has been entered on the list of law-worthy men? The writ of 1232 is directed to "Archbishops and bishops, abbots, priors, knights, freemen and villeins" (*ibid.*, p. 360); five years later the same list re-appears but with this curious alteration at the end: "Freemen for themselves and for their villeins" (*ibid.*, p. 366). The freemen are now spokesmen of the unfree. But if the unfree are to have representatives, even though these representatives be not chosen out of their own body, their unfreedom is of a negligible type and may soon cease to exist. It does not seem possible that a man should be "sold like a beast" who has thus become an integral part of the Constitution.

Yet the curious fact remains that this double, this anomalous, position of the villein was not only recognized but was enforced. He might figure in social categories as possessing responsibilities and rights, and he might rise to wealth, but this did not affect his status. It was unalterable. A hundred years later, in 1347, the Bishop of Ely set out to claim as his villein one Richard Spynk, who had been born on his manor of Duddington. Spynk was by that time a prosperous business man in Norwich, so prosperous that he complained of the serious loss of trade inflicted on him by the Bishop's action and estimated that loss at a thousand pounds (*Trans. Roy. Hist. Soc.*, vol. ix., 1895, p. 72).

Why should the Bishop have been anxious to reclaim his villein? For one reason, because labour was already getting scarce even—the date is noteworthy—before the Black Death. Already the villeins were slipping away. Lack of male heirs to succeed to the unfree holding was one cause of this, or else the evasion of the heir who should have stepped into the vacant place with all its hampering disability. The villein may have fled and could not be found; or he paid cheavage; or the lord made no effort to trace him, or lacked a record as to who among his tenants was of unfree descent. Research work into the proceedings of the manorial courts has brought to light cases in which one or other of these causes was responsible for the action, or want of action, taken by the lords, and the facts are beyond doubt (cf. *The Decay of Villeinage in East Anglia*, in *Trans. Roy. Hist. Soc.*, vol. xiv.). After the Black Death the position became sharply accentuated. There is no longer to be found in the records any continuity in the performance of servile obligations in any neighbourhood, or in any trade, or in any holding. The villeins were upon the march. It had ceased to be possible to tether them to the soil; in practice they were already emancipated.

It is to be noted that the servile life had presented all the while a curious paradox: in the first place, the slave was a slave only to his master, to the rest of the world he owed no service; in the second, the master who enfranchised him could only enfranchise him as regards the personal service due to himself, but not—or so at least it is commonly implied in mediæval legal theory—as regards his native servile condition, with the result that any freeman could subsequently challenge his judgment as being villein-judgment and not the judgment of his peers.

As example of that attitude of independence towards all the world save his master we have that curious incident in *Aucassin and Nicolete* (ed. Andrew Lang, 1905, p. 49) when Aucassin meets his father's villeins in the forest. "Fair boys," quoth Aucassin, "know ye me not?" "Yea, we know well that thou art Aucassin, our demoiseau, natheless we be not your men, but the count's." "Fair boys, yet sing it again I pray you." "Hearken, by the Holy Heart," quoth he, "wherefore should I sing for you if it likes me not? Lo, there is no such rich man in this country, saving the body of Garin the Count, that dare drive forth my oxen, or my cows, or my sheep, if he finds them in his fields or his corn, lest he lose his eyes for it, and wherefore should I sing for you if it likes me not?" "God be your aid, fair boys, sing it ye will, and take ye these ten sols I have here in a purse." "Sir, the money will we take but never a note will I sing for I have given my oath, but I will tell thee a plain tale, if thou wilt." "By God," said Auccasin, "I love a plain tale better than naught."

It is interesting to note the consciousness in the tone of the villein of what he owed to his lord, and no less of what he was protected from by having a lord. He was his master's slave, but at that great price he had purchased freedom from the rest of the world. Yet it can be easily conceived that, with the arrival of a time in the social development of the country when freedom from the rest of the world in any case belonged to the villein, he would no longer be willing to make such a sacrifice in order to gain what was already his as a matter of right. As soon as law had its grip on the community, as soon as justice could be depended upon by villeins and freemen equally to protect individual liberties, there would cease to be any necessity for the villein to have a Count Garin to befriend him and his oxen and his sheep. This spirit of independence, exercised all the while by the villein as against all masters save his own, was thus kept active enough to be used in the end even against that master.

The other villein complained to Aucassin, it will be remembered, that his life was hard and the treatment of his mother inhuman; this would have broken his spirit in the long centuries that followed had not the other side of his experience upheld him. To his lord—even himself a villein—he was only as a beast to be sold or to be sent adrift, but to all others he bore himself as a man. He lay at his lord's feet, but he faced the rest of the world erect.

While the villein was thus in this frame of mind the Black Death broke over Christendom. His condition had been steadily growing more tolerable, many of the villein class had acquired their freedom and were working for hire. Some had become free labourers giving their labour to whosoever was willing to employ them, many now paid a fixed rent for their holding. It has, however, now been proved that the commutations of rent for service had not become so absolutely general in the first half of the fourteenth century as was at one time thought.

Moreover, for many years there had been a steady advance in the diffusion of knowledge, the result of the enormous strides made by the thirteenth-century schoolmen in the realms of science and thought. From the scholars, who thronged the universities to return slowly afoot to their own districts and cities, from the familiar and informing public lecture or sermon of the wandering friar, from the spirit that the jousts of the great scholastics had aroused, was begotten the thirst for learning that provoked the Renaissance.

Add to this the appeals addressed to the people by the Crown. The literature of the chroniclers is full of the appeals of the kings to their lowlier subjects. Whenever the baronage sought to hamper their sovereigns, or curb their power, or depose them, the sovereigns appealed to the Church and to the people. Whenever war was declared, or taxation inevitable, the people and the Church—but more particularly the people —found themselves the objects of flattery and of respectful solicitation by their zealous prince. They might often doubt the sincerity of these appeals and have occasion to remark what little effect the suggestions they might make, or the demands they might put forward, had in the counsels of kings ; nevertheless, repeated sufficiently often these appeals could not fail to create in the minds of the people a sense of their power and importance. The kings first used these arguments to the people ; after a while we find the people rehearsing these arguments to the kings. Later, monarchs like Louis XI. and Henry IV. built up a public theory—older than themselves in one way, yet in another quite new and of their own manufacture—which gave the people an enhanced appreciation of their own responsibility for government.

Moreover, it is difficult to imagine that the new soldiery which Edward I. and Edward III. found so useful—the bowmen and footmen who, between them, had revolutionized the art of war and displaced the cavalry as the fighting strength of an army—would, after their triumphs in France, settle down to bond service in England in the interlude of peace. We know that the nobles who commanded them were for ever protesting against the duration of their foreign service, and continually leaving the army abroad on some pretext to hurry back home. We know, also, that by this time there were organized bands of professional soldiers who never did anything else but soldiering : nevertheless, we must take it for granted that many of the archers and foot-soldiers were bond serving men who, when the war was over, would return home to their villages. Would they return again without protest to their old slave existence?

These forces in the movement towards the independence of the villein were strengthened by the Black Death. As a result of its ravages the workman found his services in increased demand, since the supply of labour had run short, leaving him in the position of being able to command a higher rate of wages with the comfortable assurance that in the general shortage his services were indispensable at any price. The workers realized that the need of the masters was their opportunity : they got the wages they demanded or they went elsewhere. Moreover, the new consciousness of his economic importance—now made evident to the labourer—impelled him to insist that his political and social position in public affairs should receive fuller recognition. The demands of the Jacquerie and of the Ciompi, as well as of our revolting peasantry, were political as well as economic, and reflected the new social self-consciousness of the labouring classes.

Nor were the disasters that marked the French war in the latter part of Edward III.'s reign without effect: they had made fighting extremely unpopular and the disbanded soldiers were already in a dissatisfied mood before they reached their towns and villages. When, therefore, they were confronted with attempts to override their demands, and forcibly to keep down wages with prices steadily rising, the situation found them ready for any outbreak that might ameliorate their condition and, at any rate, could hardly make it worse. Nor was discontent confined to the rural districts, recruits were found among the artisan class of the towns, who formed " alliances and covines " to fortify their demands (*Statutes of the Realm*, i. 367), and who added their quota to the rising of 1381. Disorder was rife throughout the country, and in November 1381, following the collapse of the revolt, Parliament urged that among contributory causes of the trouble were the maintainers of the lords who went about in companies plundering the country districts and menacing even the towns (*Rot. Parl.*, iii. 100-117). On the Continent we know that the " Grandes Compagnies," until they were taken in hand resolutely by the Crown and driven out, were the cause of worse destruction and misery than came even from the invading armies (*cf.* Langlois in *Mediæval France*, ed. A. Tilley, 1922, p. 120).

The consequences of the awful visitation of 1348-1349 made themselves quickly felt in the labour world. The Plague had hardly stayed its ravages before a royal ordinance appeared (June 1349) with the preamble: " Because a great part of the people and especially of workmen and servants late died of the pestilence, many, seeing the necessity of masters and great scarcity of servants, will not serve unless they may receive excessive wages and some are rather willing to beg in idleness than by labour to get their living " (*Stat. of the Realm*, i. 307). In virtue of this ordinance any landless or lordless man or woman under sixty years of age could be compelled to work for any master who demanded their services ; no reapers or landworkers might leave their holdings or be received or retained by other lords under penalty of imprisonment ; the wages were to be those paid in 1346 or earlier, those who asked more should be fined double what they had asked, and the lords who offered more should be fined treble what they had offered (*ibid.*, p. 311). But the statute of 1351, the " First Statute of Labourers," which reinforced the provisions of 1349 in fuller detail and with harsher stringency, showed that " the said servants having no regard of the said Ordinance, but to their ease and singular Covetise, do withdraw themselves to serve great men and others, unless they have Livery and Wages to the double and treble of what they were wont to take to the great damage of the Great Men and impoverishing of all the said Commonalty." To the " Great Men," the landlords, this conduct of the workers seemed immoral. It was taking advantage of their necessity. This was usury though in a less blatant form. They appealed to Parliament to exercise all its coercive power, and Parliament—which was the " Great Men " writ large—adopting a method of dealing with economic and inevitable laws by legal and futile enactments made periodical resort to more and more stringent measures. Labour was to be more strictly bound to the soil and to be branded like the beast with the mark of the owner (*ibid.*, p. 367). The result was the first clear issue in English social life between capital and labour. As every fresh trouble fell on the land—bad weather, failure of the crops, renewed visitation of the pestilence, mortality of cattle—regulations were made more stringent, and conditions more impossible, with the sole result that the Government became more and more ineffective and unable to enforce its own legislation.

At last fell the dreaded blow. The revolt broke out simultaneously in many parts of the country. Was there a freemasonry of distress? Did the soldiers, disbanded from the French wars, link village to village by a common policy discussed in tent and by the light of scare-fires? Was the preaching of the friars and Lollards but a wind fanning the already kindled flames? Had the chains of villeinage since the Plague galled too intolerably a sore in process of healing? Perhaps we shall never know, for as yet the last century of research has failed to disclose the baffling mystery of the efficient organization of the Rising. Undoubtedly the irritation caused by the incidence of the Poll Tax played its part in the explosion, but the social and economic grievances of the villeins were the primary cause. They had been well on the way to emancipation ; the Black Death and the legislation which followed it bound them down again. The evasion of the old servile conditions by the villeins caused the lords to go carefully through their records and court rolls to discover who among their tenants had a legal claim to freedom. Everything combined to drive the people to desperation. The position is reflected in the demands put forward by the bands of peasants who everywhere clamoured for the abolition of tolls and of bondage, for the commutation of villein services, and for the grant of a general pardon. Revolutionary demands figure hardly at all in the petitions of the mobs that have survived. They were practical and common-sense suggestions for the removal of existing disabilities accompanied, indeed, by acts of violence and bloodshed, for which individual motives of revenge and the broached casks of wine and ale were, perhaps, more responsible than any social theories emanating from Lollard or friar. As in the case of Magna Charta it was for no idealistic principles of communism but for the remedying of concrete injustice that the majority were moved to revolt and to draw up a programme of definite reform.

But the outrages perpetrated by the mobs alienated many who had sympathy with the dreams but not with the acts of revolting villeinage, and from this alienation—which deprived the movement of outside support and effective leadership— came its collapse, engineered by trickery and stark cruelty on the part of the Government. Parliament had again recourse to its stern relentless policy of insisting that while life changed law should remain the same. The old legislation, impossible to enforce, continued to be re-enacted with increasing violence of language and corresponding impotence. Gradually—but how gradually is much in dispute—practice prevailed over enact- ment and legislation itself relaxed. By some it is contended that labour services were all but commuted in the first half of the fourteenth century, by others that they were still main- tained throughout the fifteenth. Some hold that copyholders from villeinage were not legally protected in their holding and in their emancipation from servile obligations till the reign of Elizabeth ; others again hold that legal protection was secured much earlier and that customary tenancy was fully upheld by law long before that date. But this disagreement among specialists is not, save technically, of much importance. It is at least certain that the imputation of villeinage against a family was not infrequently made as late as the fifteenth century by slanderous rivals who desired to poison public opinion against its members. The famous *Remembrance of the Worshipful Kin and Ancestry of Paston*, the work of an enemy of the Pastons, insists that this family was of unfree status, that its not far-distant ancestor, one Clement, was not only a " house bondman " [1] but had married a bondwoman and transmitted to his son and grandson lands held by servile tenure, with the result that in law none of the family could establish a lordship. As the family had by that time acquired a leading position in the country we may guess from the bitterness of the resentment

---

[1] *The Pastons and their England*, by H. S. Bennett, Cambridge, 1922, p. 1.

at the imputation of villeinage how recent was its memory and how widespread its revolt.

At the close of our period we come upon many works written in praise of liberty, urging the glories of freedom and the greatness of the rule of kings over free subjects. Not only in England (which we have elected to follow rather than any other country because the development is simpler, clearer and more uniform) but all over Christendom we have a sense of individuality deliberately cultivated, a growing search for independence, a talk of personality and of the value of life for life's own sake. Yet side by side with this we also find a greater tightening up of the authority of the landlord, increased inspection of villein service, attempts to hold down the now more restless people closer to their soil.

" The king," said Aquinas *(De Regimine Principum*, Bk. I., cap. 14), " is the doctor of the body politic making it healthy, is its merchant making it rich, its teacher showing it truth, and *by king we mean to whomsoever in the State is committed the supreme rule of human affairs."* In that sentence we may see the difference between the opening of the century and its close. It began in a period when that sentence could be written and where the concluding phrase was necessary to explain to Christians the obligations of obedience to any rule ; it ended in a period where, save in the Swiss Cantons and in Venice, the concluding phrase would not only be superfluous but might even be considered high treason.

The thirteenth century began in a society wherein slavery was accepted as normal in human life ; but from that time, and even prior to it, the conditions of slavery had been gradually improving and the line of division between freeman and bondman was becoming gradually obliterated by custom. Slavery had always been a matter of tenure rather than of personal status in the mediæval centuries, and as tenure began to be less and less the primary distinction it had been in a less organized and cohesive society, slavery or villeinage became almost disregarded in practice. The Black Death interfered with this peaceful development, renewed the idea of the importance of the distinctions of tenure to lords who desired cheap labour and sought means to restrain their labourers abandoning their work, though the question gradually again lost its significance with the Acts of Parliament remaining largely inoperative owing to the impracticability of their rigorous enforcement. At the last, however, we may again notice a tendency to insist upon servile tenure, though to discover its cause and the theories it provoked we should need to stray beyond 1500 into the literature of a succeeding age.

From Aquinas to Antonino of Florence, and thence to Savonarola, we can describe the mediæval attitude to serfdom in two sentences from the *Summa Theologica*, the first of which we have already cited but which remains as the simplest key to the whole of mediæval social thought :

I. " The distinction of possessions and slavery were not brought in by Nature but devised by human reason for the benefit of human life " (94, 5, ad 3 m)—that is, the introduction of slavery is due to the *Jus Gentium*.

II. " Without the *Jus Gentium* men cannot live together, which [living together] is a point of the law of nature since man is by nature a social animal as is proved in *Politics* i."—that is, the institution of some sort of servitude was contained in the natural law and could never be wholly abolished.

CHAPTER V

PROPERTY

As with all other social theories of their age, the ideas of the mediæval writers on Property were the inheritance bequeathed them by the Fathers. St Augustine formulated them in his *Commentary on St John*, and it was chiefly through St Augustine that the mediæval world received them, and thereby reached back to the earlier age of Christianity. The other great thinkers and writers are often quoted by name—St Gregory, St Ambrose, St John Chrysostom—but even when his phrases are not quoted verbatim, the treatises of the moralists of the Middle Ages are obviously steeped in the commonplaces of St Augustine's thought (Migne, *P.L.*, xxv., pp. 1436-1437). Gratian again, another formulator of what was older, teaches the same origin of property that had been accepted by the Church, to some extent, from the Stoics though considerably modified by the facts of Christian revelation (*P.L.*, clxxxvii., pp. 43-46). Very briefly the origin of private property was ascribed to original sin. It was held that man would have cultivated the soil even had he never sinned, for the moralists remembered that Adam, even from the beginning, was to have care of the Garden, with full liberty to taste of all the fruits with one exception. Sin did not introduce, therefore, the cultivation of the soil, but it did introduce greed—and once men were greedy the cultivation of the soil would soon lead to strife. No doubt at first all would have been in common, but little good could come of this when men's greed got the better of them. Innocence could live from a common purse, not ordinary man. Communism was a lost ideal left behind in the Garden. Between it and our world was a flaming sword. " As for riches," says Tolomeo de Lucca, " all things were in common which can only happen among the perfect " (*De Regimine Principum*, Bk. IV., chap. iv.).

We must be content to take as the doctrine of the thirteenth century what it itself had been taught ; to discuss its origins would be to go back behind our period. Gratian, who comes earlier, developed the theory which he accepted. We shall, therefore, take for granted whatever originating previous to this was accepted by the scholastics without change, and merely retold.

It is interesting to notice whereabouts in the treatises of the schoolmen we should turn for references to private property. Without irony, it was treated of under the sin of theft.[1] It should be remembered that these writers were above all theologians and moralists ; they were not themselves politicians or statesmen, but the teachers of politicians and statesmen. They dictated the principles of moral justification and action ; it was for the kings and their counsellors to carry them out.

The first thing that the reader will notice in the thirteenth and fourteenth century compilations is that they begin by treating, first the right to private property, and then the exercise of that right. These were, to them, two separate and independent ideas, always carefully kept apart. The right they based entirely upon moral or theological grounds ; its sole justification lay, they held, in ethical teaching, for so only could it be sacred and inviolable. To be unchanging it must be rooted in divine truth, in revelation, in the Christian law. If the right to private property could be defended only on grounds of utilitarianism, or expediency, or experience, then it would be entirely a matter for the statesmen to argue about, and, therefore, possibly to set aside. But in fact all the scholastics of the thirteenth century, without exception it would seem, asserted that the right to property was a natural and moral right. To their way of thinking it sprang out of the very nature of man, since it was based upon his intelligence and his will. Consequently, for them the right to property was an absolute right which no circumstances could ever invalidate. Even in case of necessity, when individual property might be lawfully seized or distrained—in the name of another's hunger or of the common good—yet the owner's right to property remained and endured. The right was inviolable even when the exercise of the right might have to be curtailed.

Secondly, this right to property had found its expression

[1] Canonists, like St Antonino, followed Gratian's order and not the order of the schoolmen.

in the institution of private property. This last, the early schoolmen looked upon as the exercise of a right. The right was itself of natural law, the exercise of that right was of positive law : " According to natural law there is no distinction of property, for this is the result of an arrangement by man which is part of positive law " (*Summa Theologica* of Aquinas, I. ii. 66, 2, ad 1 m). By positive law, we have already explained,[1] St Thomas does not mean a civil enactment, but that positive law which is native to man and yet is not absolute—the *jus gentium* which no state has ever decreed but only accepted, the law found to exist in all nations, older than states and beyond their appeal.

The argument given by Scotus shows us the way in which the problem proposed itself to the early Middle Ages : " Even supposing it as a principle of positive law that ' life must be lived peaceably in a state or polity ' it does not straightway follow ' therefore everyone must have separate possessions,' for peace could be observed even if all things were in common ; nor even if we presuppose the wickedness of those who live together is it a necessary consequence that they should possess separate properties. Still a distinction of property is decidedly in accord with a peaceful social life. For the wicked take care only of what is their own, rather seek to appropriate to themselves the common goods than leave them for the use of the community, whence come strife and contention. Hence we find it [division of property] taken for granted in every positive law. But, although there is a fundamental principle from which all other laws and rights are derived, still from that fundamental principle positive laws need not follow absolutely nor immediately. Rather is it as detailed declarations or explanations or applications of that general principle that they come into being and are consequently in evident accord with the universal natural principle" (*Super Sent. Questions*, Bk. IV., dist. 15, q. 2, Venice, 1580 ; *cf.* Albertus Magnus, in *Polit.*, ii. 2, 3, 4, Lyons, 1651, tom. iv., pp. 68-74).

We can say, therefore, that the right to possess follows from our personality, but that the method of the division of

---

[1] Chapter I., p. 15.

possessions amongst individuals follows from actual experience of human life. This division of private property is not, therefore, a sacred right. On the one hand, the lawfulness of property was definitely admitted as an ethical truth founded on Scripture; on the other, the division of property was defended not on moral grounds but for reasons of universal convenience.

Thus Aquinas in his preliminary article (I. ii. 66, 1) of the *Summa Theologica*: " An external thing can be considered in two ways: first as regards its essence, and this does not fall under man's power but God's only, Whose command all obey; secondly, as regards its use. In this second sense man has a natural dominion over external things, because by means of his reason and will he can make use of them for his own purpose, as though they were made for him. But this natural dominion over creatures, which befits man on account of his reason (for in this is he fashioned after God's likeness), was shown at his very creation, where it is written: ' Let us make man after our own image and likeness, and let him have dominion over the fishes of the sea,' etc. (Genesis i. 26)."

On the will and reason of man, wherein he is likened to the Creator, rested for Aquinas the right of man to possess and to dispose of the external creation. According to him, the good use to which man was able to put natural things justified him in using them. In other words, the existence of man in the world enabled him to develop in nature what otherwise could not be developed, what without him would never have reached the perfection which it now enjoys. Nature was created for the glory of God, would be his statement of the case, but is to be used " as though it were made for man."

The succeeding article of the *Summa Theologica* (I. ii. 66, 2) takes us a step further, for Aquinas next considers another relationship of man to external things. So far he had only decided that man has a right to use nature. He then proceeds to the next step in the argument: " Man has a twofold relation to external things; of which one is the power of producing and consuming. For this it is lawful that man should possess property." This to him is the conclusion to be derived from his first article. He maintains that the " lawfulness of private property" follows directly upon man's "habitual dominion over other creatures." He has no other argument to give in favour of private property, though when he wrote this part of the *Summa* he was in the fullness of the maturity of his mind. It was hardly more than a year before his death, at the age of forty-seven. The problem had been perplexing his own generation over in the Midi, where heretics were denouncing the possession of private property as immoral and un-Christian. Moreover, at least from his friend, St Bonaventure (whose Generalate of the Friars Minor was so much disturbed by disputes over the lawfulness of the holding of private property by Franciscans, and even by Christians), he must have learned how men's minds were agitated over this very point. Indeed, one of the popes was shortly afterwards compelled to make a dogmatic pronouncement upholding the lawfulness of private property. To St Thomas, therefore, the lawfulness of private property was a theological conclusion, deduced from the nature of man, his reason and his will.

But because it is lawful to have private property, does it follow by another theological conclusion that it is also necessary to have it? Because a thing is lawful it need not, therefore, be obligatory. Is private property not only lawful but obligatory? Must the state or the prince insist upon its retention in virtue of Christian dogma? St Thomas states roundly that he thinks not. He did argue, indeed, in favour of its necessity, and maintain that it was required by the race; he did not, however, base this assertion on the ground that the exercise of the right was a revealed truth connected with the Faith, but only on the ground that it was an experienced truth connected with the art of living. It will be clearer to give the whole article. The kind of argument used by St Thomas should particularly be noted.

"Man has a twofold relation to external things, of which one is the power of producing and consuming. For this it is *lawful* that man should possess property. It is also *necessary* for three reasons. First, indeed, because every man is more solicitous in procuring something which will belong to him alone than something which will belong to all or many, for everyone tries to escape work and will, therefore, leave to others what should be produced for the community. Secondly, because human affairs are more orderly if to each belongs the proper care of something, for confusion would arise if each one looked after everything indiscriminately. Thirdly, because thus human society is preserved in greater peace so long as each is content with his own. Hence we see amongst those who possess things in common and indiscriminately, more often than not ructions occur. The other relation to external things is their use, and as far as this goes no man ought to have anything proper to himself but all in common, so that thus each may communicate easily to another in his necessities. Hence says the Apostle: ' Charge the rich of this world not to be high-minded . . . but to communicate to others ' (I Tim. vi. 17, 18)."

St Antonino, writing more than a hundred years after St Thomas, and referring to this very passage, adds to its close these two appropriate texts of Scripture (*Summa Theologica*, i. 14, 6, 3) : " Going into thy neighbour's vineyard, thou mayest eat as many grapes as thou pleasest ; but must carry none out with thee. If thou goest into thy friend's corn, thou mayest break the ears and rub them in thy hand but not reap them with a sickle (Deut. xxiii. 24). When thou reapest the corn of thy land, thou shalt not cut down all that is on the face of the earth to the very ground ; nor shalt thou gather the ears that remain, neither shalt thou gather up the bunches and grapes that fall down in thy vineyard, but leave them to the poor and the stranger to take (Levit. xix. 9, 10)."

But to return to Aquinas, it is noticeable that for him the necessity for the division of private property is not a moral necessity arising from the absolute nature of man, but a practical necessity arising from his usual behaviour. The lawfulness of private property is guaranteed by man's reason, the necessity only by his greed. Both perhaps are equally persistent, but both need not be. Indeed monasteries existed to disprove, not the absolute lawfulness, but the absolute necessity of private property. Man then had a right to property, and further, it was expedient that he should exercise that right by the institution of private property.

The three reasons which St Thomas gave were common-places in social science. It was from Aristotle that they were derived; they continued to be copied and repeated by everyone to the end of our period, elaborated further but never added to, developed more richly but never supplemented. They deserved elaboration, for they were neatly and nicely arranged. The first was concerned with the individual as an individual—namely, the greater solicitude shown by him for what was his own; the third with the community—namely, the greater peace of human society; the second with the interrelation of society to the individual—namely, the confusion that would result were each indiscriminately to look after everything.

The last part of the article is in some ways the most practical and the most interesting—namely, the use of these private possessions—for to Aquinas the epigram of Aristotle is the epitome of Christian teaching and economics, that possessions should be private in ownership and public in use. It was a happy solution, thought St Thomas, of the extreme views of those who would have all things in common and those who would have none. Individual ownership and common use was his solution, perhaps offending both parties, for the heretics would not have allowed private ownership and the orthodox were perhaps too chary of public use. Nevertheless, as we shall see, to the mediæval mind this last was essential to the scheme of social Christendom, without which the rest was but greed made legal; nor would our word " charity " have quite covered the meaning of the phrase " public use." Private charity was not the remedy to be applied to the abuses of individual ownership. Something more drastic was in mind : the common use of what was privately owned.

Between abstract right and concrete exercise of right, then, a division was to be noticed, for abstract right was of natural law and, therefore, absolute and inalienable. The concrete exercise of that right was of positive law and, therefore, variable, the one based on the nature of man, his intellect and will, the other based on sheer experience of life. Not, however, was positive law to be taken to mean a decree of the state—save in mere matters of detail—for to such extent was private ownership, and the actual division of property into private hands, in accord with human nature that in every state it had taken place. Everywhere the three arguments had been held to be valid and private property had been retained. A society, however, in which the three arguments were found no longer to be valid would permit also the exercise of the right to be forgone. Was not religious life such a society? Did not religious life make the exercise of the right to private property unnecessary? Yet did it not leave the right to private property, even in religious, still untouched? The right then was sacred, the exercise of the right a matter of experience: private property as an institution was not opposed to nature, nor dictated by nature, but according to nature—that is, everywhere it was to be found in use. Abstractly and theoretically, however much it might be questioned as expedient, in practice it would be found alone to work. Its defence, then, was conducted by the scholastics with pragmatic arguments only.

Nor was this theory of the scholastics peculiar to themselves. It overflowed into the lecture-rooms of law, and is to be found in the treatises of Bologna as well as of Paris. Dante hints at it in his *De Monarchia*. For the lawyer, the Pope and the Emperor halved the world between them : "les deux moitiés de Dieu," as Victor Hugo speaks of them. These twin powers overshadowed the legal world, loomed out of the mist over the lives of their subjects, as Durham Cathedral and Durham Castle in dawn and twilight project themselves in ghostly shape over the streets of little houses that shelter under their shadows, and between them symbolize the dual powers, spiritual and temporal, that governed, protected and inspired the folk in that northern Palatinate. The Pope's power being spiritual was easier to enforce, and its universality and absolutism were not resented in the same way as the universality and absolutism of the imperial Temporal power seem to have been. Men were not troubled so much over what they were called on to believe as over what they were called on to do and to pay. The only aspect of the Papal supremacy against which emperor or prince was likely to set up opposition concerned such matters as marriages, or legacies, or the temporalities of bishoprics, or investiture, or taxation, in which the spiritual prerogatives expressed themselves in material terms. Belief or faith hardly ever, even in the Catharist Midi or to Frederick II., constituted a reason for dissatisfaction with the Papacy; heresy was never a fashionable royal pastime till the sixteenth century. Never the Creed, only the Commandments, really antagonized a king or emperor. On the other hand the material sway of the Emperor was a far more difficult thing to make effective in the mediæval world and was far more resented by lesser sovereigns and princes than was the Pope's spiritual dominion by subordinate ecclesiastical authorities. Moreover, the Emperor's claims lacked continuity; both his circumstances and his character made a consistent policy impossible. His circumstances—because though from time to time as its anointed and crowned representative the Emperor claimed the right of lordship over Christendom yet, since the position was elective and not hereditary, the imperial Electors who disliked these claims were able to marshal forces against them too strong to be overcome. His character—because as these claims might indeed be made effective by emperors of exceptional character, the imperial Electors, for that very reason, abstained on the whole from electing exceptional princes, and where they were successful in carrying out this principle of election the candidate they elected lost his imperial significance. Only in the case of emperors like Frederick I. and Frederick II., and later on the Emperor Sigismund, did they succeed in securing recognition of their universal lordship. Just before our period an accident made Richard I. an illustration of this: captured by the Archduke of Austria he was held up to ransom until he had resigned his crown and received his kingdom back as a fief of the Empire on payment of an annual tribute of five thousand pounds (Stubbs, *Select Charters*, pp. 252-253).

Moreover, the position of the Emperor in Christendom had become paralleled in each kingdom by that of the prince who claimed similar rights within his particular domains. The older idea of kingship in Western Europe had been of a leader of war-bands, but as the restless, shifting tribes settled down and grew into the soil the character of the king had materially altered. Even the royal title underwent a transformation : no longer was the wearer master of a tribe but of a territory, not king of the Angle-cyn but of Engla-land. And abroad throughout Christendom the same process of development was in operation, the king—in whom was vested ownership of the land on which the nation was encamped—was thereby advancing to the position in which he was to be recognized as the representative of his people.

But as it was impossible for him personally to administer the whole country he was compelled to hand over to his followers the land or stock in usufruct. The word *feudum* (derived from words meaning cattle) shows how ancient was the system, for it originated undoubtedly in days when the staple wealth was cattle ; later on it came to mean the pasture for the cattle (*i.e.* the land on which the cattle grazed) ; later still its significance lay in the distinction it set up between allodial tenure (*i.e.* absolute ownership) and feudal tenure (*i.e.* conditional ownership). These several landowners held their lands of the king in return for services in which they represented him and were responsible to him, who, as supreme landowner, was nevertheless bound by the contract which was the bond between lord and vassal, while as king he was limited by the idea of Christian monarchy contained in the coronation oath. The expression used to express the relationship of the landowner to the land was that he " held " it, he did not own it ; it was within his possession, but that possession was not absolute but conditional. The theory conceived of each holding land on terms of use and not of full ownership, whether, as one of the greater feudatories, he held of the king or, as a lesser feudatory, he held of an intermediate lord, and so on down to the very lowest in the scale of social organization who had an acknowledged place in the hierarchical ladder. Despite the failure of its enforcement this principle of contract, permeating the whole system and binding equally on king and villein, remained the theory of possession reducing all ownership of property, whether house or cattle or arms or castle or land, to mere conditional use. Gravely and soberly we may state the principle of mediæval social life in a familiar phrase by saying that theoretically the means of production remained in the hands of the community.

The Feudal System was perhaps the nearest approach to a consistent system of communism that has ever been practised on a large scale. This volume, since it deals only with the theories of the mediæval period, need not, however, describe its failure from the first, for the system did fail all the time. Its practice was by no means perfect, as other chapters of this book show, for, like every ideal, in its process of realization and practice the system became untrue to itself. But even granting this, we may still say that so perfect a communistic ideal has never elsewhere had an opportunity of universal application in Christendom. In England, where, owing to the happy accident of the Norman Conquest, feudalism had almost its best chance of success, we may see the theory at its best. Before his coronation—or else Archbishop Ealdred had refused to crown him—William the Conqueror had sworn to defend the Church and to rule justly his subjects, to enact and to observe just laws, and to put down robbery and violence. This was not regarded as a mere pious pledge of idealism. It was looked on as a legal contract. We have already quoted the statement attributed by Matthew of Paris to Archbishop Walter, by whom the same oath was exacted from John prior to his coronation, before he would crown him. The oath still survives as part of the English Coronation Service, emptied now of all meaning since the king is already ruling sovereign before he has been crowned. But coronation was then regarded as so essential to the possession of royal power that there was a persistent tendency, both in England and on the Continent, for a king to crown his eldest son even in his own lifetime in order to ensure an undisputed and immediate succession to the throne. This coronation then, which was the sanction of princely authority, was preceded by a question on the answer to which the royal prerogatives depended. The promise given not only bound the king to observe the law, but bound the people to obey the king. The social contract of the Middle Ages was not between subjects pooling their independence to beget " Leviathan, that mortal god "; it was between a people and their prince establishing the princedom on the limited terms of the contract. The release of the people from their allegiance followed automatically on the non-fulfilment of his promise by the king; when he ceased to rule according to law, his violation of a mutually binding agreement itself invalidated any claim on his part to the obedience of the people on theirs. Legally, indeed, some authority was needed to declare publicly that the contract had ceased to hold, but that authority did nothing else than declare the facts of the case, the release followed automatically. Aquinas is quite clear about this : " Against savage tyrants proceedings should be taken not by private presumption but by public authority, for since each group has from its beginnings a right to provide itself with a king, so it cannot be unjust for it, should he employ his power tyrannically, to destroy or restrain him. Nor can that group be justly accused of disloyalty, merely on the strength of its previous oath of perpetual fidelity to him, since he has himself deserved this [deposition] by his non-observance of that fidelity to which his own kingly oath committed him, he has not observed his compact with his subjects " (*De Regimine Principum*, i. 6).

The English king, therefore, possessed the " Engla-land " in virtue of a contractual obligation between himself and his people. His ownership of whatever he possessed was never absolute. He held conditionally—he did not own absolutely. He was the steward of his people. He could be discharged from his office on the ground of negligence. He was to be the mark of his people's closest criticism. We could not indeed maintain that this in practice was consistently observed, but that it was sufficiently recognized as to make it more than a mere theory; indeed it was the justification of a movement that resulted in the creation of Parliament as a legitimate court of criticism—a resort to which no English king ever turned who could afford to dispense with it.

This is the persistent principle of feudalism running through and permeating the whole of its organization—namely, a basis of property held conditionally, implying a contract. The vassals, for example, who held their lands directly of the king held them on conditional terms, as he held his kingship of the nation. Everywhere an oath—that is to say, a contract under religion—held each to his superior ; everywhere the means of production were fundamentally in common ownership but in private holding. The vassals then who were tenants-in-chief—that is to say, holding immediately of the king—received their lands from him, yet not in such a way as to allow the royal right to lapse, at any rate in theory. They owed duties to the king in return for the privilege of administering what was not absolutely their own. These duties were summed up in the two words : suit and service.

"Service" meant military service. Each vassal, to whomsoever he owed service, was bound to attend the military expeditions of his immediate lord and to bring with him the necessary equipment and armed followers according to the extent and the terms at which his holding was assessed. By personal arrangement, as we know, William the Conqueror settled with each baron (lay or ecclesiastical) the exact number of knights he was bound to provide and to lead in time of war. Subsequently, in 1166, Henry II. sent round to each of these barons—or rather to their descendants or successors—a cartel in which he required a return to be made him in writing of the number of knights which each was bound to furnish. It would, therefore, appear that there was no record kept of the original grants at the Royal Court and that these grants were possibly only verbal agreements. Some of the returns made in response to this requisition are still extant (Stubbs, *Select Charters*, p. 146). They prove, therefore, that the royal knowledge of the conditions of these grants was essential to the due administration of the kingdom.

"Suit" meant that besides military duties there were civil and political duties attached to the holding of land. The tenants-in-chief, the feudatories, lay under the obligation of attending the King's Court (*Curia Regis*). That they did so we know from the *Anglo-Saxon Chronicle*, which describes for us something of these state functions of William I. and his immediate successors. Later on fuller details are given, as in the case of the Great Council convoked by Henry II. to meet at Northampton (1165) for the trial of Becket. The King's Court, or

Curia Regis—the central institution of the Norman period, as the Witenagemot was of the earlier Saxon—was at once a royal court, a royal council and a feudal assembly, and is the germ of all our great political institutions at the present day : the Privy Council Parliament, and the Royal Courts of Justice. So fundamental was this duty of suit at the King's Court on the part of the vassals that a refusal to attend constituted an act of contumacy, often heralding revolt ; nor as a means of enforcing recognition of the royal supremacy was it always liked by the feudatories ; while, on the other hand, as the contest between Crown and baronage developed the king was not always anxious to give the barons opportunity to voice their grievances and to make combination oftener than he could help by summoning the full body of the magnates ; sometimes his advantage lay rather in treating with them singly. Sooner or later he must desire their attendance, however, for so only could the machinery of taxation be set in motion without which a mediæval king was helpless, since he " could not live of his own."

The idea at the back of taxation, as mediæval theologians endlessly insisted, was the common obligation of subjects to provide for the common necessities of their lord and of the kingdom—that is, of themselves. The money raised could only be justly applied by the authority that demanded it when it was expended for the common good of the taxer and the taxed. War would justify it, or trade advantages, or some immediate necessity that affected the whole group. Moreover, this had to be, or at first was thought to be, a merely exceptional measure to meet an exceptional need—of which the danegeld is an outstanding example—to be defended by exceptional arguments. For normal purposes of administration there were the feudal incidents—fines upon succession, the marriage of the lord's daughter or the knighting of the lord's eldest son, together with the fines levied in the administration of justice. Over and above these, the king was entitled to a limited hospitality at the hands of his immediate vassals, and in times of poverty would institute a royal progress and eat his way from one end of the kingdom to the other. Thus living at the expense of others he was able to curtail his own.

The rights of the king were reproduced on a miniature scale by the rights of his tenants-in-chief over their tenants, and so *ad infinitum*. These lesser tenants owed to their lords both suit and service, for the administration of law was the privilege of every lord the terms of whose grant included judicial " immunity " or freedom from the interference of royal officials. He was empowered to exercise jurisdiction in civil and certain criminal cases, to set on foot certain inquisitions, and to pocket the fines of the court. In Christendom generally this was the organization that linked together, beyond the borders of nationality and across them, the responsible chiefs in every part of it. The English King, it will be remembered, did homage to the King of France for certain lands that had come into his possession by inheritance through the marriages of heiresses who, by feudal custom, handed on the inheritance to their sons. Similarly the King of Scotland as Earl of Huntingdon did homage to the King of England for the English barony of which he was enfeoffed, and in so doing raised the question as to whether homage was performed in virtue of his Scottish kingdom—involving the suzerainty of England over Scotland —or in virtue of his English barony. Both relationships—that of the King of England to the King of France and that of the King of Scotland to the King of England—were made the basis of claims that contributed to the outbreak of war, but this began only when the original ideas of feudalism had lost their meaning and its forms were being used by ambitious monarchs anxious to find some legal pretext of quarrel to justify their ambition to the public conscience.

Rights of suit and service were then demanded by the greater tenants from the lesser. Gradually, however, the suit, which furnished the material of the baronial courts, lost its importance, for the reforming and centralizing kings, the great Western monarchs of European history, emptied these local courts of their prestige by insisting on the right of the Crown to intervene, by sending their own officials to try certain cases and by making their own court a court of appeal, thus super-seding baronial justice. By the time we begin our period this policy of depriving the territorial magnates of their strong local position by breaking down the close co-operation between the greater and the lesser men, and of linking up the latter with the Crown, had been steadily going on for the last century, not only in England but elsewhere, despite the steady resistance offered by the baronage and the opportunity offered them by the weakness of a royal minority. Even when we get down to the smallest territorial unit—the manor—we find that process of undermining the power of the local magnate also in operation, though it is difficult to dogmatize in matters that still remain so much in dispute. Moreover we have to meet a state of things in which practices were extremely varied, springing perhaps from a difference of origin, mixture of custom, the engrafting of similar practices upon practices not quite similar, local peculiarities, tribal memories, national custom superseding Imperial law ; all contributing to diversify what would in any case have been difficult to introduce as a uniform and absolute system. But avoiding disputed and vexed questions, and keeping to what is generally admitted, we can from the organization of the normal manor obtain a fairly satisfactory idea of the mediæval sense of property, for the manor was on the whole not so much a unit of defence or offence as a juridical and economic unit.

The manor or dominical farm had at its centre the lord's hall, which was the nucleus of the organism ; it had its estate for cultivation divided into the demesne land, or inland, for the support of the lord and his household, and the land of the village community, consisting of the dependent holdings of the tenants. The lord had his outhouses, and at a distance was the village, with its dominating church and parsonage, its rows of houses ; besides the strips of land for the plough, very often scattered about—those of the lord intermixed with those of his tenantry—there was common land, to suffer later under successive Acts of Enclosure, and the unreclaimed land, which only gradually, under pressure of an increase of population and what we may call the Ricardo theory of rent, came into cultivation.

On the strength of the manor dwelt, besides the lord, five main classes of dependents : (1) the *servants*, who did the work of the house and of the main outbuildings of the manor ; with whom perhaps we may associate (2) the *servi*, of *Domesday*, a diminishing class—only nine per cent. of the population in the days of the Conqueror—whose lot was not comparative but absolute slavery : a landless class ; (3) the *borders* and *cottars*, whose holding varied from two to five acres, who provided no oxen for the plough-team of the manor, who possessed a share definite and determined by custom in the common land, whose servile obligations bound them to put in a couple of days' handwork a week on the manor, and who might be called upon for even more than that at certain seasons of the year—a body constituting thirty-two per cent. of the population in *Domesday* ; (4) the *villeins*, constituting thirty-eight per cent of the population in the same reckoning, whose holding consisted of anything up to thirty acres, with rights of pasturage, whose obligations were : (*a*) one, two or three days' work a week on the manor ; (*b*) *precaria*—or boon-work—at the lord's special request ; (*c*) *gafol*, certain payments in money or kind or work ; and who supplied the oxen for the great plough-team. All these four classes were unfree, were tied to the soil, could not move without leave of their lord, and were technically subject to all the disabilities we have already detailed in a previous chapter. At least seventy-nine to eighty per cent. of the population or more held land therefore in various categories of servile tenure, and these four classes, by all manner of legal devices, were gradually amalgamated under the single name of " villeinage," and began at the end of the thirteenth century to escape into the fifth class of landholder, the freemen, (5) *liberi-tenentes* or *socemanni*. These held their own land, and had no week-work, only " boon " work, performed at the lord's request according to the need of the manor. Even these, however, could not sell their land nor leave the manor without permission ; some paid rent for their land. This last was the beginning of the break-down of the system. It indicated a way out. From the *liberi-tenentes* were chosen the higher officials of the manor : the steward, who presided over the courts of the manor ; the bailiff, who took charge of its agricultural organization ; the reeve, its elected representative ; these were severally responsible for the tenants on the manor and for its working.

In connection with the manor were courts: civil—such as the court-baron for the freemen and the court-customary for the unfree; and criminal—such as the court-leet. The jury system, either of presentation or of recognition or of trial, was another of the feudal burdens, and was itself merely a condition of land-holding, a repeated reminder that none owned absolutely the land they lived on or cultivated, but only on condition of suit and service. The feudal incidents of succession, etc., were again to stamp this knowledge upon the memories of all.

The villages were thus self-supporting and self-sufficing; so too were the towns, which in their way were no less manorial, being agricultural and commercial, no doubt, but also feudal units, which had purchased their freedom from king or lord in the name of a guild or corporation and, in exchange for money down or by payment of a yearly rent, had secured a charter by the terms of which the town was henceforth immune from further exactions.

The point, however, here to be noted was the permanence of the holding of land and yet of its wholly conditional nature. Whatever rent was paid was never competitive. Quit-rent, moreover, was never arranged according to the value of the land but according to the value of the services which went with the land, showing that land was looked upon as an objective thing, the ownership of which imposed obligations for the good governance and organization of the people who lived upon it: that this ownership was conditional upon the discharge of the duties, and that succession-fines were intended as a reminder to each inheritor by how frail and how personal a tie his heritage was secured to him. The whole fabric rested not only on contract but on custom —*i.e.* on status. Into whatsoever status you were born you remained, upon conditions older than you and over which you had no control, but also on the proper fulfilling of which depended your possession of your property in land or in arms.

The lord was looked upon as performing public services, for which he received fees: thus he had his right of taxation, his fees for the use of the oven and of the mill, his dues arising from the market or the court; nor could any market or court or mill, or even oven, be used other than his. This feudal system has been defined as " government by amateurs paid in land rather than by professionals paid in money." But this is not quite accurate ; for, first, the feudal lord was a professional, and secondly, land itself was money—it was the wealth of the age. But more happily it has been described as " a graduated system based upon land-tenure, by which each lord judged, taxed and commanded the classes next below him."

Now this is sufficiently true and comprehensive to show how little the notion of ownership of land had as yet emerged. The nation was represented by the king. He in turn let the lands which the nation had entrusted to him to certain individuals on the condition of their paying rent in the form of governmental work, not only of military service but also of suit to the King's Court, with the performance of judicial functions. By subinfeudation this letting of land was continued through every grade of society on similar terms of rent. The land of the Middle Ages was, therefore, never sold but only let out on hire.

But this system was slowly broken down. The king, the Church, the nobility and the common people all attacked it. The king naturally opposed it, for his desire was always to break down the independence of the feudatories and to effect direct contact and establish personal relations with their vassals as well as with his own. The nobles, and more particularly the Church, were also inconvenienced by the perpetual demands of the king for their services in war overseas and for their attendance at his Court, which often came to mean the exaction of extortionate aids and subsidies. It became more and more to the convenience of both parties to substitute money for personal service, and advantageous to secure justice from the royal courts, which were steadily reabsorbing those rights and jurisdictions which the baronage had vainly struggled to retain. The objections of the common people became vocal and operative after the Black Death—enhancing the value of their services—had enabled them to demand higher wages, which attracted the unfavourable attention of the landlords to the growing emancipation of the agricultural classes. The working population had become considerably reduced, with the result that there was insufficiency of labour to meet the demand. Under the old manorial system few—save perhaps the servant-class and the remnants of the *servi*, if even they— had been required to give up the whole of their time to others ; no one was without the possession, if conditional, of some land, though almost all were unfree. The *liberi-tenentes* in the eleventh century amounted to hardly five per cent. of the whole population.

With the Black Death came the stampede of labour : it sought its natural market and clamoured for the best terms. The Statutes of Labourers, initiated by the Ordinance of 1349, were the reply, determining the wage of labour, reducing the obligations and the cash wages to the old service for which they had been in certain cases substituted, and punishing masters as well as labourers for any infringement of the decrees. They were inoperative. It was found impossible to stem the tide. Trade unions of labour were formed against which further legislation was levelled. In the first year of Richard II.'s reign we learn of these unions, which "gather themselves together in great routs and agree by such confederacy that everyone shall aid to resist their lords by strong hands" (*Statutes of the Realm*, 1 *Rich. II.*, cap. 6). The resistance of the working class was met by the insistence of Parliament on the accustomed services, the denunciation of the growing demands of labour for a higher wage as usury, and the statutory fixing of the price of food.

But this legislation broke down under the competitive greed of the masters and the revolt of the men. The peasantry were aided in their escape from villeinage by the need which the lords had of money, caused by greed and encouraged by luxury. The anxiety of the labouring classes to escape from the life of bondage made them willing to buy themselves out ; and the discovery of the lords that hired labour was cheaper and easier to get inspired both sides to come to terms. Money was beginning to take the place of land as the symbol of power, and with money came, curiously, the sense of absolute ownership. Men, whether a town or a noble or a villein, bought their freedom, and with freedom naturally conditional ownership ceased, for it was precisely the conditions that were sold, and with the lapsing of conditional ownership absolute ownership emerged. With absolute ownership came the desire to increase personal holdings of land, and this desire dominated the evolution of political history, for from it sprang both the series of Enclosure Acts (though the earliest of them, the Statute of Merton, dates as far back as 1236) and of monastic spoliation which ended in the establishment of the Reformation and the rule of the squire.

The English peasant then—and his example was followed everywhere else in greater or less degree—in gaining his liberty lost his land. Indeed it may almost be said that the social theories of the Middle Ages made a complete antithesis between the freedom and the land of the villein class. The landless man was an exception in mediæval society ; the earlier the society the more exceptional was he ; yet the freeman was as rare as the landless man, while the man in whose power it was to leave his holding and his lord and his trade was only the landless man and no other. Even the free tenants were in practice tethered to the soil. Land, because of the demand for service made upon its holders as a condition for holding it, meant a loss of personal freedom to whomsoever it belonged. It owned the men and not they it. To be free in your choice of dwelling meant only to be dispossessed of dwelling. You were a traveller in the world, and to travel well you must travel lightly ; you must jettison your cargo to ride free in the storm ; the heath of the world was beset by robbers who carried you off into captivity with your booty—you could only escape from their clutches by having no booty. It was an age in which you were perpetually faced with the cut-throat menace : " Stand and deliver. Your land or your freedom." The surrender of one or other was essential to your life. Thus under stress of the Peasant Revolt the lord became a landlord ; and the result of the first great strike was to dispossess the strikers of what they had in order that they might gain what they lacked. Competition came to stay in place of custom ; freedom of work and opportunity was granted in place of fixed and regulated service ; absolute ownership was substituted for conditional ownership but was narrowed to a very few. All the ranks of society had once owned some land but none without doing service for it; now the majority lost their land in exchange for money, and those few into whose hands it came did less service for it, or less obvious service. The majority forgot that they had surrendered it, the few forgot that they had not always owned it. Labour of its own free will forced the lord to take over from it all its land. Labour was the prodigal who demanded cash down for the portion of his inheritance that he might go into the far country of freedom; perhaps he has ever since had to envy the brute beasts of his lord their tranquil and unanxious lives, their fixed services, their weekly work and their home-lands.

It was money, then, that altered the attitude of the mediæval mind to property, though the mere substitution of money for land did not at first destroy the older theory of conditional ownership. Land was too cumbersome, when commerce began to extend and spread over Europe, to be of value, too immovable, too inelastic. Hence the substitution of money for land was welcomed eagerly. Yet at the beginning the basis of the substitution was not the value of the land surrendered, but the service and suit which the land entailed. It was hardly, therefore, the land that was sold, because the notion still endured that the land in itself did not belong to the holder of it, it was his only conditionally and as it were on trust: so that the idea of service still survived even when money began to be the new basis of state organization. But this could not and did not last. The idea of service grew fainter, and in a while the exchange of money was no longer equivalent to the service due from it or to anything else than the value of the land. The land was sold or bought and not the servile or free tenure that the custom of the land carried. Land began to be thought of as a thing in itself. It was owned directly, and absolute ownership began.

All this was not done at once; and even when done its full meaning was not apparent, even to those who suffered by it. In the Peasant Revolt of 1381 we find that the rioters demanded the cheaper rent of land—namely, at fourpence an acre—showing certainly that there was still a desire to own land; but it is difficult to see what this reduced cost of land would have effected in the life of the nation had it been carried into force. It is quite clear from the manorial records that the chief desire of everybody was to get away from his holding. The lords who were now landlords bought larger properties, the size of the individual properties growing considerably in extent right up to the time when the monastic spoliation completed the process of the steady enrichment of the few. But as far as the worker was concerned the decay of villeinage seems to have meant the decay of land-holding in permanent tenure; there was henceforward little fixity of succession, perhaps little security.

The monographs that have been written in these last years seem consistently to show that the population shifted a great deal and that whether the land had been free or been encumbered by servile tenure it proved impossible to secure for it uninterrupted family ownership. It looks as though this hereditary ownership had been the custom throughout the previous centuries only because it could not be escaped, and that the people remained stationary only because they were not allowed to move away.

But it is the effect of this on the theory of property that we are considering, and it was bound to be great. Yet while the principle of feudalism had been that the whole of the land belonged to the king as the representative of the nation, but was let out to individual use on the condition of suit and service, the theory of the mediæval thinkers seemed at first sight almost the reverse of this, for St Thomas Aquinas and all the doctors of scholasticism reprobated the teaching of Plato, who favoured common ownership and individual use. Over and over again, as we have already shown, the ideal was propounded and preached that there should be individual ownership and public use—*i.e.* private possession concomitant with almsgiving on a very large scale.

The hordes of beggars, the canonization of mendicancy in the person of the Poverello of Assisi, the enthusiastic reception given to the friars, and earlier to the Hospitallers, satisfied the mediæval conscience, which held that wealth was not to be looked up to with too much deference. Moreover, it seemed to mediæval society that only by lavish distribution of your super-fluous means could you escape the denunciations of riches contained in the Gospels. Private ownership could only be tolerated at the price of the public use of its more than necessary possessions. This is a doctrine that is to be found everywhere in the pages of the orthodox mediævalist.

But once you leave the orthodox mediævalist, you find that one or other of these institutions gets attacked, or becomes exaggerated, to the destruction or the loss of the other. Take, that is, as the normal proposition, this saying: "Private property is lawful but only if the precept to give alms is added to it." That was the patristic defence of property, reaching the Fathers through the Stoics, and passed on by them to the mediæval world. Then note how each part of this proposition was attacked:

1. Wyclif and his followers threw over private property as a general institution and attacked the widespread begging and mendicancy of the pilgrims, though the Poor Preachers of Lollardy were, as beggars, little distinguishable from the friars in many of their ways. Wyclif disliked the friars, but copied them. However, his prime theory was the famous Dominion of Grace, whereby he endeavoured to uphold the principle that only the just could possess property. He was not a clear thinker and his treatises are very puzzling to follow, for though he has the style of the scholastics of his day he has none of the simplicity of his contemporaries.[1] Perhaps he found that actually his teaching could not well be defended, for he had to invent so many devices for explaining away his original proposition that in the end it meant little more than the power of goodness to enjoy riches without possessing them. His followers, who were not philosophers, preached his original proposition, without troubling over the refinements of thought which had emptied it of its explosive quality. It was precisely its explosive quality that made it so suitable for propaganda and so intensely popular. Wyclif, however, since John of Gaunt was friendly to him and John of Gaunt was rich, entirely disowned the

---

[1] The amazing plagiarisms he perpetrated can be seen in Loserth's *Johann von Wicliff und Guilelmus Peraldus*, Vienna, 1916.

doctrine of communism then being preached, and accused the friars of having been the authors of it. Yet there can be no doubt that the Lollard preachers did denounce property and riches, and were affected by the ideals of Gospel poverty to the verge of denying the righteousness of individual possessions. It is interesting to see how the Lollards following Wyclif threw over private property and would have abolished begging.

2. The Spiritual Franciscans, on the other hand, earlier than Wyclif, denounced private property indeed but preached mendicancy. No follower of Christ, they thought, had any business to take scrip or coin, for they urged that the Scriptures never showed Christ holding money in his hand. He looked at it, worked a miracle for St Peter to find it for the tax-collector, but never possessed it. Instead, He had not where to lay His head. The work of St Francis was to them not so much the founding of an Order as an appeal of a lover of Christ to all men to go back to the Gospel of Christ. They declared that not only was he right himself in his appeal but that anyone who refused to follow him was refusing to follow the greater Master. Did not Christ go barefoot, for the Magdalen was able to wash His feet at table? Had not the Christian equally to follow the Master, renouncing, denying himself and still more his possessions, and carrying the cross? Almsgiving was, therefore, the beginning of wisdom; to give to the poor all a man had was the necessary condition of Christian spiritual life, incumbent upon all who would be saved. Property was paganism, poverty was of the Faith, not as a counsel of perfection but as a command. So serious was the matter considered that a commission of cardinals sat to discuss the point, and some of the treatises sent for their inspection are still extant. The Papal decision accepted the findings of this commission, and the Fraticelli were condemned as heretics for denying the right to property. The Pope adopted the report and declared that poverty was not of universal obligation : it was a perfection for such as were called to it but it was not a precept.

3. Towards the end of our period we begin to get a new party which will have nothing to do with almsgiving. The Reformation, with its general worship of efficiency, could not

abide the " sturdy beggar." He seemed a wastrel, indeed was one; and in the hurry which always accompanies an age of crisis, when men have neither patience to bear with what they dislike nor leisure to think out their principles to the full, begging as such became denounced as an evil, and private property became regarded as the stable institution of a nation's life. Our period ends on that note. Tongues and pens are busy over the vast development of trade, urging, pushing, forecasting. We are in the glow of the Renaissance, of vast commerce, international and world-wide. Everywhere there were dreams and visions of trade. Columbus had gone West to search for it and Vasco da Gama had gone East; the spirit of wealth was stirring. But trade is based in practice on the need of the individual to possess what he has amassed. Take from man the fruits of his own labour and he will have no stimulus to labour at all. Communism makes most people indolent; they are only desirous of sharing the profits of their neighbour and of not having to produce any for themselves. That is the economic teaching at the end of the fifteenth century, the new version of the old arguments which Aquinas had borrowed from Aristotle. Hence trade was one of the strongest of the new forces in favour of absolute ownership, since the more thoroughly you own, the more motive have you for endeavouring to add to your possessions. Also, by way of consequence, the mind that trades becomes in time a mind that holds and never lets go. Trade is based upon absolute ownership and insists upon extending it.

Another influence in the same direction was the new teaching, begotten of the classic revival—the worship of the individual. To live is to be yourself. In graceful Latinity this was preached, expounded in the universities, and wholeheartedly practised. The magnificence of the Renaissance was the result of it: the carelessness of the cost so long as to-day provides the best we can produce. Wealth was the condition of the new culture; only princes, church or lay, could afford to humour the scholars, to provide them with manuscripts or marble or an audience. Psychologically the vast importance of the individual became the leading motif of the new teaching; the humanists were as a whole a most egoistical, conceited and self-opinionated body of men, whose quarrels with each other and whose praise of each other were interminably full of self. It is impossible to find in the mediæval time anything to parallel that general Renaissance spirit. Certainly it was an acquisitive age. Princes must have wealth to buy culture, living or dead ; scholars must have wealth, for they were in their own eyes so necessary to the world that their every whim must be satisfied and their freedom from financial anxiety must be wholly assured.

The old theory of property as conditional upon service has broken down. It will survive amongst the theologians and canonists. Giovanni Dominici, Antonino of Florence, Savonarola and Sebastiano dei Maggi will insist upon this as the bedrock of social existence, but their voices are drowned in the universal clamour for wealth and possessions, and the right of each man to do as he willed with his own. The ceiling of St Mary Major, in Rome, is covered with the first gold brought from the new continent. It would hardly have been decorous in such gilded surroundings to preach the gospel of poverty, to denounce the greed of men, to speak of property as only compatible with Christianity when it had been recognized that the first claim upon it was not that of the man who made it but that of the man who needed it.

In a well-known sentence, later by a hundred years, we hear of this island as once " famous throughout all Christendome by the name of Merrie England ; but covetous inclosers have taken this joy and mirth away, so that it may be now called sighing or sorrowful England " (*The Humble Petition of Two Sisters : the Church and the Commonwealth*, by Francis Trigge, London, 1604). It is not easy to justify this praise of the earlier mediæval Christendom as full of " joy and mirth," for we meet with many tales of distress and hardships, from Aucassin in the thirteenth century to Savonarola's sermons in the fifteenth. But there is this to be said, that the miser who figured so largely in the earlier period was only a moneylender—he owned little else than wealth ; whereas the new landowner was much more than that, he had power, for he sat in Parliament and made the laws. But at the end of our period the two are one.

PROPERTY

Latimer's famous sermons give a wonderful account of the new order of things. They show us property as a new force, giving men " a stake in the country," letting them deal as they will with their own, uprooting the older notion of land hired out for service and producing trade and art and individualism.

The Mediæval Age is an age of groups and guilds, of communes ; the ending of it passed into a period of intense personal self-development. Men no longer held, they owned.

CHAPTER VI

MONEY-MAKING

In the *Life of Savonarola*, by Burlamacchi (Lucca, 1784, p. 69), there is a pathetic passage in which he defends his own entrance into what might be called politics, and endeavours, at least against a brother friar, to find justification for himself: " It saddeneth me to see that my fiercest foe is likewise clad in the habit of St Dominic. That habit should remind him that our founder took no small part in worldly affairs ; and that our Order has produced a multitude of saints and holy men who have been engaged in the affairs of the state. The Florentine Republic cannot but remember the names, illustrious in their annals, of Cardinal Latino, St Peter Martyr, St Catharine of Siena, and St Antonino, all members of the Order of St Dominic. To be concerned with the affairs of this world, in which God himself has placed us, is no crime in a friar, unless he should enter into them without the aim of lifting them to higher purposes and without seeking to promote in them the cause of the Faith." No doubt with the same intention friars and other theologians of the thirteenth century gave their minds to the problems involved in the art of trade, and sought to find answers to questions that arose from the evils which seemed in their philosophy to be almost inherent in the whole business of money-making.[1] Their ideal of what trade should be was certainly good : " By divine providence," writes Humbert de Romans (Serm. xci., *In Nundinis*, p. 561), " it has so happened that no country is self-sufficient to the point of not needing the goods of any other country. From this follow three excellent results, one is humility . . . ; another is friendship, for diverse countries need each other's help and thus friendliness is occasioned, a blessing to mortal kind ; a third is the support of human weakness, for as the mechanical arts help many men to support themselves, so from trade in shops many are able to

---

[1] *Cf.* W. J. Ashley, *Introduction to Medieval Economic Life*, 2 vols., 1889-1893 ; J. E. T. Rogers, *History of Agriculture and Prices in England*, 7 vols., 1866-1902 ; P. Boissonade, *Le Travail au Moyen Age*, 1921.

support themselves, lawfully, too, if the trade be rightly carried on." This passage dwelling on trade as a unifying influence, which shows already the effect of the teaching of Aristotle, could be paralleled by quotations from many other contemporary sources; an interesting reproduction of it at greater length and more beautifully developed can be found in the *Summa Moralis* of St Antonino (I. i. 3, 3, *cf.* II. ii. 16, 3). It will be as well to continue the quotation of De Romans a little farther since the passage betrays what the earlier Middle Ages feared as the all but inevitable accompaniments of trading : " However it can happen that lying and fraud and usurious contracts are occasioned in marketing, and men sell their souls for gain, a detestable avarice. . . . And some merchants, kept by their voyaging so long away from their wives, seek satisfaction where they should not. . . . And some are careful enough to keep the laws of the market which man has made but are not so careful to keep the laws which are from God. . . . And other sins are committed in trade, non-observance of feasts, contentions, disputes. . . . Indeed, may we not truly call the world itself naught else than a great market-place where we trade at our stalls with the talents lent us by God. As quickly as the booths close with the ending of daylight, is the ending of our trade. Joy comes as quickly, is as quickly gone. So was the trade of Tyre, as Ezechiel tells us in chapter twenty-seven, for markets are an ancient mode." There was always this dread of evil in the mind of the moralist however highly he might dream the ideals of commerce to be.

In a passage of considerable length, the introduction to his *Commentary on the Politics of Aristotle* (Parma edition, pp. 366-367, vol. iv., 1866), St Thomas Aquinas argues out the possibility of a science of Political Economy : " As the philosopher teaches in Book II. of the *Physics*, art imitates nature. The reason of this is that the relationship between two or more principles determines what shall be the relationship between their various effects and workings. Now the principle of whatever is effected by art, is the human intellect which is derived from, and is in some way a reproduction of, the divine intellect, and this divine intellect is the principle of whatever is in nature; so that the processes of art must imitate the processes of nature and whatever is effected by art must imitate something in nature. And as, when the master of an art produces a work, his apprentice, whose business it is to learn his art, watches him so as to be able to produce a like work himself, so the human intellect, which derives its intellectual power from the divine intellect, must watch the world about it and learn from the workings of nature how to reproduce such effects as it desires. Man, the apprentice, must watch God, the Master, his art imitating God's. Hence it is that the Philosopher says that, were art to do what nature does, it would have to do it in nature's way, and were nature on the other hand to do what art does it would do it as art does it. So nature does not perfect art but supplies the principles and in some sense shows the model for the artist to copy. Art indeed can look at nature and use it for the perfecting of its own work, but art cannot perfect nature. We can say then that the human intellect only knows nature, but both knows and creates art. Thus it comes about that the human sciences that deal with nature are speculative; while those that deal with art are practical— that is, not only watch nature but also work after nature's model.

"But it is the way of nature to proceed from the simple to the complex, for we find invariably in the workings of nature that the most complex is the perfection, completion, and end of the others, as is clear in every whole in respect to its parts. The mind of man, therefore, in its artistry must no less proceed from the simple to the complex as from the imperfect to the perfect. But the human reason has to direct not only things which fall under man's use, but even other men who are themselves ruled by reason, and in both it must proceed from the simple to the complex: (i) in those things which fall under man's use, as when out of wood ships are built or houses out of wood and stone; (ii) in other men, as when out of men a single community is formed. Since, however, in these communities there are many degrees and grades, that community is final which is a State and is sufficient of itself for the lives of its citizens; this is the most perfect of all human communities.

And since those things which fall under man's use are ordained to man as their end (and the end is of more account than the things ordained to that end), necessarily the State is the highest and most perfect end that can be known or devised by human reason.

" We accept, therefore, four principles of political science from this book of Aristotle. *First* indeed the necessity of it, and this because, out of all those things which can be known by human reason, some body of doctrine must pertain to the perfecting of human reason which we call philosophy. Since, therefore, this ' whole,' which is the State, is itself subject to human reason, there must be a body of political teaching (or civil science) complementary to philosophy. *Secondly* we can accept its definition, for practical sciences are distinguished from speculative science in this, that speculative sciences are ordained solely to the knowledge of truth but practical sciences to the doing of work. Therefore this science must be a practical science, for a State is not only something known to human reason but something affected by human reason. Again, since reason sometimes produces effects in external matter in a transitory way proper to the mechanical arts (as in carpentering, shipbuilding, and so on), and sometimes produces effects purely within the producer of them (as taking counsel with one's self, choosing, willing and the like) which belong to the moral sciences, it follows that political science, which considers the proper ordering of men, is not contained under the sciences which make things, the mechanical sciences, but under the sciences which do things, the moral sciences. *Thirdly* we can accept the importance which he attributes to political science in regard to the other sciences, for the State is the noblest of those things which can be constituted by the human reason, for to it all other human communities are ordained. Again, since every unit constituted by the mechanical arts out of those things that fall under man's use is ordained to man as to its end, and since that science is the noblest which is busied with the nobler and more perfect object, necessarily political science is the noblest and most architectonic of all the practical sciences, since it deals with the final and perfect good in human things.

Thus it is that the Philosopher at the end of Book X. of the *Ethics* says that philosophy, since it deals with human things, is completed by political science. *Fourthly* it will be seen from what we have said that we accept the method and order of this science. For just as the speculative sciences when considering some unit arrive at a knowledge of the whole from the consideration of its parts and principles (because these manifest its capacities and activities), so must this science arrive at a knowledge of the State from the consideration of the parts and principles that constitute it, since these manifest its capacities and activities. Nor does its work stop here, for, since it is a practical science, it teaches man how to make the State ever more perfect, for this is the necessary consequence of its being a practical science."

It seems worth while to quote this passage in full since it shows how, to the mediæval mind, philosophy was justified in concerning itself with trade and commerce.[1] These were to them practical sciences, comprised under civil science, and they were necessary to, and completed, philosophy itself. They were arts because directed by reason, and were to be copied from nature, which equally with reason was derived from God. The other Aristotelean divisions of political economy Aquinas also adopted. Thus in *Lectio* v., p. 348, we find the art of acquiring money (*pecuniativa*) divided from the art of using money (*æconomica*), and this distinction set between them : " The art of acquiring money is subordinate to the art of using money, not so much by way of providing material for it as by way of providing tools for it. For money and every kind of wealth are merely economic tools." Moreover this comparison and opposition are explained by taking as an example the difference between the art of making combs for the textile trade, "which is the providing of tools," and the art of preparing wool, "which is the providing of material." "Those, therefore, that abound in what is strictly speaking necessary for life are richer than those that abound in mere money " (p. 389).

The prime distinction, therefore, that must be borne in

---

[1] *Cf.* T. F. Tout, *Medieval Town Planning*, 1917.

mind as the determining and guiding distinction in all mediæval
political and economic science is the distinction between those
arts that are subordinated to another and those arts which are
not. If you give an art a purpose you have given it a limitation ;
unless you give it a purpose it will have no limitation. This
simple philosophic concept, elaborated by Aristotle, is for
example the sole human argument which Aquinas urges against
usury : " The art of amassing wealth which is solely concerned
with money is infinite, as we can prove in this way. The desire
of the end of each art is an unlimited desire, but the desire for
those things which serve the purpose of the art is a limited
desire, for it is limited precisely by that purpose as its rule
and measure. But the object of the art of making money is
merely the making of money, and to this there can be no limit.
Political economy, however, which is concerned with the using
of money for a definite pupose, does not seek unlimited wealth,
but wealth such as shall help towards its purpose, and this purpose is the good estate of the home " (*ibid.*, pp. 390-391). For
the mediævalist, then, the whole justification of trade lay in the
intention of the trader. If his prime object was to make money
he was sinfully engaged in his profession ; if his object was to
secure enough money to live on, and to help forward the good
of his neighbour, he was lawfully engaged in his profession,
though further questioning would follow as to the manner in
which he traded.

The pursuit of wealth had a limit, because the purpose of
acquiring wealth was the good estate of the home ; if it were
possible for that purpose once for all to be assured, and if the
good of one's neighbour or of one's nation did not otherwise
demand it, trading should be given up or handed over to
others. Merely to engage in commerce for the purpose of
making more money was not a sufficient justification, for
money should be only a means to an end. To make it an end
in itself was to spoil man's life, because life thenceforward
became robbed of definite purpose. This might seem a mere
point of philosophic speculation without serious effect ; yet its
effects were definite enough and designed. The following
quotations from the *Summa Moralis* of St Antonino show how

the theory was operative and not merely academic. Philosophically, in the *Summa Moralis* of St Antonino, the idea is thus expressed: " The object of gain is that by its means man may provide for himself and others according to their state. The object of providing for himself and others is that they may be able to live virtuously. The object of a virtuous life is the attainment of everlasting glory " (I. i. 3, iii.). " If the object of the trader is principally cupidity, which is the root of all evils, then certainly his trading will be evil. But that trade (as natural and necessary for the needs of human life) is, according to Aristotle, in itself praiseworthy which serves some good purpose—*i.e.* supplying the needs of human life. If, therefore, the trader seeks a moderate profit for the purpose of providing for himself and family according to the condition becoming to their state of life, or to enable him to aid the poor more generously, or even if he goes into commerce for the common good (lest, for example, the State should be without what its life requires), and consequently seeks a profit not as an ultimate end but merely as a wage of labour, he cannot in that case be condemned " (II. i. 16, ii.). " To acquire by labour the amount of food sufficient for preserving one's being requires only a moderate amount of time and a moderate amount of anxiety " (IV. xii. 3, i.). There is undoubtedly the touch of the tranquillity of mediæval moralizing and of its impracticability in that last phrase.

Moreover, trade as such, and work as such, were considered a blessed thing. " In the first days of the Order," says *The Mirror of Perfection* (cap. xxiv., p. 205, Dent, London), " when the friars dwelt in Rivo Torto, near Assisi, there was amongst them a certain friar who prayed well and did not work, who would not ask for alms and used to eat well. Considering these things the Bl. Francis knew by the Holy Spirit that he was a carnal man and said to him : ' Go thy way, friar fly, since thou wilt eat of the labour of thy brethren and be idle in the work of God, like a lazy and sterile drone which profiteth nothing and laboureth not, but eateth the labour and profit of the good bees.' And so he went his way. And because he was carnal, he sought not for mercy nor found it."

In the introduction to *The Little Flowers of St Francis* (translated by Professor T. Okey, Dent, London) the same gospel of work is taught again in the famous Testamentum (5): " I worked with my hands and desire to work. I steadfastly will and desire that all the friars work at some honourable handicraft; and as for those who know none, let them learn, not for the sake of the price of their labour but for example and to eschew idleness. And when we can obtain nothing for our labour, then we can have recourse to the labour of the Lord, begging alms from door to door." In the *Regula Prima* each was ordered to work at the trade he had learnt, unless it had been scandalous work or was likely to imperil his salvation; nor was poverty to be so straitly interpreted as to prevent each retaining the tools necessary for his work. In the case of necessity, however, and it would seem only in such case, the friars were "to beg as do the poor." So we read that Brother Giles (p. 151), "being on a time in a friary at Rome, was minded to live by bodily toil, even as he was ever wont to do since he entered the Order, and he wrought in this wise. Betimes, in the morning, he heard Mass with much devotion, then he went to the wood that was eight miles distant from Rome and carried a faggot of wood back on his shoulders, and sold it for bread or aught else to eat. . . . Friar Giles did any honest work for hire and always gave heed to holy honesty."

What was meant by honest work is revealed to us in a glimpse by a mediæval writer : " Lady," said the tumbler turned monk, who was solemnly turning head over heels before the statue of the Blessed Virgin, "this is an honest performance. I do this not for mine own sake, so help me God, but for yours, and above all for the sake of your Son " (*Our Lady's Tumbler*, p. 10. London, 1909).

We can, therefore, lay down as the first principle of mediæval economics that there was a limit to money-making imposed by the purpose for which the money was made. Each worker had to keep in front of himself the aim of his life and consider the acquiring of money as a means only to an end, which at one and the same time justified and limited him. When, therefore, sufficiency had been obtained there could be no reason for continuing further efforts at getting rich, whether as merchant or beggar, except in order to help others :

" Ac under his secret seel treuthe sent hem [Merchants] a
 lettre,
That they shulde bugge boldely that hem best liked,
And sithenes selle it again and save the wynnynge,
And amende mesondieux theremyde and myseyse folke
 helpe,
And wikkid wayes wigtlich hem amende ;
And do bote to brugges that to-broke were,
Marien maydenes or maken hem nonnes ;
Pore peple and prisounes fynden hem here fode,
And sette scoleres to scole or to somme other craftes ;
Releve Religioun and renten hem bettere ; . . .

Forthi biddeth nought, ye beggeres, but if ye haue grete
 nede
For who-so hath to buggen hym bred the boke bereth
 witnesse,
He hath ynough that hath bred ynough, though he have
 nought elles :
Satis dives est qui non indiget pane." [1]

The second principle was that the trade or commerce must be carried on honestly and well. Ruskin quotes an inscription found in a church at Venice : " Around this temple let the merchant's law be just, his weights true, and his contracts guileless." That this was often not the case is clear from many sources. Tolomeo de Lucca observes at the end of the thirteenth century : " Victuals that are sold are often not pure and therefore have not the same nourishment value as home-grown produce " (*De Regimine Princip.*, Bk. II., cap. 5). At the end of the fourteenth century, under the heading " Falsitas," John Bromyard asserts : " Scarcely does any simple or trusty person come up from the country to buy in these great cities without meeting that herb [of falsehood] ere he return home " (*Promptuarium*

---

[1] *Vision of William concerning Piers Plowman*, Skeat, Oxford, 1924, Passus VII., ll. 23-32, 84-87.

Praedicatorum, Lyons, 1522, vol. i., fol. clxxxii.). In the *Summa Moralis* (pars iii., tit. 8, cap. 4) St Antonino gives us a list, long, detailed and technical, of the various kinds of dishonesty practised then in the staple trades of Florence.

But the fullest statement as to fraudulent practices is perhaps to be found in the treatise on court keeping—*Modus Tenendi Curiam Baronis*—printed by Wynkyn de Worde about 1510, but belonging to a much earlier date:

" Also of all comyn bakers amonge you that make unholsom brede for mannes body and kepe not the assyse ye shall do us to wete."

" Also of all bruers and tapsters that brue and kepe not the assys and sell by cuppes dysshes and bolles and by mesures unsealed do us to wete."

" Also yf there be ony amonge you that useth double mesures, that is to saye a grete mesure to bye with and a smaller to sell with or useth fals ballaunce or weyghtes yerdes or in dysceyte of ye kynges people shewe us."

" Also of all bochers fysshers or ony other vytelers [that] sell vytayles corrupte and not holsom for mannes body or sell to excessyvely ye shall doo us to wete of theym."

" Also yf there be ony regratoures or forstallers amonge you that bye in the waye to bye corne or ony other vytayle at ye townes ende or in ony other place to make the chepe thereof derer do us to wete of them."

" Also yf there be ony myllers among you that use to take excessyve toll otherwyse than they ought to do by ryght ye shall do to wete."

" Also yf there be ony vagabondes or hasarders or robbers amonge you that wake on ye nyght and slepe on the day and haunte customable ale houses and tavernes and routes aboute, and no man wote fro whens they come ne whether they shall [go] ye shall do us to wete of them and of theyr recettoures."[1]

While giving the procedure to be followed, the *Modus Tenendi*

---

[1] Published by the Manorial Society, 1915, pp. 8-10. " Also they say that K. sane and healthy is a common vagabond who wakes at nights and sleeps through the day and does no work, therefore . . . " (p. 21).

contains information as to prices : " The stewarde shall make
the baylyfe to make an oez et dicat. All manner of men that
wyll bake brede to sell, loke they sell four loves for iiii*d*. and
ii loves for ii*d*. And loke ye kepe the assyse. All manner of
brewsters that wyll brewe to sell, that they sell a galon of ale
of the best for i*d.ob*. and other for i*d*. and other for halfpeny,
and kepe the assyse, and that no bruer sell out no burthen tylle
the ale founder hath assayed thereof and set a pryce thereupon.
Upon payne of forfeyture etc."

The mediæval thinker seems to have discerned a third
principle in economics—namely, that there should be a just
price at which articles should be sold, and that this just price
was determinable, and should be determined, by law. The
above quotation from the *Manner of holding a Court Baron* is a
practical illustration of this principle. But it is also necessary
to remember that the moralist, to whose department economics
were at that time assigned, formulated his theories in the light
of abstract principles of justice. He was dealing with justice,
therefore had only to lay down principles. It seemed to him
therefore that individuals engaged in trade were not likely
to sell at the lowest price compatible with a due margin of
profit, but at the highest price they could extract from the
customer. It hardly entered his head to take into account
competition as a factor in reducing prices, because the practice
of the guilds ruled competition almost entirely out of the
market. The real danger in mediæval commerce was the
formation of rings of merchants—or even one merchant—
who, by buying up the whole of a commodity, could hold up to
ransom the public, who must needs buy it, and yet could only
buy it from the sellers at their price. Partly then as the outcome
of experience, and partly as the result of this abstract reasoning
about justice, the practice grew up throughout Christendom of
fixing " the just price," a legal price, beyond which, or below
which, no valid sale could be effected. It was the principle of the
taximeter applied to the market-place. Legislative assemblies
fixed—not the railway fare, as now—but the reasonable charge
to be exacted for the chief necessaries of life.

The moralists were, however, perfectly aware that the price

could not really be justly fixed at an absolute figure. St Thomas, in the thirteenth century, and St Antonino, in the fifteenth century, both say this quite definitely. Thus, in the *Summa Theologica* : " Sometimes the just price cannot be determined absolutely (*punctualiter*), but consists rather in a common estimation, in such a way that a slight addition or diminution of price cannot be thought to destroy justice " (II. ii. 77, 1, ad 1 m), and no less explicitly in the *Summa Moralis* of St Antonino (iii. 8, iv.) : " No certain rule can be given as to the amount of gain allowed, but let it be settled by the judgment of an honest man " (*cf.* also ii. 1, 16, iii.).

Efforts, therefore, were made to ensure that the just price when settled by the state should be so fixed as to be adjustable to the cost of living. The assize of bread under Henry II., for example, established wages on a sliding scale based on the price of bread. Moreover, it was admitted that the forethought of the seller, in the purchase or production of his goods, should be taken into consideration, and consequently that he must be allowed to make money out of his ability. He might lawfully add on to the just price a fair remuneration for his trouble in the management of his business and for his prudent fore-thought in buying, and thereby securing for himself, a sufficient supply of his commodity. The price, therefore, was not ab-solutely arbitrary but was based on a calculation by prudent men (St Antonino would have preferred it fixed by the state, *Summa Moralis*, pars iii., 8, 3, iv. ; pars ii., 1, 16, ii.), due allow-ance being made for the ability, time, and forethought of the merchant.

" The middleman," says Aquinas, " is one whose business consists in the exchange of things. The exchange of things is twofold : one natural, as it were, and necessary, whereby the commodity is exchanged for another or money is taken in ex-change for a commodity in order to satisfy the needs of life. Such-like trading, properly so-called, does not belong to the middleman, but rather to housekeepers or civil servants who have to provide the household or the state with the necessaries of life. The other kind of exchange is either that of money for money or of any commodity for money, not on account of the necessities of life, but for profit; and this kind of exchange, properly speaking, regards the middleman. The first kind of exchange is commendable because it supplies a natural need. The second is justly deserving of blame because considered in itself it satisfies the greed for gain which knows no limit and tends to infinity. Hence trading, considered in itself, has a certain debasement attaching thereto, in so far as, by its nature, it does not imply a virtuous or necessary end.

"Nevertheless, gain, which is the end of trading, though not implying by its nature anything virtuous or necessary, does not in itself connote anything sinful or contrary to virtue, wherefore nothing prevents gain from being directed to some necessary or even virtuous end, and thus trade becomes lawful. Thus, for instance, a man may intend the moderate gain which he seeks to acquire by trading for the upkeep of his household or for the assistance of the needy; or again, a man may take to trade for some public advantage—for instance, lest his country lack the necessaries of life, and seek gain not as an end but as payment of labour " (II. ii. 77, 4).

The dangers of trade, and, indeed, the moral difficulty of making profit-taking in trade fit into the scheme of the Gospel, were constantly before the eyes of all mediæval writers, whether they were rulers, or theologians, or poets, or lay chroniclers:

"Falsenesse for fere thanne fleig to the freres,
And gyle doth hym to go agast for to dye.
Ac merchantz mette with hym and made hym abide,
And bishetten hym in here shope to shewen here ware,
And apparailled hym as a prentice the people to serve.
Ligtliche lyer lepe away thanne,
Lorkynge thorw lanes to-lugged of manye.
He was nawhere welcome for his manye tales,
Over all yhowted and yhote trusse;
Tyl pardoners haued pite and pulled hym into house.
They wesshen hym and wyped hym and wonden hym in
    cloutes
And sente hym with seles on sondayes to cherches,
And gaf pardoun for pens poundmel aboute . . .

Spiceres spoke wyth hym to spien here ware,
For he couth of here craft and knewe many gommes.
Ac mynstralles and messageres mette with hym ones,
And helden hym an half-yere and ellevene dayes.
Freres with faire speche fetten hym thennes
And for knowyng of comeres coped hym as a frere.
Ac he hath leve to lepe out as oft as hym liketh,
And is welcome whan he will and woneth wyth hem oft." [1]

Again : " Note that there are some in this world who live by sin, as usury or theft or rapine or fraud or lies or other evil ways ; and these for the most part are rich laymen. . . . Others there are who live on just means but got by the labours of others and not their own, entering into the work of husband-men whose labours they devour at their ease; and these for the most part are clerics and religious and rich folk. . . . Others live from just labour and these are husbandmen living on manors. Note that this was the life which first we lived on earth. This is our penance given us at the beginning, our business keeping man from sins he would otherwise commit, the toil that tames the rebel flesh " (Humbert de Romans, Serm. lxxviii., *Ad laicos in villis*, p. 494).

De Romans speaks elsewhere of many in hostels, " who alas ! receive others to hospitality not out of holiness or poverty, but for greed of money," and who even after having wrung money out of them treat them ill, " promising them in the beginning good quarters, good food, good beds and so on, and not giving them," or " extorting money from them themselves or by their wife or sons or servant," or " at the end presenting too heavy an account," or " introducing bad company into the house to attract guests," or " giving unfit food and making the guests ill," or " using false measures," or " decrying rival taverns," " therefore more truly should they be called victims rather than guests " (p. 495). " Workmen," he added, " oftentimes defraud their masters," or " spend whatever they

---

[1] *Vision of William concerning Piers Plowman*, Skeat, Oxford, 1924, Passus II., ll. 210-232.

have earned during the week in taverns on feast days and so always remain poor " (p. 500, *Ad operarios conductivos*).

We learn, too, from him how little in practice could the just price, legally fixed, be insisted on : " Though markets and fairs are terms often used indiscriminately, there is a difference between them, for fairs deal with larger things and only once in the year, or at least rarely in the same place, and to them come men from afar. But markets are for lesser things, the daily necessaries of life ; they are held weekly and only people from near at hand come. Hence markets are usually morally worse than fairs. They are held on feast days, and men miss thereby the divine office and the sermon and even disobey the precept of hearing mass, and attend these meetings against the Church's commands. Sometimes, too, they are held in graveyards and other holy places. Frequently you will hear men swearing there : ' By God I will not give you so much for it,' or ' By God I will not take a smaller price,' or ' By God it is not worth so much as that.' Sometimes again the lord is defrauded of market dues, which is perfidy and disloyalty. . . . Sometimes, too, quarrels happen and violent disputes. . . . Drinking is occasioned. . . . Christ, you may note, was found in the market-place, for Christ is justice and justice should be there. . . . Thus the legend runs of a man who, entering an abbey, found many devils in the cloister but in the market-place found but one, alone on a high pillar. This filled him with wonder. But it was told him that in the cloister all is arranged to help souls to God, so many devils are required there to induce monks to be led astray, but in the market-place, since each man is a devil to himself, only one other demon suffices " (Serm. xcii., *In Merchatis*, p. 562).

From this it will be seen that the evils of trade were thought to spring from a wrong principle or motive on his part who entered upon it, that it was precisely the intention of the trader which had to be put right, and that therefore economics became a moral question to be solved only by a moral answer. Trade was sinful if conducted for sake of gain or greed. Goods, therefore, or wealth could be turned to evil by being evilly produced, or evilly distributed, or evilly consumed (St Antonino, *Summa Moralis*, II. xii. 1 ; iv. 14, iv.).

There is a treatise on Usury attributed to St Peter Celestine, the Pope whose fame has rested largely on his resignation of the Papacy. Why this attribution has been thus made it is impossible now to say, but it is morally certain that Celestine V. was not its author, and that so neat and canonical an arrangement of the teaching of the Mediæval Church on usury could not have come from the mind of a Pope whose agony it was to have to deal with these matters of practical or speculative law. It is to be found in Bigne's collection of *Latin Fathers* (vol. xxvi., p. 853), and as it is a very compact treatise we will give it almost in full. It is written in short, concise paragraphs consisting of single sentences, or, at most, of two or three.

CHAPTER I

Usury is gain derived from something owing or exacted. Hence there is no usury if the additional profit be freely given or freely offered. Usury can be committed in number, weight, and measure.

He who has gone bail for another and has had to give usurious gain to the creditor to meet the bail, can seek it from the debtor.

If what you owe me at a certain date is not paid me, and if in consequence I have to go to a moneylender, who will lend only at usury, you have an obligation to pay me back my original loan and in addition what I have had to pay in usury.

Take the case where merchandise to-day is worth five pounds and at the end of a period is sold for six, it is not usury if there be a doubt according to the common custom of the merchandise as to whether it is worth more or less during the period covered by the purchase and the sale; but it is better not to indulge in such transactions. If at the end it is sold for a great deal more than it cost, that is usury.

Again, sometimes a penalty is attached to a contractual loan for the punishment of the contumacious debtor; that is not usury, if the penalty has been fixed with the consent of both parties so as to ensure payment of the debt by a certain date under penalty.

If I have sold a field with a proviso that whenever I pay a certain larger price I can buy it back again, this is not a loan and the buyer can take his gain without fear of usury, unless this had been done *in fraudem legis*.

If a man lend money at one hundred with the hope of getting back one hundred and ten, and is willing to suffer the loss of both, this is no usury. He who pledges an old crop in order to receive one newer and better commits usury.[1]

CHAPTER II

In seven cases usury is lawful according to Canon Law:

(1) When a layman abuses a benefice assigned him, the Church or someone in her name can receive it in pledge and gain a profit, so long as this be the only way the Church can get possession of it.

(2) When he who goes bail for another pays that debt, he can demand usury from the debtor.

(3) When canonical usury is asked—*i.e.* a penalty imposed by a Canon which demands more than the mere principal.

(4) When it is asked for not as usury but as interest, as in contracts of good faith; and this I understand to mean when the interest is really part of the thing itself or when it is asked for not to secure gain but to avoid loss.

(5) In mortgages in which more than the sum originally lent can lawfully be asked.

---

[1] In the *De Confessione* of Robert de Sorbonne, in the same collection, p. 357, the point of this last remark is expressed more clearly: "The priests distinguish: says the penitent, 'If I buy a definite amount of corn and sell it and make a gain, that is usury; but if I buy all the crop and sell it and make a gain that is no usury, for I may gain or lose.' To this the confessor answers: 'You must distinguish; if the money were given, not when the final sale was made but when the grain was delivered, in August say, and this was the agreement, good. Moreover even if it was only given later there is certainly no usury; especially since the seller asserts that he gave freely on the chance in August and took all the risk on himself. If, however, he was bound by his contract that the buyer should receive in August and had no right to it till then even if he had wanted it earlier, he can freely give his money to the seller and he would do well, if he were in need.'"

(6) By reason of the increase which the thing itself has produced of its own nature.

(7) From one's father-in-law when the dowry has been held back, the interest is not to be reputed usury.[1]

CHAPTER III

If a Christian receive usury from a Jew he must repay it to the persons from whom the Jew took it and notify the Jew.

Whoever pays usury can demand it back again.

A usurer is bound to restore his usury and whatever he has gained, because whatever comes from a tainted source is tainted.

The wife of a usurer is bound in the same way as the wife of a thief—namely, that she cannot eat of its fruits without having the intention of repaying the usury.

Here you have the chief cases—as well as their solution—that would arise out of practices that might appear doubtfully to fall under the ban of the Church. The evil of usury was taken for granted, because the practice was forbidden in the Scriptures. The divine commands repeatedly expressed in the Bible sufficed for the guidance of those generations. But usury meant the taking of gain for the use of money or any other form of wealth. How then could trade be justified, for certainly trade involved selling at a profit? This was a real difficulty of conscience which was argued about throughout the Middle Ages. The normal answer was invariably the same. You may trade at a profit, you may not trade for a profit. Your object must not be primarily to make a profit, but primarily either to earn your living or to help your fellow-men. It is, as has been already stated, in the first instance a matter of intention. This intention was essential, theologians believed, because it gave a purpose, and therefore a limitation, to the making of money. To make money for gain was wrong because there could be no limitation

---

[1] Note in these cases the principle laid down by St Thomas Aquinas in his treatise *De Usuris* (tom. xvii., opus 66, Parma, 1864): "No act can be lawfully excused from evil unless the excusing circumstances empty the act of evil: similarly danger, etc., cannot make usury allowable unless they make it cease to be usury."

to it : never could there be a reason to cease making money, never, therefore, a limit to the amount of your money, whereas all the world admitted that, once you had provided adequately for yourself and your own, whatever remained over and above was not yours at all, but belonged to the poor. It must be given to the poor. There was attached to it a *jus pauperum*. The rich man might select his particular form of charity, but to some charity, divine or human, all superfluous wealth must go. To the mind of the Middle Ages this satisfied the teaching of the Scriptures : the substitution of a moral purpose for mere indefinite making of money.

The practice of lending money was naturally even more difficult to justify. It was worse than mere trade. Hence the many denunciations of the mediæval Jew whose trade was moneylending. It is sometimes stated in defence of the Jews that in England, for example, they could not enter the guilds and were, in consequence, driven into moneylending for a living, but we know that in 1268 Benedict the Jew was admitted by the Mayor of Winchester to "full membership of the liberty of the city and citizenship and guild rights in the Merchant Guild with all the privileges pertaining to the same liberty." [1] We may, nevertheless, take it for granted that this would be but a rare occurrence ; ordinarily the Jew was allowed to practise certain learned professions—medicine, for example —but not commerce. Thus driven out of trade the Jews turned to moneylending, by which they soon found themselves able to attract a large circle of clients, clerical and lay and, above all, royal. It is commonly stated that the first-known usurer was a French rabbi, Jacob Tam of Rameru, in 1146, but, the practice once started, its ramifications must have developed with great rapidity, for the "Ordinance of Jewry," by which the whole business came under regulation in 1194, shows the hold the Jews had by that time secured over their clientage and the strength of their position in the public life. By the thirteenth

---

[1] It seems curious that the writer who makes the assertion that Jews were not allowed into the guilds (G. H. Leonard, *The Expulsion of the Jews by Edward I.*, in *Trans. Roy. Hist. Soc.*, vol. v., 1891, p. 103) should himself have cited this instance to the contrary (from Kitchin's *Winchester*, p. 115).

century their prosperity, coupled with their immunity from restrictions binding the Christians, had roused popular feeling, which rose in proportion to their growing wealth and the increasing number of those in their debt. Popular dislike coincided with the adoption of public action against them. In 1240 the Caursines—moneylenders from Cahors—were expelled by Henry III. from England ; they had made themselves unpopular and for the same reason—that they were owed money and strove harshly to recover it. When the Jews of 1270 ventured to petition the king to be allowed the custody of Christian heirs and advowsons in default of payment, public feeling was much excited and Edward I. was subsequently urged to follow the example of his father and expel the Jews. The Statute of Judaism (1275) endeavoured to deal with them short of proceeding to this extremity ; it forbade the practice of usury and urged the Jew to engage in commerce and handicrafts, for which facilities were now given them, together with liberty to hold land—for a period, however, not exceeding ten years, and with exclusion from all feudal privileges springing from land tenure. This legislation naturally proved useless ; it was hardly possible for the Jews skilled in one trade to turn successfully to another, and thus handicapped on all sides they turned for a living to clipping the coin. Urged by a papal rescript to take further action, the king then fell back on an attempt at their conversion, promising to every convert full liberty of residence and trade. Dominicans and Franciscans were dispatched to argue with them ; only a few tried this way of escape from a hopeless position, the rest stood firm. With the failure of this last attempt to settle the " Jewish Question " Edward I. in 1290 banished the Jews from England under circumstances of considerable hardship and distress. By this time the Jews, whose position had largely rested on their usefulness to the Crown at a date when no mediæval king could " live of his own," had been superseded in usefulness by the Italian financiers, whose improved methods of finance rendered them of greater service than their predecessors.

Simon de Montfort had already, in 1260, expelled the Jews from Leicester, and Grossetête, then Archdeacon of Leicester, wrote to the Countess of Winchester to explain that this had been done in order that they might no longer oppress Christians unmercifully there by means of usury (*Epistolæ R. Grossetête*, Rolls Ser., p. 33). This attitude of hostility to usury was a consistent one throughout our period, and on the expulsion of the Jews the hatred against them was largely transferred to the Italian financiers who took their place. In 1376 the citizens of London petitioned for the expulsion of the Lombards "whose ostensible calling rendered them most liable to the suspicion of usury" (*Trans. Roy. Hist. Soc.*, vol. v. (1891), p. 129, note 9).

The Church, as we have already seen, did allow, under certain conditions, the taking of interest for money lent, and was always wider in her interpretation of these conditions than were the laity. Dante, for example (*Inferno*, canto xi. 17), and Chaucer (*Prioress' Tale*, l. 5) were far more severe than the canonists; Matthew Paris again, though a monk, was much more severe than Aquinas the theologian, as may be seen in his *Greater Chronicle* under the years 1235, 1251, 1253, 1254, etc. Shakespeare, who inherited the Catholic tradition, is equally strict in his rendering of the mediæval doctrine in the *Merchant of Venice*. Even English law was stricter than canon law (Round, *Ancient Charters*, p. 90; Gross, *Gild Merchant*, vol. ii., p. 50).[1]

Nor was the Roman Church singular in her attitude, for the writers of the Orthodox Eastern Church held precisely the same views. In an *Oration against Usurers*, Nicolas Cabasilas, Bishop of Thessalonica in the fourteenth century, attacks the lending of money at interest as a practice contrary to Christian teaching, and, condemning the Jews for their preoccupation in the business, he replies to the arguments put forward in their defence by an exposure of the fallacies therein contained. Other sins require effort, only "to the usurer no labour can be ascribed, no dangerous business. He alone grows rich without doing anything for it" (Bigne's edition, vol. xxvi., p. 169). "But I have helped the poor," says the Jew. "Yes, but you did not take up your trade for that. It was an accident of your trade. If by that means poverty was put from their door, yours is not the merit. Certainly your help relieved them, but not

---

[1] *Finance and Trade under Edward III.*, ed. by G. Unwin, 1918.

your injustice. No one blames you for lending, only for lending with usury. This does not relieve poverty, this causes it. Can you really call this humanity and the care of the poor? . . . The law never allowed princes or priests to lend money at interest. . . . But, says the Jew, we are no use at farming, nor at merchandise, nor at begging. 'What else then can we do? But do not thieves say this and the women of the streets? . . . There is only one point at issue, is usury lawful? But surely we may take interest from those who freely offer it? . . . Are you so sure that it is freely offered and not compelled by necessity? If so freely offered, why is a bond drawn up? Why the law invoked but that you may have the law's support?" (*ibid.*, pp. 170-172). The argument of the *Oration* is the counterpart of the teaching of the Western Latin Church.

Bromyard, under the title " Usura " in his *Promptuary for Preachers* (Lyons, 1522, vol. ii., fol. dcxxxiii.), tells a story for pulpit use which illustrates the popular attitude and makes us wonder whether the preacher might not be responsible for the narrower interpretation by the layfolk of the canons against usury. " A certain preacher," he said, " knowing that many usurers were in his congregation asked if there were any usurer present in the church. To this no one answered. He then asked if there was a drain-cleaner present. To this a man answered that his trade was such. Look, said the preacher, how vile a trade must usury be when the vilest trade admits its existence and is not ashamed, while the usurer dares not in his shame publicly own himself a usurer."

The increase of trade, however, while it did not alter the attitude of the Church to usury, did alter her attitude as to what particular cases fell under the ban of usury, and opened up possibilities under which interest might be safely taken. Nor was this surprising, for the new problems of trade could not really be referred for solution to the older decisions. St Thomas himself dealing with the new case—corresponding to the modern holder of dividends—in which several shareholders contribute money to a venture which they do not personally conduct—such being the position of the financier who does no more than put money into a business—absolves them from the taint of usury. They do not lend money, he argues, but rather risk it in a common enterprise : " He that entrusts his money to a merchant or craftsman so as to form a kind of society *does not transfer the ownership of his money to them,* for it remains his, so that at his risk the merchant speculates with it or the craftsman uses it for his craft and, consequently, he may lawfully demand as something belonging to him part of the profits derived from his money " (*Summa Theologica,* II. ii. 78, 2, ad 5 m. ; cf. *ibid.,* 62, 4). Again when there is danger of the whole merchandise being lost, as at sea, to ask for interest on money lent to the merchant himself is not to be classed as usury. Whenever, in fact, by delay or other means, the lending of money meant a loss to the lender, this circumstance was held to justify the taking of interest.[1]

Thus Edward I. gave one thousand pounds to the Frescobaldi " in recompense of the losses and risks which these merchants suffered by reason of the delay in repayment of the aforesaid debts " (Bond, *Archæologica,* vol. xxviii., p. 141, n.7). It was considered that these circumstances removed the taking of interest out of the category of usury, for interest here represented, not " the breed of barren metal," but compensation for discomfiture, or risk of discomfiture, caused to the lender. To repeat : the sin of usury lay in the unlimited and unlimitable nature of its demand, and the fact that it unjustly deprived the worker of his profit, for the man who made money by handwork had a right to the full value of his profit, since this increase was due entirely to his labour. Consequently, if the money with which he purchased the instrument or material of his labour were lent him this did not entitle the lender to demand a share of the profit, since it was the worker's labour or forethought that alone made the money fruitful. The lender was entitled to what he had originally lent, and to no more. The sole title to interest that could be admitted lay, not on the ground of the fruitfulness of the money lent, but on the loss which the lending of it had occasioned him : interest ceased to be usury only when it was compensation.

---

[1] *Cf.* St Antonino, *Summa Moralis,* pars iii., tit. 8, cap. 4, 3 ; Wilson's *A Discourse upon Usury,* ed. by R. H. Tawney, London, 1925.

In the same way we can say that practically the only other form of interest allowable was a return for risk or danger. You could not indeed demand usury, but you could gamble on its chances of success. You insured, you made bets, you played your game of hazard, ready to meet in a proper spirit the failure of your "argosies," and on the other hand to share amongst your fellow-gamblers the proceeds of the success should any come of it. You, as the financier, became a fellow-worker with the shipmen, not merely because you had contributed money to the enterprise, but because the same uncertainty made you partners with them—the menace of loss to you and to them in shipwreck. You passed, through your spirit of adventure, into the ranks of the merchant; your risk gave you the freedom of the craft. You entered thereby into the guild.

Meanwhile the number of books dealing with trade, its facilities and the policy that should actuate its encouragement, increased steadily from the fourteenth century onwards.[1] Already the *Dialogus de Scaccario*, under Henry II., had urged on the king and the royal officials their responsibility for the good of the whole people under their charge, not least in finance. Taxation should not be used merely as a means of raising money, but in order to stimulate trade and, therefore, the wealth of the people. It was a part of royal administration to see that trade was developed. Indeed, the *Dialogus* definitely stated that the wealthier the people the wealthier would be their king. The plea was irresistible. Edward I. entered into the hopes of the writer of the *Dialogus* and framed a policy built on the principle laid down in it. His public acts of administration had frequent reference to trade, both of import and export, and his treatment of them, though at fault, represented at least a gallant attempt to benefit his subjects by the careful administration, organization and encouragement of trade.

Limitations which hampered it were often enough imposed on trade, but the motive which actuated their imposition was to benefit rather than to restrict it. Bromyard complains (*Civitas*, fol. lxxxviii.*b*) : " In sea towns, where foreign merchants come

---

[1] L. F. Salzman, *English Industries of the Middle Ages*, 1923.

over in ships, they are not allowed to sell freely to all but only to the more important folk, whence comes great mischief, so that (*a*) cities grew poorer, for the merchants come there no more, and where there were twenty ships now there are scarcely five, and (*b*) so that not all can buy but only the more important folk, who sell still more dearly to the citizens and cause much distress." Already the controversy had started as to the best policy to be pursued in connection with foreign trade; the policies of free trade or of protection were already argued out alternately, and acted on by successive kings—or even by the same king—in successive divergent ways.

But into the intricacies of "the Staple," shifted from England to foreign ports and then back again, we need not enter. The social economic theory in its main features remained the same, it was but the practice that varied, following experiments to discover the best means, whether by making the tariff payable at the foreign or at the home port, of shifting the burden of taxation on to foreign shoulders. The cry raised was that the foreigner must be made to pay, and yet at the same time that he must be induced to sell here as cheaply as possible. The struggle to combine these two results continued to disturb the peace of many kings.

It must not be thought, however, that England was either singular or unique in having rulers who sought thus to develop the trade of their subjects. Everywhere throughout Christendom the same desire was to be found, least effective perhaps in the Empire only because the domestic power of the Emperor was so much less than that of other national sovereigns. In regard to France, to the free cities of Germany and Italy, to the kingdom of Spain, to Sicily, to Flanders, a mass of material has now been published showing us that everywhere the commercial projects of their subjects were recognized as meriting the encouragement of kings and senates. The growth in royal taxation had increased so that wherever royal authority had done its best to nourish trade it now reaped its own reward.

Theories on the value of money and the necessity for good coinage had also their learned exponents, most famous of whom was Nicholas Oresme (*d.* 1382), Bishop of Lisieux, who in 1373 first translated into French the *Politics* of Aristotle. His work on the revision of the coinage was translated into English early in 1400; in its Latin form its name was *De Mutatione Monetarum*. His rival theorist was Philip de Mezier. In the *Red Book of the Exchequer* there is a *Tractatus Novæ Monetæ*, a later and very interesting work.[1]

Generally, however, we can say that trade and commerce, like the arts and crafts, were regarded as needing both the direction of a good conscience and the motive of a good purpose. First, then, the intention must be right, for man is a moral agent, who works for an end proposed to him by himself. His end in this must be especially his own livelihood and the decent accommodation of himself and his family.[2] Secondly, the work itself must not be evil or forbidden, either absolutely as wrong in itself, or relatively as wrong for him : thus trade or commerce would have been considered relatively wrong when conducted by a cleric. Thirdly, all work must be pursued with discretion, adapted with prudence to each one's needs and capacities, and not overstepping the times and days appointed by divine law or just human law.

Again, the work of each man's choice should be that particular work to which he was led by his natural inclination and aptitude (St Antonino, *Summa Moralis*, iii. 8, 1). Delight, Aristotle was quoted as saying, perfected a work, and so whoever was attracted to a work—not in itself evil—ought, because it suited his powers and gave him pleasure in the doing of it, to carry out that special work, for it would then be better done, and he would arrive the more surely at the perfection of his genius. Albert the Great maintained that each man had his own humour, begotten of his complexion, and that this should guide him in the choice of his profession : " for the melancholy become poets, and the placid turn moralists, and the sanguine take to natural science, and the choleric pursue mathematics or metaphysics " (*ibid.*, i. 16, 1). So it was believed was each man led, one to mechanics and another to art, because of a

---

[1] Rolls Ser., part iii., pp. 991-1010. Perhaps by Walter Bardes, *c.* 1398.
[2] *Cf.* St Thomas Aquinas, ed. by C. Lattey, S.J., 1925, Cambridge, pp. 186-193.

natural instinct implanted by divine Providence in the soul for the perfect development of man's work on earth.

This natural instinct of man to labour at something was thought bound to be fulfilled, for were he not moved to the toil of his hands he would die. 'Without labour the land would not bear fruit, and the land, in the taming and culture of it, tamed man himself, and made him cultured. Again, necessity had compelled man to adopt pastoral work and to practise weaving and spinning and the arts essential for his clothing.

On the other hand not necessity, they thought, but greed in fallen human nature had invented commerce. In this, too, mediæval writers followed and quoted Aristotle, seeing in trade something in itself vile if its sole purpose were but gain. Yet they insisted that, though in itself degrading, trade could be turned to noble use, and made to serve the purpose of supporting a home and of helping the poor, and that these objects redeemed it from its baseness and, indeed, gave it a dignity which in itself it lacked. That the Ishmaelites should have been the first traders mentioned in Scripture (Genesis xxxvii. 28) did not help them to look upon it with any deeper respect, for the descendants of Ishmael were in their reckoning the Saracens. Indeed "the cursed Mahomet, whom they venerate as a prophet and almost as a god, was himself first a trader, and then in process of his wickedness, helped by a certain heretic called James, he deceived those ill-taught and bestial men by means of pestiferous doctrines. Moreover, since they are the enemies of Christianity they do business with Christians only that they may pervert them to their own deceits, therefore has the Church by her decrees (Nic. 4, Clem. 5, John xxii.) forbidden traders to take merchandise to those lands under pain of papal excommunication and other penalties " (St Antonino, iii. 8, 1). Moreover the mediæval theologian was confronted by a much-quoted text of St Chrysostom : " He that buys a thing in order that he may sell it, entire and unchanged, at a profit is the trader who is cast out of God's Temple " (*Summa Theologica*, II. ii. 77, 4, ad 1 m). Several writers were puzzled by this stern saying, and endeavoured to explain it by explaining it away. It is clearly to be seen that they found themselves hard put to it to defend the compatibility of trade with the teaching of Christ. Even when they praise it, their praise does not ring true, they are not whole-hearted nor quite at their ease in their advocacy of it ; and the canon lawyers were as unfavourable to commerce as the moralists, with the result that the fierce denunciations of the Fathers of the Church figure as much in the *Decretum* as in the *Summa*. Yet somehow the facts were too much for the theories, and gradually the merchants came to be recognized as men who need not necessarily be judged to be in sin : " But this business is full of perils and deceits and seems *sometimes* inseparable from usury " (*No. Extra de usu c. in civitate et c. navigante*).

Vanity was suggested as the third cause responsible for human arts. An example of this was silk-weaving, for though holy men and women—as kings and queens—had woven these " soft garments " the number of those who abused these gifts of God were thought greater than those who did not. The result of this opinion was to fill mediæval literature with plentiful denunciations of the vanities of dress, not altogether perhaps misplaced either as regards men or women. From the reign of the Conqueror the dress of the women hardly changed in England till the reign of Edward III. ; thenceforward the changes grew in fantastic exaggeration, till they culminated in the Yorkist period when, under the impulse of fashion, both men and women lost all sense of beauty or moderation and placed the achievement of strange and weird effects before everything else.

Besides good intention and good work, it was urged that labour demanded of the labourer constancy and perseverance. The worker should have in his mind a good purpose, and should choose that art towards which his natural genius drove him. But these were not sufficient unless they were sustained by his steadiness and thoroughness. Pope Anacletus was cited as having said that in every art perseverance was the mother of invention (Distin. 8 3, *Nihil*). We have, therefore, to be grateful to the preachers of that time who insisted so much on this, for to the thoroughness of the workers we owe whatever of their masterpieces have survived.

Again, in producing work, the honesty of the labourer was preached, and for any fraud in its production he was held bound to make restitution. Though human law permitted base metal to be mixed with precious metal, almost up to fifty per cent., divine law required the information that this had actually been done to be understood clearly by the purchaser before the seller could be held exempt from blame (*Summa Theol.*, II. ii. 77, 1, ad 1 m). In art work, only the master's work was to be declared as by the master, and the pupil's work must not be sold in the master's name. In alchemy, false gold must not be sold in place of true gold; "but if by alchemy true gold is produced, then this may be sold as genuine, for nothing prevents art from using natural causes to produce true and natural effects" (*ibid.* 77, 2).

A broker, whether in business or in matrimonial causes, must be careful to be exactly truthful, quoting his goods or his clients not above their true value but as he knows them to be: "not saying the girl is rich, when he knows her to own nothing, nor modest and good, when he knows her to be wanton and ill-tempered, for these lies would cause grave damage to his neighbour" (St Antonino, *Summa Moralis*, iii. 8, 4, i.).

One by one each trade is described by St Antonino, with its dangers, its fraudulencies and its noble purposes, each indeed in St Antonino's day having its guild and organization, its laws, customs and penalties.[1] Nor did he forget to note amongst them the sailors "risking their lives, sharing immense labours, commonly the worst of men and the most blasphemous, praying only when the storms are on them, promising repentance in a fear that is wholly servile, and when the danger is past [he concludes, not without a smile, I think, in his metaphor] returning to their vomit, troubling neither about God nor holy things" (*ibid.* § 10).

Amongst the crimes of the artists he enumerates the pictures that provoked to lust, not because of their exquisite beauty, but because of the direct suggestion of evil shown in their arrangement of nude figures; the pictures that were heretical,

---

[1] Cf. *English Nouveaux Riches in the Fourteenth Century*, by Alice Law, in *Trans. Roy. Hist. Soc.*, 1895, vol. ix.

such as " the monstrous representation of the Holy Trinity as a man with three heads," or " the Annunciation in which the child Jesus is shown descending into the Virgin's womb as though He had not been formed of the substance of her virginal body," or " Jesus as a child learning His letters from a book, for He was never taught of men," or " midwives sitting near the manger for the Mother who remained a virgin," or " the apocryphal dropping of her girdle by Our Lady in her Assumption to St Thomas because he could not believe that she were really dead," or " the foolish introduction of comic elements into the pictures of the Saints, a monkey, or a dog in pursuit of hares or such like, especially by illuminators," or their working on feast days, or their overcharging, or " most of all the use of bad paints which lose their colour, and the habit artists have of never completing what they have begun " (§ 11).

Musicians were blamed for their frivolities and foolishness in the sacred psalmody, for their extravagancies at weddings and festive occasions, for the lasciviousness of the words they sang. Yet their trade was sacred and a good invention. It was akin to that of the actors, as useful and as dangerous, giving men joy and sometimes leading to great sin : " but because in our time sacred plays are so interspersed with buffoonery as to be almost irreverent, it were better that they were played neither in a church nor by churchmen " (§ 12).

Last in the pageant came the farmers and husbandmen, the dwellers in country districts. St Antonino thought as little of their morals as he did of those of the townsmen—crafty, deceitful, drunkards, dancing even in church on feast days, " and, under the dreadful lure of fishing, which is not of itself, however, a forbidden art, missing Mass." " They curse their beasts in moments of anger, are often evil-livers, blunt in conscience, seldom going to confession, rarely receiving holy communion, ill-teachers of their children, often given to sorcery and superstition, little attending to the commandments of God, in short living like beasts and like beasts sometimes in their death " (§ 13).

The production of wealth was, therefore, in the judgment of

the mediæval moralist always fraught with peril, and difficult to achieve without dishonesty ; its just distribution, which was studied and debated under the term of property, was equally dangerous to handle. In the times of the greatest luxury and licentiousness the woes against the rich were always brought up and rehearsed : " Woe to you rich " was engraved on one of the papal coins. But the making of fortunes and the holding of them, fortunes in money or in land, went busily on—not least stimulated when Edward III. married all his sons to heiresses and thereby incidentally left the way open for party quarrels amongst the royal princes and ultimately for civil war. The just consumption of wealth was also much discussed, the morality of luxury trades, the amount of money that should be given in alms, the scale between a man's own needs and the needs of his neighbour, when he might legitimately refuse to part with money in the name of the decent requirements of his own family : " It is not sufficient that a man give alms, he must also take trouble to give them in the right way " (*Summa Moralis*, II. i. 24, iv.). So again the justifiability of taxation figured as a subject of mediæval social and moral discussion. Certainly it was agreed that it should not be employed for political purposes (*ibid.*, II. i. 13, iii.), in order to impoverish your rival and drive him from the state—a not infrequent habit of the Medici. Equally certain was it that you could levy the " customary " dues of your kingdom ; you could even raise an additional tax to meet an exceptional circumstance. But you might never raise taxation above its customary rate merely for the greater glory of your name, in terms of wastefulness and selfish luxury.

Other questions, as their titles suggest, are reviewed at length in Walter of Henley's treatise on *Husbandry* (edited by Eliz. Lamond, *Trans. Roy. Hist. Soc.*, N.S., ix. 215), in the *Libell of Englishe Polycye*, in the *Debate of Heralds*, by Charles Duke of Orleans (1458-1461), and in Fortescue's *Commodities of England* (ed. by Lord Clermont).

CHAPTER VII

WAR

THE subject of war was naturally much discussed in early Christianity : whether or no a follower of the Crucified Master could take up the profession of arms or, under any circumstances, kill his fellow-men. In early commentaries on Scripture the point can be found debated with more or less agreement as to the ultimate conclusions. These conclusions were more clearly thought out and stated by St Augustine than by any other writer, arriving as he did towards the end of the line of Great Fathers and the heir to their literary and intellectual riches. It was from St Augustine, therefore, that Gratian quoted authoritatively in the *Decretum* on the Christian theory of war. It was from these quotations in the *Decretum* taken from St Augustine that the thirteenth-century schoolmen derived their own teaching ; and it was to these quotations again that the fourteenth and fifteenth century canonists returned for the solution of the new problems of war that confronted them.

For it is noticeable from the end of the fourteenth century that, as the art of war developed and methods altered, armies came into being, and local companies offered their services to the highest bidder, moral problems involved by war increased in complexity, consequently that books written to deal with it multiplied. Some of these tractates have vanished, and are known to us only by name or citation, but a great deal yet remains. To open the pages, say, of St Antoninus, who died in 1459, is to meet with a mass of references to names and theories and contrary opinions that cannot but impress the reader at least with the increased interest shown in this problem of the morality of war.

By the thirteenth century the idea of nationhood had become sufficiently developed to constitute itself a leading idea in policy and, consequently, a leading cause of war. The speculations which the Greeks had pursued on the origins of civilization, and the theories elaborated, especially by Plato and Aristotle, naturally became at this date of increasing interest. John of Salisbury (1180) had already developed his own political ideals.[1] Aquinas, in his commentaries on Scripture, in his philosophical and theological treatises, and in his commentaries on Aristotle, pushed still farther the conclusions of his predecessors. For him, as for Aristotle, the city was the political unit, the self-governing and self-sufficient city. As far as the necessaries of life were concerned it was "a perfect community"—perfect, that is, in the sense of complete. Yet though in this material and absolute sense able to stand by itself, nevertheless, for other reasons—not the least of which was fear of foes—the city found that it needed the support of other cities, "whence came into existence the kingdom" (*Comment. on St Matthew's Gospel*, lect. xii. 2 and *De Regimine Princip.*, Bk. I., cap. i.).

Already the larger sense of patriotism and the cosier sense of home were appearing in literature, otherwise dry and scholastic, for the Middle Ages were emotional only under discipline. Thus St Thomas talks of the Kingdom of Sicily like a good patriot when he speaks with feeling of the land "in which we are born and bred" (*Summa Theologica*, II., ii. 101, 1).

He then proceeds to argue that this aggregate of cities which had constituted itself into a kingdom (whether St Thomas thought that historically nations began by way of social contract, or whether he is merely spinning the threads of an Aristotelean metaphysical concept it is impossible to say— as a Neopolitan he had almost every reason to hold it to be good history) had its own definite purpose in forming itself into a union. It had certain evils to escape by federation or confederation, it had good objects to promote and maintain. It desired to avoid war and to secure peace. But what is meant by peace? The notion—the philosophical concept—of peace as

---

[1] *Policraticus*, ed. by J. A. Giles (1848).

[2] Reference can profitably be made to Duval, *La Doctrine de l'Eglise sur la Guerre au Moyen Age* (in the volume *L'Eglise et la Guerre*, published in Paris, 1913), and to Vanderpol, *La Doctrine Scholastique de la Guerre* and *Le Droit de Guerre d'apres les Theologiens et les Canonistes du Moyen Age*, both published in Paris, 1915.

understood by the mediæval writers must be grasped before it is possible to understand their philosophical concept of war.

" Two separate concepts are discoverable under the word peace—namely, first, that two or more things or persons should be united, and that, secondly, they should agree " *(Comment. on the Divine Names of Dionysius,* cap. xi., lect. 1). Thus Aquinas held it to be quite possible for things to be united and yet not to be at peace, and possible for them to agree and yet not to be united: " If a man agrees with another, and yet not freely but under compulsion of some threatened evil, such agreement cannot be called peace " *(Summa Theologica,* II. ii. 29, 1, ad 1 m). Or, as St Thomas again describes it, "concord implies that the desires of those in agreement coincide, but peace adds to this the implication that those in agreement desire to coincide in agreement " (II. ii. 29, 1, ad 3 m)—that is, then only is there true peace when everyone not only is in agreement but wishes to be in agreement. "Therefore," he continues, " it is clear that dissension, or the break-up of peace, can be due not only to the opposition between one man and another but to the crossed purposes of the same man. The dissension which opposes man to his fellow is the contrary of concord, the dissension which opposes him to himself is contrary to peace."

This idea of peace should be remembered, because it shows how morality or gospel teaching was accepted as the basis of life's relations. The desire for concord was the basis of peace, and this desire must itself be based on eternal principles in order to be permanent. Human society was, therefore, not yet secularized. Politics were held to come under the eye of the theologian, for the art of them could be reached through virtue and, in their perfection, only through virtue. Politics were never to the mediæval thinker or writer or speaker a " game " or a " dirty business." Politics may often have been degraded in practice, but not in theory; political science, as we have already seen, was held to be the completion and crown of the life of philosophy. The perfect philosopher must be a king. And do not the carved portals of Chartres, when you think of them, show such a sermon in stone? The virginal monarch,

beardless and radiant in his youthful beauty, wears on his untroubled brow the calmness to which philosophy has schooled
him. The older kings have more hardly purchased it by life,
their long knowledge is shown in their very beards. We know
how they have found wisdom, but the young one amongst them
has already reached their maturity by the way of vision. " Peace
is no other thing that the union of all desire. Thus to unite a
man is the property of God, because divine love alone is great
enough to engage all a man's desires and divine love is no other
thing than God. For God knows how to gather into one all
desires and affections, since God is love and love is the bond
of perfection " (Aquinas, *Commentary on Epistle to the Hebrews*,
cap. xiii., lect. 3).

For this purpose, therefore, though perhaps beyond their
knowing, cities came together and kingdoms were formed and
princes were set to reign. The ruler was no policeman deputed
to keep order ; his purpose was a divine one : he was a divine
minister. The Emperor no less than the Pope, though in another
sense, was the Vicar of God. Dante tells us of his ideal of
monarchy ; it is the ideal of St Augustine's *City of God*, of
Aquinas' political writings. " Sufficiency of corporal goods,"
writes Aquinas, " and of the life of virtue is the end of human
confederation ; but since the life of virtue is itself ordained to
something infinitely higher—namely, the blessed vision of God
—this ultimate purpose of individual human life must be also the
ultimate purpose of any human confederation. The end of the
State is, therefore, the Vision of God " (*De Regimine Principum*,
i. 14-15 ; iii. 3, 10). The Prince, " to whose keeping is committed the care of the state," must, therefore, take charge
of the interests, temporal and indirectly eternal, of each " city
or province or kingdom over which he holds sway " (*Summa
Theologica*, II. ii. 40, 1). He will find that peace is produced
amongst his people by ordered government : " Peace is indeed
the tranquillity of order ; but order means that each part is
fittingly chosen and proportionately placed. Peace, therefore,
comes when each is in its proper place " (Aquinas, *Comment.
on Matt.*, v. 10).

With this keen sense of the beauty of order, of the divine

purpose behind political life, of the magnificence of peace, the notion of war came as a mental or academic difficulty. Already everyone was sure that fighting was lawful to a Christian ; but this common knowledge and practice was difficult to fit in with the rest of Christian teaching. Thus most of the problems of the thirteenth century were problems of thought and not of conduct. They knew a man could fight with a clean conscience, but they were interested in discussing how this fact could be made consistent with the so-obvious meekness of the Sermon on the Mount. "These precepts," answers Aquinas, "are always to be kept in our hearts to give us the proper frame of mind, so that a man be ready not to resist or even not to defend himself, if circumstances demand this of him for the common good " (*Summa Theologica*, II. ii. 40, I ; *cf*. ad 2 m, and ad 3 m).

But the *De Eruditione Principum*—that work of doubtful authorship which we have attributed to Vincent de Beauvais, rather than to Guillaume de Perault—is more opposed to war than was St Thomas, or at least much more at pains to show its evils. " Christ's triumph was won," he says, " by sweetness and not by swords. The world is full of evils certainly, but in such a world patience is the best protection. It is the impatient man who alone really is unarmed. To secure this patience remember Christ's sufferings, and that these were allowed by God precisely to His best-loved Son, and that in our patient suffering and in weakness is His power most made manifest, and that thus we shall achieve an exceeding weight of glory " (Bk. VII., cap. ii.). In chapter eight the author proceeds to develop one by one all the manifold miseries begotten by war and the little good that comes of it : " It produces little good and it wastes much more than it produces. . . . Moreover it is inhuman that a Christian should make war on a Christian." This is proved at great length in the ninth chapter, wherein is shown how Christ was born in a time of universal peace while angel voices sang of peace, how He preached peace and sent others to preach it, how He was our peace. " Wise men, then," is his conclusion, " avoid war. The distance indeed between peace and war is so great, that in every difficulty there must be some shorter cut to peace than going all the way round by war to reach it. It is reached more surely by giving than by taking."

This feeling against war blazed out at times into Crusades of Peace, such as that started by Giovanni de Vicenza[1] in the summer of 1233, a strange medley of idealism and wildness that ended in disaster. But at Bologna, where Giovanni first preached his glad tidings, his success was immediate; the magistrates bade him remodel their constitution according to the law of love, of universal brotherhood, which was the burden of his message, the breaking down of old feuds and animosities. From Bologna he went to Padua, thence across to Feltre, Verona, Mantua and Brescia, everywhere meeting with the same enthusiastic reception, and arousing the public conscience to the iniquity of the general state of war prevailing between city and city, and between the different factions within each city. Finally he persuaded all these and other cities to send representatives to a great meeting, to be held on the 28th of August 1234 on the plain of Pagnara, three miles outside Verona. Invitations to this meeting were dispatched several months ahead by a deliberate arrangement, that a considerable time might elapse between the sermons and the meeting in order that the enthusiasm of the people might be duly tested. But the numbers that subsequently assembled proved the reality of the movement, contemporary chroniclers—like Parisio di Cereta—giving four hundred thousand as the estimated figure. It was not the number of the people, however, but the importance of those thus brought together that gave the movement an appearance of success. Twenty of these little cities attended with full solemnity, even sending their *carroccios* to testify how formally the city pledged itself; some of the greater families—like the Este—came at the head of their men, while the Patriarch of Aquileia and nine bishops represented the Church. To these thus gathered together, Giovanni, a preaching friar, held forth on the evils of war, its un-Christian character when waged between Christian men, and the blessings of peace. Gregory IX. sent a special letter to the assembly, and

---

[1] *Johann Von Vicenza und die Italiensche Friedesbewegung*, 1891, Freiburg.

this too was read, and the ceremony ended in the formation of a League of Peace to which all these Lombard cities subscribed. Like so many other mediæval peace meetings it was cemented by a marriage—namely, between the Lord of Este and a daughter of Alberic, Lord of Romano, both of whom had been the leaders in a country feud.

But Giovanni, now under the excitement of his success, lost his sense of prudence—at least, so it would appear from the rhyming verses, embedded in chronicles, which tell us of his fantastic claims to lordship over the cities that had joined the League. He demanded absolute power, and even the titles of secular rule; he began to interfere and take sides in political disputes; he assumed an autocratic position of authority over the clergy. This last appears to have been his undoing. The Benedictines of Padua roused their city to resist his encroachments, and the apostle of peace retaliated by arriving with armed forces to quell the insurrection. At first triumphant, he was afterwards defeated and captured, and ended at Bologna in monastic quietude his " withered dream."

Many years later, John Bromyard, the English Friar Preacher, under the heading of " War," in his *Summa Prædicantium* (Part I., fol. lxix. 1522), tells us what was thought in England of these Lombard cities and their endless quarrelling : " The Lombard wars are for the most part entered into without the public authority of the state, only at the instigation of one party, the dominant party, of the state. Nor have they a just cause for their wars, but merely the opposition of Guelph and Ghibelline; nor a right intention, but merely the lust for lordship." In using this example, Bromyard was explaining to his readers what war should not be like, for he had just previously quoted from Aquinas (*Summa Theologica*, II. ii. 40, 1) the three conditions required for a just war : the authority of the state, a just cause, and a right intention—namely, to avoid evil and to pursue good. This triple requirement was violated in every particular, so it seemed to him, by the Lombard wars.

In seeking for a philosophic basis by which to justify the morality of war, Aquinas himself went back through Gratian (Causa 23 of the *Decretum*) to St Augustine : " Just as princes lawfully defend the state with the sword against domestic breakers of the peace when they punish wrongdoers . . . so they have the right and the duty to defend the state by means of war against alien enemies "; this is a quotation given in the *Summa Theologica* (II. ii. 64, 2), and copied from the *Decretum*. And again : " The safety of the state must be preserved, for without it would come many violent deaths and evils innumerable, both spiritual and temporal" (quoted, II. ii. 40, 4 and 31, 3 ad 2 m, and in the *De Regimine Princip.*, i. 13 and 14): and finally, in dealing with offensive wars as well as defensive wars, Aquinas cites and accepts this other phrase from St Augustine, which again had been cited by Gratian : " Just wars are commonly defined as those in which injuries are avenged against the city or nation that has been guilty of them, either because they neglected to punish the mischief committed by their citizens or to restore what their citizens had injuriously taken away " (II. ii. 40, 2).

These principles of Augustine, with which his mind perfectly agreed and which he deemed to have been logically established, Aquinas used as the basis of his own treatise on war. War was the defence of peace ; only in this way could it be justified : " All who make war seek through war to arrive at a peace more perfect than existed before war " (29, 2, ad 2 m); " No one seeks peace to stir up war, but war to establish peace " (40, 1, ad 3 m) ; " The carnal wars waged by Christian folk are to be referred to the divine spiritual good of men as their purpose and end" (10, 3, ad 3 m) ; " It is lawful to attack one's enemies in order to restrain them from sins which are doing hurt to their good and the good of their own neighbours " (83, 8, ad 3 m).

Cardinal Cajetan (1469-1508), Luther's opponent and the greatest of the commentators on the *Summa* of St Thomas, sums up this idea of war which St Augustine elaborated, Gratian handed on, and Aquinas accepted and taught to succeeding Christian writers : " He who wages a just war acts as a judge proceeding against a criminal " (II. ii. 40, 1).

It may make the attitude of mediæval moralists to war between Christian people clearer perhaps if we notice the conspectus of Christendom as it appeared to St Antonino (1389-1459), midway between Aquinas and Cajetan. He divides the world of his day into Romans and non-Romans : " First of all, amongst the Romans are all those who obey Rome. Then there are some who do not obey Rome in all things but who live by the laws of the Emperor and hold him to be the lord of the world, as do the Lombards. There are some again who neither obey the Emperor nor live his laws and who claim to do this in virtue of a privilege, as does Venice. Others, again, neither obey him nor live his laws, in virtue of a definite convention, as do the Papal cities, who claim exemption from the Empire by the gift of Constantine, who handed the temporal juris-diction of them over to the Popes. In addition to these there are the non-Romans, who do not obey him, for instance the Greeks, who claim to have an Emperor of their own. Of these, again, some, like these Greeks, are allied with us against the Turks ; with some we have nothing to do, as the Jews ; with some we are at peace, as with the Tartars, for our merchants go to them and theirs come to us ; with some we are at this time at war, as the Saracens, and more recently the Turks. Would indeed that they were not encamped on a part of Christendom !" (*Summa Moralis*, Venice, 1571, iii. 4, ii.).

Over this medley of states the Pope had some suzerainty, the precise nature of which varied considerably with the in-dividual Pope, or rather, not so much did the nature of the suzerainty come into dispute as the grounds on which this suzerainty was based. In the *De Regimine Principum* (i. 14) Aquinas bases it on the ultimate destiny of man—namely, the divine purpose of human life—for since this was a moral and spiritual matter it was part of the duty of the Pope to see that this end was not violated by Christian princes, but helped forward and developed by them. Since then the purpose of human government was a spiritual good, and since spiritual goods were ultimately put under Papal care, by the direction of Christ, as final arbiter the Pope had an obligation to insist on the carrying out of the due purpose of political rule.

Thus the heresy of a prince, or his aiding and abetting of heresy, or his lapsing into infidelity, since these failings were considered to make impossible the fulfilment of this purpose, would be sufficient grounds for his being dispossessed of his princedom. This required, however, the declaratory judgment of the Pope before it could be acted on. The Pope judged thus the sovereigns of Christendom (II. ii. 12, 2). He was not their feudal head, for the Emperor had that position ; but, as the supreme guardian of the rights of God, he could interfere juridically to decide whether or no they were fulfilling the purpose of their princedom, to the due observance of which they had in their coronation oath sworn to devote themselves. The need of this declaration of the Pope before a prince could be deposed was insisted on by Aquinas, because he held very strongly to the principle that infidelity was not incompatible with lordship. Dominion in grace, which Wyclif had attached primarily to the possession of private property, had been attached by some eminent canonists to the political power of rulers. The famous canonist, Cardinal Henry di Susa (died 1271)—more famous perhaps under the name of Ostiensis, his cardinalate being attached to the Bishopric of Ostia—maintained (*Summa Aurea*, i. 34 and v. 6) that no infidel had any right to rule, that heresy and infidelity of their very nature destroyed all right to dominion of any kind. Innocent IV., equally great as a canonist, denied this, and held the contrary (*Apparatus ad Decretales : De Voto*)—namely, that only a definite sentence of the Pope could deprive an heretical prince of his jurisdiction, precisely because the Pope was the sole ultimate guardian on earth of the divine rights and obligations of men in their spiritual and temporal capacities.

Aquinas followed Innocent IV. No one can make war on pagans " in order to compel them to believe," only " in order to compel them not to obstruct the exercise of the Christian faith " (II. ii. 10, 8 and 11). Hence the religion of pagans and Jews was to be tolerated, " either on account of some good to be obtained thereby or at least to avoid some evil " (II. ii. 10, 12 and iii. 65, 10 ; especially worked out in detail in the *De Regimine Hebræorum*, addressed to the Queen of Cyprus, Parma edition, vol. xvi., Opusc. 17).

" As soon as anyone has been juridically excommunicated

on account of apostasy from the faith, by that very fact the faithful are absolved from his dominion over them and from their oath of allegiance which bound them to him " (II. ii. 12, 2).

Here as elsewhere St Antonino, coming very much later, is able to elaborate the process and the possibilities of war and arbitration : " If the Emperor makes war on the Pope, his subjects are not bound to follow him against the Papacy, for the Emperor is the defender of it [advocatus] and bound by his oath to protect it. Indeed the Pope could on this account release the Emperor's subjects from their oath of allegiance to him. If the Pope declared war against the Emperor, or against a heretic or a schismatic, all must obey him for he is the lord of all. If a king made war on the Emperor, or the Emperor on a king not subject to him, no one except the Pope could be referred to as the common lord of both. The Emperor and the king would sin if they went to war in spite of their adversary's offering to make satisfaction for what had been ill-done. If an earl attacked the king, the king could reply by force of arms ; but no earl should make war on his sovereign without first appealing to the Pope, or, when both earl and sovereign are his subjects, to the Emperor. If an earl makes war on an earl, the victim must appeal to their common king. Were a vassal to make war on his lord, it would be treason ; and in this event the feudal followers who join with their immediate lord against their common overlord are liable to the penalties of treason, for feudalism cannot be used as an excuse for breaking the bond of loyalty due from subjects to their king. But should one baron make war on another baron, and call out his men, and should the king of the first baron also himself declare war on his own account against another king, the feudal followers must obey the immediate summons of their lord and not the immediate summons of the king " (chap. ii., § 3).

The need for precautionary statements in the fifteenth century will be clear to all who remember the constant and elaborate feud-letters, or challenges, addressed by individuals to kings or to one another : " Most serene and most gracious Prince, Frederick, King of the Romans [Emperor Frederick III.] I, Henry Mayenberg, make known to your royal grace that from this time I will no longer obey your grace, but will be the enemy of your country and your subjects, and will do them as much harm as possible. Dated at Yderspewgen, the Wednesday before Palm Sunday." We know that the Lord of Prauenstein declared war on the city of Frankfort because a young lady of that city refused to dance with his uncle; that a challenge was sent in 1450 by the baker and domestics of the Margrave of Baden against certain imperial cities; and another in 1462 by the baker of the Count Palatine Louis against Augsburg, Ulm and Rothwell; one in 1471 by the shoe-blacks of the university of Leipzig against the provost of the university and sundry other members of that body; one in 1477 came from a cook of Eppenstein, and his scullions, dairy-maids and dish-washers, to Otto, Count of Salms (Coxe, *House of Austria*, i., pp. 306-307).

Duelling was generally forbidden; but the canonists disputed whether under certain circumstances it might not be lawful. There was always before them the Scriptural example of David and Goliath. Was it not lawful, therefore, to engage in single combat and so end a war, for this would amount to "ordeal by battle." The famous *Gloss* (1 Kings xvii.) of Nicholas de Lyra (*d.* 1340) was thought to favour this, provided always it was undertaken with the authority of the state and not as a means of deciding a purely civil dispute. But Raymond of Pennafort, and Alanus whom he cited, convinced Antonino that a duel was not permissible even in the name of the state; St Thomas was also cited by him as disapproving even of the ordeal by heated iron or boiling water (part iii. 4, 4, 11).

An interesting note on tournaments is to be found in a sermon of Humbert de Romans (Bigne, Bk. II., Serm. lxxxv., p. 559): "It is to be noted that in tournaments, to which come many who greatly need instruction, a sermon is extremely useful provided an audience can be collected, for it is written in Eccles. xxxii. 6: 'Where there is no hearing, pour not out thy words.' To find matter for this, note that although tournaments are forbidden by law because of the danger to bodies and souls, as often happens, there are some things there to be wholly reprobated, some to be tolerated, and some to be approved. About the first, note how some nobles spend so much money on tournaments that they ruin themselves and their houses and their families. . . . Some seek there only the vain renown of valour and so forth. . . . Some go thither, a thing far worse, for no other reason than to revenge themselves on their rivals, or, against the law of tournaments, to make gain out of doing ridiculous things before the crowd, or to frequent places of ill-fame. . . . About the second, it is to be remembered that to fight for justice is justifiable, especially justifiable in defence of the justice of the state, supremely justifiable in defence of the justice of God. Hence to acquire skill in arms so as to be the better fitted for the defence of justice (for without practice no productive art can be effectively attained), it is lawful to frequent tournaments. . . . About the third, note that sometimes at tournaments knights urge one another to use in the service of the Cross and of God the powers hitherto put to the service of vanity. This certainly makes tournaments commendable. Some too take care to avoid folk of evil fame and jesters, and to keep away from evil actions and the occasions of unchastity."

The conclusion, therefore, reached by St Thomas is that war is justifiable on three conditions : that it is declared by the public authority of the state ; that it has a just cause ; that the intention of those who go to fight is right (II. ii. 40, 1). It will be remembered that these were the conditions cited by Bromyard from St Thomas as affording ample justification and requiring no further argument. Similarly St Antonino repeats St Thomas's expressions verbatim ; Vittoria also, and the rest of the scholastics down to the end of the period, make use of the identical expressions of the *Summa*. To the three conditions, however, later writers sometimes add, that the war should be properly conducted. But St Thomas was not thinking of the conduct of war, but rather of the declaration of war : " Whoever is attacked because of some fault of his deserves to be attacked."

Bromyard then adds (Part I., fol. lxix.) the conditions of right fighting—namely, that it demands on the part of the combatants a desire for the glory of God and the good of one's neighbour, faithfulness without treason, mercy and all the other virtues. The possession of these seems rather an exhaustive list of requirements on the part of the soldiery, but, as Bromyard remarks, a soldier who has them all is never afraid ; it is sin that terrifies. Yet it must be admitted that his postulates are hardly likely to be fulfilled : " If, in the armies of modern times, all those in mortal sin were sent away, there would be very few left. This would not really matter, for the few good left would defeat a larger force composed of the wicked."

It is a relief to pass from Bromyard, who is often interesting but nearly always impracticable, to St Antonino, who is above all else the practical thinker. His long service in the confessional, his large dealings with men of all sorts and kinds, from beggars to princes, his phenomenal memory, his close study of canon law, make him the most valuable writer after Aquinas, and the most sane, particularly on subjects in which abstract arguments are not required. He was " Antonino the Counsellor " to his own generation ; and it is pre-eminently in that capacity that he sits down to write his treatise on *War* (iii. 4, 1-4).

He looks first of all at the soldier's life, for this portion of his great work is devoted to the treatment of every condition of life, its obligations and dangers. The profession of soldiering has never, he declares, been condemned by the Church, but that was because it was judged from its ideal standpoint, as seen in St Sebastian and St Maurice and St George. The soldier should aim at virtue, should abstain from whatever is contrary to the law of God or man, and should undertake only just wars. The treatise thus is eminently practical. It is not so much war, as the soldier, that is the theme of it.

By insisting that the soldier should aim at virtue, St Antonino explains that he means the soldier to recognize, for example, that courage is a virtue and that virtues are a divine gift. The good soldier is good precisely because of his intrepid bearing, and this is secured him by grace. Grace also it is that enables him to keep faith with his enemies when it seems that he can least afford to do so, to take no mean advantage of them, to interpret truces as generously as possible, to show clemency to the defeated, in manliness never to fail. " God," he says rather finely, " alone can make us men." When he insists that the soldier must avoid unlawful things he has his practical explanation to make of this : " to abstain from robbery, uncleanness, blasphemy, drunkenness, sacrilege, and other vices which to-day are only too plentiful." The picture he draws of the warrior of his day is scathing in its faithful portraiture of the fifteenth-century hired soldiery of Europe : " The elaborate paraphernalia, the careful commissariat, the golden armour, the inlaid shields and extravagant workmanship of every weapon, suggested a banquet rather than a fight." [1] Hardihood was forgotten as the soldier's virtue, war had lost its solemnity, it was no longer even a game : " In certain places the custom was for the knight on the eve of his consecration to spend the night in prayer." That is the spirit he would have liked to see revived. He notices sadly that it has gone.

In a just war the soldier is something more than a mere fighter ; in such a contest " neither the general nor the people is so much the author of the war as its minister." To die in such a quarrel is blessedness, yet it is possible for hate to be engendered in a just quarrel. What then? Did that not ruin the moral excellence of the warrior? Did it not make his action sinful? Was he not in consequence bound to restitution for all damage done in such a spirit? No, answers Antonino, hate would undoubtedly make the fighting lose its spiritual merit, as every good action would be deprived of its merit if it were done in an evil frame of mind, but that does not imply any obligation of restitution, unless in consequence of his hatred the soldier has done more damage than was necessary for his purpose.

Again, under the heading of the justice of war, we are reminded that no war is just unless declared with the public authority of the state ; but this declaration of the prince is not

---

[1] This description recalls the contrast drawn in the *Chronicle of Lanercost* (cited by J. E. Morris, *Bannockburn*, 1914, Cambridge University Press, p. 57) between Edward I.'s manner of going to war and that of his son, Edward II. : " Edward I. . . . had been wont to visit the saints of England, to make them rich offerings, and to commend himself to their prayers. . . . [Edward II.] did nothing of the sort, but coming with pomp and curious retinue he seized upon the goods of the monasteries en route. . . ." It would suggest that the degradation of war had set in a century earlier.

necessary to justify a man fighting a defensive war : " because man has a natural right to repel force with force in the defence of himself and his own, so long as he uses no immoderate amount of force. Pope Innocent III. even justified immediate defence on the part of a guilty nation when the invading nation had made no attempt to secure redress by other means than war, though even to recover one's stolen property by force is illegal without previous recourse to law " (Dist. 1, *Jus Gentium*). This is interesting, for it shows us that Innocent regarded Christendom as composed of separate nations governed by one law, and as much the subjects of that universal law as individual members of a state were subject to its authority. The appeal of the injured nation was first to be made to Emperor or Pope before recourse was had to armed intervention. Certainly Innocent III. was able to secure this from France and England, though he claimed to be no judge of feudal rights (*Decretals*, ii. 1, 3. Cf. *Epis.* iv. 17, 13 ; *Epis.* vi. 163, Migne, *P.L.*, 215).

St Antonino even declares that a ruler who is negligent in defending the rights and possessions of his people is bound to make restitution to them for whatever unjust loss they may sustain at enemy hands. But even when the war is just, no general and no soldier may despoil "clerics, religious, pilgrims," nor by convention " agriculturists, traders, or peaceful citizens " (cf. *Extrav. de Treuga c. Innovamus*), though he admits that this conventional non-interference with non-combatants is very much a matter of debate. St Antonino quotes Henry Boich as having made a distinction between conventions deliberately entered into between nations and conventions imposed from above by canon law. Conventions deliberately entered into between nations bind one nation only so long as the other nation observes them, conventions imposed by canon law are not quite so simple to deal with, for they have an obliging force independent of the deliberate acceptance of them by the polity of nations. Hence if one nation disregarded them it did not follow that the other nation was equally free, therefore, to do the same. Boich made a further distinction between canonical conventions which were permanent, and those that were merely temporary. The first could not be abrogated—such as the non-despoiling of clerics, religious and pilgrims; the second depended upon the observance of them by the adversary—such as the non-despoiling of " agriculturists, traders and peaceful citizens " (Dist. 95, *Esto*).

Whoever, therefore, knowingly injured any innocent person in war was bound to restitution, whatever might be the contrary custom. But those were not to be held innocent who directly or indirectly helped the guilty side of an unjust war. Makers of munitions, or adherents of either side, who directly or indirectly took part in the war, ceased to be innocent if their side acted unjustly, and forfeited the right to claim the privileges of non-combatants.

If, on the other hand, the war were just, it was lawful to destroy enemy property under the authority of the prince; but it was not lawful to do so under private authority. If this last had been done, then the individual destroying the property was liable for the damage done, even supposing his side in the quarrel to have had just cause for declaring war. But circumstances might arise which made it difficult for the soldier to be sure whether his side be right or no. What should he do if after all his efforts he remained unconvinced of the justice of his side? Could he fight in a doubtful cause? In his answer you have St Antonino, the practical counsellor, confronted by a state of affairs different in many respects from the social order known to his master St Thomas. Both, indeed, were familiar with the old feudal levy, which marched under the summons of its immediate lord : " If after discussion with experts there is still doubt about the justice of the war, the soldier is excused from evil when he is merely following his lord, for in doubtful matters a man should always obey, but the lord is not excused, says Raymund, 23, q. 1, *Quid culpatur* " (St Antonino, iii. 4, 2, ii.). But St Antonino had also to deal with another type of soldier—the paid soldier, who followed no feudal lord but a captain of his own choosing, like the bands that, under the Sforza or Hawkswood, offered their services to the best payer, or like the new national arm recruited on a system of voluntary service and paid an agreed sum per day or month out of the Royal Exchequer. Such a hired soldier, it seemed, had no such excuse as the retainer had, for he could not plead obedience to justify a doubtful conscience. Consequently St Antonino decides that "the professional soldier may not enter on a war only doubtfully just, nor can he be absolved by a confessor so long as he remains voluntarily on that side " (*ibid*.).

Are the Crusades a just war? By what right were the territories of the infidel invaded? A pertinent question even in the fifteenth century, with the indomitable Pius II. assembling his fleet and troops at Ancona to launch an attack on the Turk. St Antonino answers from history that the Roman Emperors waged a just war on the Jews after the death of Christ and captured the Holy Land. This had been unjustly attacked by the Turk and conquered, and could, therefore, be lawfully recovered by his own Christendom which had succeeded, according to Dante, to the rights of the older Rome.

But, after all, if the lawfulness of war depended on the assurance of public authority there would still remain a difficulty, for what exactly constitutes that public authority? By what right, for example, did the Emperor claim even a shadowy suzerainty over free cities and nations? Or again, was it ever likely that a Pope would allow the lawfulness of a war waged against him by the nations that lay over the Alps? Was not the mediæval dream, flaming so picturesquely on the walls of the Chapel of St Maria Novella, in the cloisters which St Antonino knew so well—for he himself had once lived there among his Dominican brethren in far-off days—already no more than a dream? Had not the vision ceased wholly? Was it not buried in the pages of Dante's *De Monarchia*? Did men now take Sigismund really seriously in his pretensions, as Dante had taken so seriously Henry VII.? St Antonino was not living in the days of Aquinas, and the old theories of his master had gone, he knew, beyond recall : " Before declaring war recourse must needs be had to the supreme authority of the Prince ; to-day, however, since peoples no longer recognize the superiority over them of any other nation, *de facto*, it is no longer necessary to appeal to him. Every day people declare war on other people without recourse to anyone over them " (*ibid*., cap. ii., § 2).

In the actual conduct of war, however, many points might arise to cause perplexity. " If a general issues an order that no one under penalty of death shall venture to attack the enemy, and if one knight does attack the enemy, and defeat him, is he free of the penalty? No, certainly he is not free, for no good result can excuse an evil action, and disobedience in war is a grave evil. But the general can certainly remit the penalty, for a leader cannot be bound to fulfil every threat " (*ibid.*, § 3). Again, if in war the leader of the opposing army be captured, what could be done with him? The picture rises of the endless Italian wars, the marches and counter-marches, the sham assaults, the assassinations, the beheadings and all the treacheries of false victory or false defeat : " If he agrees not to resist, he should be pardoned, unless from his pardon greater evils be feared." St Antonino there touches on a point that had inflamed mediæval historians, the beheading of Conradin by Charles of Anjou. This could have been justified only on such a supposition as he mentions—namely, that Charles had grave grounds for believing that the continued existence of the heir of the Hohenstaufen would prove a perpetual menace to peace. Such was the argument of the Archbishop of Florence, who refused to commit himself to either side. He had the verses of Dante ringing in his ears ; he had heard the matter discussed by the Medici ; it would come under discussion again when, but a generation later, the French marched down upon the south.

But supposing a professional soldier wishes to join an army, what motives must he have? Sufficient, justifying motives, clearly these. But what exactly constitutes a sufficient motive justifying a man in offering his services in war? Could he join an army out of a sense of the glory to be won? Yes, answers the Archbishop, if the side he espouses in the war had justice. He appreciated the love of glory as a grave, satisfying motive, but he considered that glory was inseparable from justice.

Was a soldier morally justified in joining an army out of hope for rich booty? Certainly not, he replies. This was not a grave enough reason for fighting. If a war were just, could a monk or cleric take up arms? This question of the cleric in war had embroiled St Gregory with the Emperor only in the

reverse sense of the right of the soldier to turn monk. But the
Pope was a temporal prince, and had temporal states to guard,
and was wont to send cardinals and bishops as his legates.
These might find themselves at the head of armies. Was
this right? Or again, could the state lawfully compel the cleric
to join the combatant ranks? St Antonino first sets out the
answers given to this question by various canon lawyers, and
then gives his own decision last.

First of all, then, some had argued that in a defensive war a
cleric could take up arms freely, and even be compelled to take
up arms by the prince. This opinion was opposed by many and
finally abandoned by the canonists. The next point argued was
that at any rate with a merely defensive weapon, not an offensive weapon, a cleric might be permitted to take part in a
combat; he might be allowed to defend, not to attack. But
the canonists would not accept this proposition either, since it
was almost impossible to distinguish between such weapons. A
shield could be distinguished from a sword indeed, but when
was a sword used only defensively? Might not an attack be
really the best defence? The third stage was reached when
both these positions were surrendered, and it was declared that
the prohibition to the clergy to fight was a mere regulation
of canon law, and that since the Pope had supreme authority
he could allow or disallow it as he thought well. The law
was a human and ecclesiastical command enforced by human
penalties, and could therefore be abrogated by the same human
and ecclesiastical power that had imposed it.

Finally the lawyers, under the influence of scholasticism,
turned philosophers and decided that a cleric could not fight,
but that he could exhort others to fight. It might happen that
in no other way could an army be saved (II. vi.). The Crusades
had almost invariably ended disastrously when the clerics interfered with the soldiers and decided on the objective or on the
plan of campaign, nevertheless, in certain cases unless a cleric
took command of an army it might lack direction and be
destroyed. Hence he could not fight directly, but indirectly he
might be compelled to fight. Circumstances had to be judged
accordingly. The legal irregularity was certainly incurred if a

cleric killed anyone : " He could not even kill a pagan, lest this irregularity be incurred ; at the most he might urge others to fight better ; he might even throw stones at the enemy and other such missiles, so long as he was sure that no one would be killed, as Innocent notes in *Extravagant de Restitutione Spoliorum* " (§ 6). In general, then, clerics when ordered even by their princes to fight must refuse. Was it to be imputed to a cleric if he made no attempt to escape his assailant but waited for him and in his own defence killed him ? " Undoubtedly, for the text of that Clementine which said, ' *when death cannot otherwise be avoided*,' expressly prohibited killing in self-defence by a cleric, unless all other means had been exhausted. But I believe that in this case every circumstance must be weighed, the danger of flight, the conditions of the person escaping and of the person attacking, because, for instance, if flight were likely to be as dangerous as remaining, I do not think that the killing should then be imputed to him as a crime."

The final decision of St Antonino against permitting the clerics to fight gives the reasons advanced by Aquinas and all the other scholastics :

(i) Such actions interfere with the spirit of prayer and con-templation expected in a cleric.

(ii) As ministers to the Passion of Christ in the Mass it ill became them themselves to inflict death on others.

(iii) Their presence in warfare could only be justified when they came to succour, console and exhort.

A characteristic difficulty of the Middle Ages—one which was discussed by nearly all writers—was the morality of stratagems in war. Was it ever lawful to deceive the enemy, to lie in ambush, to pretend to attack in one place when the main attack was to be delivered in another, to wear wrong badges, and feign to be his friend, or the troops of his ally? It was characteristic of the Middle Ages that, side by side with their brutality and cruelty in war, and their almost incessant occupa-tion in it, the moralists should have devoted themselves with considerable amount of patience and acumen to these ethical aspects of warfare. Truth to tell, the moral side of any action however ordinary or however unethical in itself, was of perpetual interest to them. The science of morals was the gift of the thirteenth century to Christendom; till then the Fathers had but written isolated treatises on individual moral questions. The nearest approach to a moral science was to be found in the homilies of St Gregory on the Book of Job. Aquinas was the first to compose an ordered *Summa* in which ethics were adequately treated as part of the science of theology. Antonino was the first to produce an extensive work wholly devoted to ethics. From Antonino sprang the moralists proper, whose descendants, worthy and unworthy, were so pitilessly—and sometimes so unfairly—lashed by Pascal. But no one more than Antonino gave definite form to the shapeless science of morals. He founded it not on Aristotle but on Gratian, because as a boy he had learned the whole of the *Corpus Juris* by heart.

On the dispute as to whether deceits were permissible in war, Antonino was brief and to the point. He quotes Aquinas (II. ii. 40, 3). No one should tell a lie nor make a promise to the enemy and then not fulfil it; but no one was obliged to reveal his plans to the enemy. He had every right to conceal what he did not wish the enemy to know beforehand.

Again the calling in of infidels in aid against a Christian enemy was debated, and by quotations from Nicholas di Lyra (*d.* 1340) and Giovanni de Napoli (*d.* 1330) the matter was decided. The moral obligations incurred in making treaties with the enemy, or rather compositions of indemnification, were also discussed, and the question asked whether these could be made without consulting those who had suffered damage through the war. In general it was answered that the opinion of those who had suffered should be sought personally and their consent gained before the compositions were valid or could be legally enforced.

Could a man or an army forestall a threatened attack? Defensively make an offensive movement to save life or property menaced? To save life, it might be done. Violence might be forestalled by violence, because life once lost was not recoverable. To save property, however, it should not be permitted, because property or territory could be recovered or indemnified.

In this last case it was thought that there could be no absolute need of immediate offence, but to preserve life was another and immediate affair. So true was this that to save your life you could forestall violence by violence even in a church, " for human life is of more value than the safeguarding of a church from pollution " (cap. iii.).

In his last chapter Antonino treats entirely of reprisals and their permissibility. He argues the point from the expression " mystical body,"[1] connoting the whole nation at war against the enemy as a single whole. The expression is interesting, for it shows that the concept of a people as a moral unity had become accepted. By " the mystical body " he means that the nation is to be considered as a moral person. He was, of course, applying a term of dogmatic theology—even of Scripture—by way of analogy, to political and social national life. It is evident then that by the fifteenth century this concept had passed sufficiently into ordinary speech for Antonino to use it without explanation, knowing certainly that the term would be immediately understood.

Taking this concept of the moral unity of a nation at war as true, St Antonino said that he thought reprisals allowable, though only rarely, and in order to avoid or prevent very grave harm. Even then, however, there were certain classes of the community who might not be touched : clerics, students, ambassadors, merchants, pilgrims and women. These were sacred and might never be attacked. The roll-call of the Archbishop sums up a pageant of the mediæval world : the busy workers, the long line of travellers, the internationals, those aloof, or who should be aloof, from the local prejudices and penalties of war and its incidence.

But with these exceptions St Antonino did allow reprisals, even against people who were innocent, provided the evil to be avoided, or prevented, was certain and very grave. He admitted, however, that the matter was highly disputable and that some canonists were absolutely against him—noticeably

---

[1] It is also used (with reference to the *Corpus Juris*) by Giovanni da Legnano (who died in 1382 and lies buried in the Church of S. Domenico, at Bologna) in his *Tractatus de Bello*, ed. by T. E. Holland, 1917.

Giovanni di Belviso. Many names are quoted in this discussion : Domenico di S. Geminiano, Guido and Giovanni Francesco di Vercelli—the difficult moral problem was evidently well to the fore in the universities. No doubt the ethical question became more insistent as the idea of the moral personality of a nation gained ground. Before Grotius or the international lawyers had taken the matter up their postulates had been already accepted ; what the later school did was to bring clarity to ideas already widely spread.

By the time we get to the year 1500 we find that almost all the problems perplexing the earlier Middle Ages have been cleared up, but also that fresh problems have arisen owing to the new conditions of Christendom—namely, through the war of aggression arising out of the new discoveries, and the wars of conquest originating in the name of religion, or nationality, or culture, or adventure, or trade. Not that the Middle Ages had not similar wars to their discredit—for the wars of mankind have almost invariably originated in one or other of these five motives—but earlier wars were cloaked under cover of legal and dynastic disputes.

In his *Commentary on the Politics*, St Thomas expounds from Aristotle the causes that lead to civil war, noting, from his experience at many courts and in many cities, those undoubtedly answerable for some of the wars of his own Italy : " Another cause is unlikeness ; for when there dwell in the same city people who have not the same customs or traditions there is sure to be trouble unless they have come to some agreement or lived together for a long time. First, it is clear that those who have different customs are inclined to different purposes. Secondly, from this springs a divergence of intention or will. This is the cause of civil war. Hence it will be seen that where the city is composed of a heterogeneous population there is danger of endless civil war. . . . A city is not composed of men who have chosen their citizenship but of men who are born there " (*On Politics*, v., lect. 2). This is an admirable explanation of the restless wars of many an Umbrian city, with its tangled skein of Teutonic noble and Italic burgher, their ceaseless quarrels till the aristocracy had been expelled or absorbed, or the warring factions swept momentarily away by the advent of the Tyrant.

" In some cities civil wars arise on account of the lie of the land. For it may happen that a district is not suitable for one city but rather for many. Now the ordered union of all that goes to make up a city gives it its unity and stability. If one of these be ill-fitting the result will be revolution, so that even geographical conditions may make or mar the unity of a state " (*ibid.*). Here is another commentary in which may possibly be read the history of that contest between Florence and Pisa for the control of the mouth of the Arno, the history of the little hill-cities of Italy, with their poor means of communication dooming them to isolation, and to subsequent subjection by a more powerful neighbour, only to break away whenever occasion should offer. So Florence fought with Pisa, so Assisi maintained the long struggle with Perugia despite the cruelty with which its successive efforts at independence were punished.

We may then perhaps group all motives for war under religion, nationality, culture, adventure and trade. Certainly all these causes figure in the mediæval period, but such pretexts were not then acknowledged as justification for war, with the exception of religion under the name of a crusade. To satisfy the mediæval conscience some other reason must be forthcoming, some legal justification adduced. A mere legal quibble might suffice where less conscientious princes were concerned, but this at least would be demanded, otherwise it would appear as though the reign of law were threatened. The mediæval world, as we have already insisted, can only be comprehended as under the inspiration of law. Consequently, in its eyes trade was no valid reason for war, nor national expansion, nor love of adventure, nor the imposition of a higher culture. Hence the wars between England and Wales, between England and France, or Scotland, were waged under legal quibbles of sovereignty, or interpretations of Salic law, or feudal obligation and precedent. The adventure to Ireland was cloaked under the solemnity of a Papal bull. Whatever we may judge the ethical value of such pleas it must not prevent us from recognizing their existence if we are to understand the thoughts and motives for action of that age.

Its wars were conceived as wars of justice; toward the end of the period we begin to hear of wars of freedom. The same quibbles are resorted to, and cases trumped up that seem to us in our long-distant impartiality to be mere pretext and deliberate self-deception. But perhaps wars are always thus. They suddenly blaze up or are intentionally provoked. It is only later that excuses are discovered or elaborated by the patriot, who, it may be, knows very little of the inner truth of things.

By 1480, when Francesco Vittoria was born (*d.* 1546), other currents, we perceive, are entering the main stream of the ideas of peace and war. The influence of St Thomas and St Antonino is still unmistakable: their words are quoted and their names invoked, their theories are the foundation on which others build. Vittoria had his own influence on Suarez, even on Grotius, and through them on the modern world. The two principal treatises of his which deal with this matter are *De Jure Belli* and *De Potestate Civili*.[1] He was a Spaniard, a Dominican friar, a public preacher; he lived to see the wars against the Indians of Central and South America: new problems, there-fore, and new solutions are to be found in his works.

He accepted with barely any discussion the points declared by Aquinas. They have definitely become commonplaces that all admit.

War is permitted if it be just—that is, *if*

(1) declared by the public authority of the prince;
(2) for a just cause—*i.e.* against injustice, postulating on the part of the enemy some fault or crime;
(3) carried out with a right intention—namely, to establish the good and to prevent evil.

In a war that is just, subjects are bound to obey the call of the prince to serve; clerics, however, might not take up arms; stratagems were permitted, but no lying, and sworn promises must be observed; booty was the property of the just belligerent in compensation for his losses.

[1] *Relectiones XII.: Theologicæ in duos libros distinctæ*, Lyons, 1587, lect. vi.

Again Vittoria definitely adopted the opinion of his time when he laid down that offensive war alone required an authoritative declaration by the prince. Defensive war could by reason of its occasion be waged without further sanction than the fact of the presence of the invader on invaded territory: " As regards defensive war there can be no doubt, for one may always repel force by force " (*De Jure Belli*, § 3). If the justice of the war were beyond doubt then the obligation to obey the call of the prince would be correspondingly grave. This obligation varied in inverse ratio with the doubtfulness of the justice of the war.

Moreover, the power to kill was declared by Vittoria to belong to the state by divine right. This again had been the teaching which the Middle Ages had inherited from the early Church as interpreted by the Fathers from the epistles—so they held—of St Peter and St Paul. But such a power was necessarily a highly responsible one, since it affected the gravest of all human rights—the right to live—and should be committed only to such as could be trusted to use it without injustice. We may perceive that by this time " the mystical body " of the state had developed into the nation's moral personality, for the collective responsibility of the whole people was definitely acknowledged by Vittoria. The Respublica was answerable for the acts committed in its name (*De Potestate Civili*, § 12). The sense of the public conscience had been made alive to its own position in the national life ; the character of government, its composition, the authority of the prince, the whole political situation, were now realized to touch the moral responsibility of the citizen. Savonarola's sermons were permeated with this thought ; Henry VII. of England was to feel its sting.

Vittoria, therefore, when he dealt with the justification of war saw this so clearly that he formulated the principle: " There is but one just cause of war, the violation of a right " (§ 13). This is put neatly. It sums up the scholastic argument, such as Aquinas argued it, or Antonino accepted it, and sets out in a terse formula what they had laboured more roundly to explain.

Moreover, he is not afraid to reject " increase of glory " as a motive for war, though Antonino had admitted it. Perhaps by glory the two writers did not mean quite the same thing; at any rate, it evidently seemed to Vittoria a dangerous admission on the part of the earlier writer, since the word was vague and self-complacent, and calculated to give an opening to national pride and self-assertion. Naturally, therefore, he renounced also as just motive for war the extension of empire and differences of religion. Implicitly this was again a contradiction of earlier mediæval teaching, for crusades were always admitted as lawful, even if writers occasionally denounced them as futile. But it is to be remembered that the original object of the Crusades was not to convert the Saracen or the Turk, but to rescue the Holy Land, and that they were not therefore based upon differences of religion but upon " the violation of a right." Thus it will be recalled that St Antonino considered, first, that the conquest of Palestine by Titus had been a just war ; secondly, that the inheritance of the Roman Emperors had descended to the Popes and Christendom, and, therefore, thirdly, that the invasion of the Holy Land by the Saracen and Turk had been an unjust aggression. Yet the Crusade against the Toulousain and its heretics had certainly as its basis " a difference of religion," though the popes never urged war as a method of converting the heretic, but as a means of preventing the spread of infection. The attitude of Vittoria represented then certainly a gain in clearness if not an advance in ideas.

But the discoveries in East and West by Vasco da Gama and Columbus had opened up new possibilities of conquest, disclosed new territories and a new motive for war. We have already hinted at it under the name of culture ; it was perhaps unconsciously some desire to impose a higher culture that precipitated the war against the Midi and its gnostic Antinomians. In Vittoria's day it was deliberately proclaimed as a justification for war, but condemned by him : " Christian princes have no authority whatever to punish crimes committed by barbarians, even though they be against natural law, nor can the Pope give them authority to do so, for he has no jurisdiction over infidels." Here definitely is the restatement of an old pronouncement, for St Thomas had already laid it down when, referring to the pagans dwelling within Christian nations, he upheld their right to hold property; to legal justice; to the practice of their own faith. But Vittoria had arrived at the same conclusion from another angle. He had to deal with the excuse put forward in his own day that the right of conquest can be founded on the evil lives of barbarians, and that for the sake of giving them the truths of Christianity their territory can be taken from them.

It will probably not be questioned that zeal for the spread of Christianity was one of the dominant motives influencing public opinion in favour of these expeditions, and that to the end it was this missionary spirit that continued to predominate in Spain. Elsewhere, religion was made a mere cloak, or at least an excuse to justify what was primarily undertaken for reasons which might not so profitably be divulged.

When he comes down to the details of the conduct of war Vittoria is less original. He quotes the canonists as Antonino had done, repeats the same conclusions almost verbatim, at times with hardly the variation of a phrase. For example: " The enemy's goods may be seized to the amount of the expenses of the war and of the damage unjustly inflicted by him " (§ 17) is to be found also in the *Summa Moralis*, and the various points raised by earlier writers are similarly proposed and answered. The only difference is in the style, the scholastic method has given way to a more literary treatment, and in place of *Summæ*, or summaries, we are now reading treatises, consequently the phraseology strikes us as more vivid and modern, as though the writers knew our world. " Even in wars with the Turk it is not permissible to kill women and children. In wars amongst Christians, peaceful tillers of the soil may not be killed, nor the civil and unmilitary population, for all are to be presumed innocent, unless found guilty. Strangers similarly, travelling through the country or dwelling there, are not to be considered implicated; nor priests nor religious unless found with arms " (§ 35). This is again the contention of Antonino which he himself had accepted from a previous age; it was part of that primitive " right of nations " the validity of which the early Church had taken from the Stoics, and which the scholastics—Aquinas, Scotus and the rest —so strongly defended. We may, perhaps, observe in the pages of Vittoria the development of the idea of mercy. By this time the observance of the old Truce of God had definitely lapsed. Even in the time of St Antonino it had ceased to be binding, it belonged to another age. (*Extrav. de Treuga et Pace*, cap. 1, is the reference he gives in chap. ii., § 9. It suspended all war between Advent and the Octave of the Epiphany, between Septuagesima and the Octave of Easter, between sunset on Wednesday and sunrise on Monday.)

The conduct of war, therefore, in the time of Vittoria had entered on a more ruthless stage protected by none of these conventional limitations which had once justified their purpose by the creation of an ideal of justice and of peace. The later age, though an age of greater cruelty and of methods of torture, the direct result of the refinements of the Renaissance—for an age of refinement does not mean the disappearance of cruelty, it merely makes its tortures more exquisite—had at least attained to an idea of mercy when the war was over : " When victory has been gained and even after the danger has passed, the guilty may lawfully be done to death. . . . It is not permissible in a general revolt to execute a whole population. . . . The punishment must be proportionate to the crime " (§ 47) ; " When victory is gained, it must be used with Christian moderation. . . . The victor must look on himself not as a prosecutor but a judge . . . reducing to a minimum the disaster and misfortune that have overtaken the state, the more so as among Christians the fault lies for the most part with the princes " (§ 60). Save for that last phrase the rest might be taken out of the *Summa Theologica* or the *Summa Moralis*, it conveys the same teaching expressed by the older writers with more formality and precision. Undoubtedly, however, there is a new note of compassion in the framing of the ideas, the emotions are more freely expressed, sentiment is permitted to enter.

There remain two other quotations to be given from Vittoria before we leave him, illustrative of that development both of compassion and of cynicism so frequently to be found allied :

" Cases of good faith, even in an unjust war, may often occur amongst the soldiers " (§ 59)—so much for his compassion. It is the idea of the fault of war, lying "for the most part with princes," expressed in another way. " War cannot be just on both sides at the same time, except in the case of invincible ignorance " (§ 32), is an example of the writer's gentle cynicism. Perhaps, however, it is his compassion and not his cynicism that prompts his utterance of things like this.

Yet, when all has been said of war and war's justice, and when every precaution has been taken, that when justly declared war shall also be justly waged, it remains certain that throughout the Middle Ages all writers were in agreement on this, that war was something foreign to the spirit of Christ. The liturgy of the Church spoke of war as something dreadful, a woe comparable with pestilence as a scourge of man's sin. " Give peace in our time " was to be found, in the Cluniac revival, at the end of the Divine Office said by the religious in their choir. " Peace and true concord " was implored in the Litanies of the Saints as something to be divinely bestowed upon Christian princes— the desire of the hearts of those in prayer. The " Mass in time of war " speaks of ferocity as war's necessary accompaniment, and beseeches that the Sacrifice once offered may avert such evils from mankind, may give peace speedily and put an end to war.

But the sense of war's futility was also present to the mind of the mediæval writers who knew that its fruits have seldom been satisfactory to either side : "it costs more than it gains," as one of them said. He writes also (*Summa Prædicantium*, vol. i., fol. lxxi.) : "Although it is true that the object of war is peace, nevertheless peace is more secure when it is obtained by councils rather than by arms." The fruitlessness of treaties seemed, perhaps, due to the fact that they closed a war rather than that they opened an age of peace. Innocent III. has things as strongly written against war, and as strongly in favour of arbitration, as anyone (Migne, *P.L.*, vols. ccxiv.-ccxvii.) ; his influence on the whole was certainly in favour of peace.

" Good men," writes De Romans, "are wont to labour without respite for peace, exploring every method whereby the discords of men may be brought back to peace ; not giving up the pursuit because peace flies from them but using every effort to overtake it in its flight " (Serm. lxxxviii.). It is but just to recognize both the exaltation of peace and the frequency of war as simultaneous phenomena in the Middle Ages working side by side.

The Church ministered to both ideals, and had theories in defence of peace and of war. The schoolmen had most to lose by war, hoped that their persons might be safe from capture, but could not hope that they might escape the rigours of a siege, the famine and plague so often the outcome of war. The lawyers were determined that war should only be waged lawfully, in accordance with their principles and consonant with their approval; they conceived it as almost within their purview that they should judge the justice of the war as well as of the treaty with which it should end.

The rise of the professional soldier was responsible for the transformation of war towards the close of the Middle Ages. That influenced more than anything else the problem of the morality of warfare. This development, together with the developed sense of the moral personality of the nation, were the determining factors that made each successive schoolman or lawyer look at war from a slightly different standpoint than that of his predecessor. Social theories were gradually discarded as the simple gave way to the complex, with the result that new social ideas were bound to emerge. The new sense of the identity of the nation with its prince and ruler was political rather than social, but the conception of the " *corpus mysticum* " of the nation as an individual and moral personality did more than all other to alter the social system of the Middle Ages. Developed along the lines which it subsequently pursued, it helped to create nationalism, a political force, and to break feudalism, a social organization, to complete the break-up of Christendom under the guidance of the principle " *cujus regio ejus religio.*" St Antonino does not tell us whence he borrowed it, but it is to be found even in the *Decretals*. More important is it that we should note that by his time the idea had arrived. More than any other purely philosophic concept it led the race away from mediævalism to the modern world.

CHAPTER VIII

CHRISTENDOM

It seems impossible to conceive of the social theories of the Middle Ages without some reference to the idea of Christendom which all the while served as a background to them. For the people of that time religion or the Faith ran through the whole of life, in the sense of being inextricably entangled with it. The teaching of Christian tradition was not always lived up to nor ever lived up to perfectly, but the Church as the institution which in their eyes had been given them to be the living embodiment of that teaching could never wholly be put out of their lives. In the village, the church as a building was the centre of the village life, round it and in it moved the important events of life, individual and communal. It had no rival. Even in the towns, where at the beginning of the thirteenth century there were less visible signs of the domination of the Church, it was impossible to get away from the influence of the Faith. However much the mediæval preacher might inveigh against the evils of men's lives, and however distressingly he might lament the ignorance and superstition of so many even of his audience, he could not but be conscious that life nevertheless was lived in surroundings that for ever bore witness to the Faith. That was indeed the very tragedy of religion to him—the nearness of the symbols and the aloofness of the things.

From the point of view of the student of social ideals, it is necessary to remember that Christendom to the men of that time was a single and living organism, and that Christendom was conterminous with the Catholic Faith. The use of the word Christianity was common indeed, but on the whole Christianity and Catholicism were synonyms to the mediæval mind. Humbert de Romans (*De Eruditione Religiosorum Prædicatorum*, ii., p. 459) says: "This name Christian was derived from *Christ*," and he refers also to "that Christianity which every Christian ought to have." Here Christianity is not so much looked on as an institution but as a practical life, a form of life which every Christian ought to be living. Bromyard, on the other hand (under "Falsitas," fol. clxxxi., Lyons, 1522), uses the word as we use it and speaks of "the beginnings of the Christian religion . . . the beginnings of Christianity."

We also have the expression applied not only to a form of life (as in our phrase, "It does not say much for his Christianity," where we mean "his Christian spirit"), and to a definite form of religion (as in our more ordinary use of the word in the same sense as Bromyard used it), but to all those (again in the modern sense) who call themselves by the name of Christ: "Amongst Christians are some true Christians holding the true faith about Christ (*de Christo*), and some pseudo-Christians holding a false faith, however they are both alike in their Christianity (*similes tamen sunt ambo in Christianitate*)" (Humbert de Romans, Serm. lxi.: *In Inquisitione Hæreticorum*, p. 554).

On the whole, however, this last is an unusual though by no means isolated use of the word Christian, for ordinarily it would seem to have been confined to those who belonged to the sees in union with Rome. Already Rome was the centre of the Faith, the Pope was the common father of Christendom, the Roman Pontiff had plenitude of power (*omnimodo potestas*), to use a phrase of thirteenth-century reference which Grossetête often repeats (*Letters*, etc., p. 436). Even though he may be treated with scant respect, his interference with local patronage keenly resented, his demands for money publicly commented on and denounced, and his bulls require royal sanction before they acquire legal force in the realm, there was very little opposition to him as the unique court of dogmatic appeal, the one power whose prerogative it was to "determine" doctrine for Christendom. Into the origins of this power it is not necessary to go. It had already been long accepted by the Western nations.

Beyond the borders of Christendom were first of all the pagans, the Moors, Saracens and Tartars, and later the Turks; also there were the northern peoples of Europe along the Baltic coast who so long retained their old heathen deities and whose colonists in Russia came into touch with the West through the trade centre of Novgorod.[1] Trade indeed and war were the chief reasons why the mediæval Christian could never forget the existence of these large tracts of heathendom. It is certain that he never knew how large these pagan countries were in proportion to his own nor how thickly they were populated. He knew of China : for in England we had already for two or three centuries absorbed Chinese words into our language—like silk and ginger. But he could not have realized how small a portion of the world had even heard of the name of Christ.

Nearer to him were the Greeks, whose shrinking empire still, till within fifty years of the end of our period, centred round Constantinople. These Innocent III., in his letter to the Emperor Lascaris after the sack of his city by the Latins, speaks of indeed as " Christians," though he condemns them for having "striven to rend the seamless robe of Christ " (*P.L.*, 215, xi. 47). The Pope also spoke of the Greeks as Christians when he wrote to the clergy in Constantinople (ii. 203). Throughout our period efforts were made intermittently to heal the schism between West and East. But it was only towards the close of it that an official reconciliation took place, and even then the reunion was short-lived. Within a few years of the Decree of Union with which the Council of Florence (1439) ended, the Easterns had again repudiated their acceptance of the Roman Primacy; when Constantinople fell the Emperor was in communion with Rome, but his bishops had ceased to consider themselves so. The sack of Constantinople by Latin Crusaders in 1204 at the opening of our period, its brutality and evil violence had made the memory of the Latins hateful to the Greeks. Yet from 1204 onwards to the final repudiation efforts by Rome at reunion continued to be made.

There is a remarkable work by Aquinas, *Contra Errores Græcorum*, in which he sets out to prove that the early Greek Fathers and Councils had from the beginning accepted the Roman Primacy, and in which he cites passage after passage from those authorities in support of the various conclusions into which his arguments are divided. But the interest of the book centres mainly in the Introduction, in which he describes

[1] *Chronicle of Novgorod* (1016-1471), *Publ. Camden Ser. Roy. Hist. Soc.*, 1914.

the difficulty of translating doctrine from one language into another, and almost hints that in his opinion some differences at least in points in dispute are due to the transliteration of words from Greek into Latin thereby incorporating mistranslations of doctrinal expressions. As an example, he quotes the word "substance" as the exact Latin equivalent for ὑπόστασις (a standing under, a substance) and then explains that while both Greeks and Latins believed there to be three hypostases in the Trinity, the Latins would not say there were three substances in the Trinity because in Latin the word substance had come to mean nature. It was, as he repeats in the *Summa Theologica* (i. 33, 1, ad 1 m, 2 m, 3 m), sometimes through a misunderstanding of the exact meaning of technical phrases that heresy or schism began.

The third body of non-Catholics who had to be taken into mediæval consideration were those who lived within Christian territories—that is, Jews and heretics. The attitude of Christendom towards the Jews was affected by local panic or national distress; but in the main Christians were tolerant of Jews precisely because the Jews made little or no effort to convert Christians to their own beliefs.[1] The heretic on the other hand, whether an individual professor in a university or a member of a group-organization, was nearly always a propagandist, for that reason the Church and the people made a distinction between them. If the Jew was hated, it was less for his religious beliefs than for the power his financial interest gave him, though he was never allowed to forget that his race had crucified Christ. On the other hand the attitude, both official and popular, to heresy was due entirely, or almost entirely, to opposition to its religious beliefs.

The mediæval thinker, therefore, formulated his scheme of these outside his own body by grouping them under two main divisions: unbelief, which is primarily a sin against faith, and schism, which is more particularly a sin against charity.[2]

---

[1] Moneta, *Adversus Catharos et Valdenses*, Rome, 1743, Bk. V., cap. xiii., p. 519.
[2] Cf. *S. Thomas Aquinas*, ed. by C. Lattey, S.J., Cambridge, 1925, pp. 227-246.

Unbelief itself could be considered again either in those who merely did not believe the Christian Faith or in those who deliberately resisted it. St Thomas was careful to explain that those of the first sort—namely, who merely did not believe— were not sinners on that account, for their unbelief was to be attributed not to any personal failing on their part but to the effect of original sin which they did but inherit. Hence, in their case, want of faith was not to be attributed to actual sin. At the Judgment of God they would never be condemned on account of their paganism or heresy, but only for whatever they had otherwise done amiss. These, therefore, were not referred to again in the *Summa*, because Aquinas proceeded at once to consider as unbelievers only those who deliberately resisted the Faith. This is the universal attitude of the mediæval Church to unbelief.

Unbelief, then, was to be considered a sin when it is a deliberate resistance to faith. This again can be subdivided into those who resist it before having accepted it, and those who resist it after acceptance. The first were pagans, deliberately refusing to believe. The second were (1) Jews, who rejected it after having accepted it in figure; and (2) heretics, who rejected it after having accepted it in reality. Of these three, though the pagan taught more wrong doctrines than the Jew, and the Jew than the heretic (except the Manichean who held worse beliefs than the Jew), Aquinas considered that the heretic was really the worst because he " corrupts the Christian Faith."

How were these to be dealt with? Aquinas is as rigorous as any of the mediæval writers. He is as usual, however, very careful in his use of words and he expresses his mind with perfect clearness. He lays down as his guiding principle that over those who had once accepted her teaching the Church had spiritual dominion, but that she had no spiritual dominion over those who had not. Hence over heretics she claimed the right to legislate ; she did not claim any right to legislate over pagans and Jews, except a temporal dominion if these lived in territories that fell under Christian jurisdiction. Heretics owed her both spiritual and temporal allegiance ; neither pagans nor Jews (*i.e.* even those who deliberately resisted the Faith) owed her spiritual allegiance directly—at the most they might owe her a temporal allegiance.

On the basis of this distinction, Aquinas proceeded to lay down his main propositions, which again were the commonplace teaching of the mediæval scholastic writers :

(i) No one should be compelled to accept the teaching of Christianity, for it was a matter for the individual will. Even children should not be baptized against their parents' wish. It would have been a double sin to have interfered with the authority of parents given them by God over their children and to have given responsibilities of the Faith to a child whose subsequent upbringing in the Faith could not have been effectively guaranteed. No one, therefore, should be forced into the Faith.

(ii) Anyone could be compelled to carry out the teaching of Christianity who had once accepted it. To enforce this seemed as simple a business to the mediæval mind as to enforce the fulfilment of any other contract. A man who bound himself by promise to the Catholic Faith had made a definite compact which at once carried with it legal obligations, enforceable at law. But supposing he could no longer accept that Faith in conscience? At any rate, he could be compelled to fulfil his contract. The Christian religion was a fundamental law of Christendom. If, then, contracts of a human nature were to be enforced by the law whether the contractors of them still believed in the things they had undertaken to do or not, then contracts of a divine nature had no less binding force.

To the objection that this was an unwarrantable interference with the human conscience the mediæval thinker would have replied that he had no desire to touch the conscience ; he agreed that no one should be compelled to accept the Faith, only that he could be compelled to carry out the Faith he had sworn to obey. Heresy was for them almost in the same category as treason. Indeed the law of heresy was deliberately modelled on the law of treason ; this is asserted in the *Directorium* for the use of Inquisitors drawn up by Nich. Eymeric (Venice, 1604, p. 117). No one could be compelled to belong to one state rather than another : but having sworn allegiance to a state, he could be compelled to fulfil the obligations of his allegiance. This at any rate seemed a fair parallel to the mediæval concept of the Church. The Church claimed absolute sovereignty over every soul which had once accepted its teaching. Thus was Christ in His Majesty set at the royal porch of each cathedral, the supreme Ruler and King of men.

If the heretic wished to return to the Church, he must be received back : nor could there be any limit to the number of times he might be reconciled. There was, of course, a reference in this to the controversy that at one time threatened to disrupt the early Church, as to whether a penitent could more than once be readmitted to communion. The question went back to a time before the practice of frequent confession had been introduced. The Mediæval Church had, however, no difficulties on that score and was willing to absolve the penitent any number of times.

But while the heretic was to be reconciled any number of times, he could be punished after the first relapse. Sacramentally there was no limit placed to his return ; as often as he repented, he was to be reconciled. Yet it seemed to the mediæval mind that this did not in any degree affect the lawfulness of punishing him, because the difference between the guilt of sin and the punishment due to sin was widely acknowledged— for example, in the teaching on indulgences. An indulgence could be granted only to one who had repented and been absolved from his sin, and it consisted in the remission of the penalties which were still due to sin even after it had been forgiven. Similarly, heresy repented of was forgiven but the penalty due to this sin remained. This penalty at the first offence was normally passed over when the heretic sought reconciliation ; it was normally inflicted after the first relapse.

The reason for this was given by Aquinas. The Church was not like God and could not read men's inner conscience. She could not, therefore, determine whether the relapsed sinner who desired a second reconciliation was really sincere or not. She did not deny his sincerity, but thought she could not be sure of it (II. ii. 2, 4).

After this first relapse, therefore, according to St Thomas and the other scholastics, he could be handed over to the secular arm for the death penalty wherever the death penalty was in vogue. Where men were put to death for counterfeiting the currency of the king there could be no illogicality in putting them to death for counterfeiting the divine currency. But the purpose of the penalty was not only to punish, it was also to prevent false doctrine being taught, it was to prevent the circulation of falsehood. Repeatedly it was explained that no heretic was ever handed over to death or punishment in order that he might be converted; he was put to death in order to prevent him poisoning other souls (*Summa Theologica*, II. ii. 23; *Sent.*, iv. 2, 3, ad 5).[1]

Reiner, "once an heresiarch now by the Grace of God priest in the Order of Preachers, though unworthy," in his treatise, *Contra Waldenses Hæreticos*, written in 1254 (Bigne, p. 262 *et seq.*), speaks of the punishment of heretics. "First they are to be punished by excommunication. . . . Then by deposition. . . . Thirdly by military force in order that, if otherwise it cannot be done, by the mailed fist all his goods may be taken from him. . . . It is safer that this should be done by the special edict of the prince than of the Church lest the Church should appear to be acting in this way out of cupidity or revenge" (cap. x., p. 274). He quotes naturally the famous decree of the Emperor Frederich II., in 1224.

Secondly, there was the sin of schism. By this was meant the refusal to be subordinate to the Pope and to be in communion with those who were subordinate to him. Schism did not necessarily imply heresy, though often the two went together. It was difficult to conceive the refusal of subordination to the Papacy as arising from any other motive than a disinclination to accept its doctrinal authority on one point or another. The concept of mere spiritual subjection to the Holy See was so obvious to the mediæval mind, and so little liable to offend in an age when feudal society rested on the basis of subordination and service, that the idea in itself was not likely to provoke opposition. An easy instance of the truth of this can

---

[1] *Cf.* Moneta, *Adversus Catharos*, p. 515.

be seen in the career of Wyclif. As the protagonist of the national feeling against Rome, under its material aspect of taxation, he was exceedingly popular. At Bruges in 1360 he voiced the public opinion of many of the bishops as well as of the Court. As an apostle of disendowment, his doctrine received a measure of support. It was a philosophical justification of what subsequently befell the Church: the famous parable of the owl and the feathers in the House of Lords in 1370. But as an apostle of theological views against the power of the priesthood, against transubstantiation and the papal supremacy, he lost popular support at once and his strength fell away. There was hardly any opposition at any time, until the very end of the period, to the spiritual supremacy of Rome in the West. When the separation from union with Rome came about, it was in its origin due largely to despair of the Papacy. Men grew impatient because the popes, though they maintained unquestioned supremacy, yet did nothing to reform the admitted evils in the Church until the breach had actually occurred.

The effects of schism, as distinguished from heresy, were discussed by Aquinas. Sacramental power was not lost by schismatics. It could be handed on to successors. This might happen even in the case of heretics, unless their heresy denied the efficacy of any particular sacrament; but neither, it was considered, were able to use their powers lawfully. Moreover, lacking the authority to use the power they possessed, they could have no valid jurisdiction and could neither impart absolution nor give indulgences.

The schismatic, like the heretic who had once been of the body of the Church, still remained under her spiritual jurisdiction.

It has been necessary to give these details despite their theological nature, in order to understand the attitude of the Church and of the people to the dissentient Christians of their day. They envisaged the world as a Christian world: to a large extent their theories did not touch the outer circle of heathendom. Within Christendom, however, Faith was the fundamental point of life. Religion was considered as primarily the acceptance of a series of doctrines which in themselves implied and definitely stated the existence of God and of an invisible world pressing close in on and, in some measure, entering into the normal life of man. The apparitions of saints and demons were taken for granted by everybody as normal and natural. To what extent these apparitions were thought to be really objective and corporeal it is difficult to be sure, though Aquinas carefully explained how they might be corporeal. The existence of this supernatural world and its relationship to man and man's relationship to it was the fundamental concept of religion.

A secondary concept of religion implied that a form of life was required of the individual which should correspond with this fundamental concept. His actions should be as Christian as his beliefs. This secondary concept was held to be the expression of the primary concept. It was not the essential constituent of religion, but rather its effect, due, proper, and of obligation.

In his sermon to the brethren and sisters of the hospitals (Serm. xl., pp. 475-476) Humbert de Romans gave the contemporary judgment of the thirteenth century on the value of good works : " For material in preaching to these it is well to remember that amongst all the works which can be performed in the service of the Creator, the most excellent are the works of mercy, according to that verse of the Psalms : His mercies are above all His works. This is to be interpreted not only about the works He did Himself but also about those done in His Name. Moreover, amongst all the works of mercy, the most excellent are those which are performed on the sick poor. . . ." He proceeds to speak of the reasons for this, and also of the defects that were to be found in hospitals and were to be denounced by the preacher. Sometimes the sick, he said, were not well received when they arrived, or not cared for after they had been in the hospital a long time ; sometimes too much money was spent on the officials or staff ; even a chance visitor would gain the impression that the hospital was being conducted for their sakes, and not for the sake of God or the good of Christian folk : " The rich man who is sick is not in need—that is, he is not destitute—because he has whatever is necessary; but the poor man who is sick is needy as well as poor, lacking now even what is necessary."

Again he urged on the doctors never to perform an operation " that is doubtful without grave consultation and deliberation. So let them deal faithfully with their patients as to cause them as little expense as possible; let them take a moderate fee (*salarium temperatum*) that their consciences be not hurt. Above all let them beware of doing aught in their art against God in themselves or in others, lest whilst they heal bodies they kill souls, others or their own. Finally, let them have not as much confidence in their medicines as in their prayers, and let them have most in God."

Whilst, therefore, insisting upon good works and acts of charity and benevolence, the mediæval school of thinkers perpetually laboured the point of faith as being fundamental and primary, out of which good works should spring spontaneously. Hence they arrived at the conclusion, formulated theologically, that " perfect love was not possible without perfect faith." You could not love God properly unless you knew God properly, for the God you loved might never really exist, being only the creation of your fancy. But you could not know God properly, God as He is in Himself, apart from faith. Consequently the service of God and the love of God, and therefore the due and proper love and service of the brotherhood, were all dependent upon accuracy of faith—*i.e.* of dogma. The heretic was, therefore, unable to know and serve adequately God or man. This principle of the schools seemed proved to the schoolmen by the heretics whom they knew, whose gospels were largely subversive of the due service of man. These gospels they wished, therefore, to prevent from spreading; as much, so they thought, for men's sake as for God's; or rather for the sake of truth.

The repressive policy of the Mediæval Church and of the state was based upon this consideration, which itself rested on this fundamental principle of religion—namely, the existence of a supernatural world and man's relation to it. Ethics were the result of dogma; conduct was only the expression of religion; accuracy of faith must precede true charity.

But there lurked in their minds all the while an uneasy feeling that repression, however justified as a principle, was yet unsuccessful as a policy. Efforts were made by individuals to be rid of the office of Inquisitor. The Dominican Order asked to be relieved of the unpleasant task in the thirteenth century [1]; the Pope only agreed to reduce their sphere of work, and handed over part of it to the Franciscans. That some modifications were gradually introduced by the Inquisition into the process of trying heretics seems very sure; that the Inquisition gave justice, where the populace would have been far more summary and expeditious, is again equally sure. But the business of repression irked many minds. John Mandeville (John of Burgundy? *d.* 1372) in the fourteenth century shows us his mind; for it has often been the happy device of travellers, when they wish to point out the defects of their own civilization as they see it, to depict in glowing phrases the virtues of a far-off nation, so that incidentally their readers may be shamed into realizing the defects by force of contrast. So Tacitus in the *Germania* exposed rather the evils of his Rome than the real virtues of the Germany of his day. It was a genuine picture not of what the Germans possessed but of what the Romans lacked. Similarly Mandeville had his own views to convey in the following description of the Great Chan of Cathay: " He passeth all earthly princes. Wherefore it is great harm that he believeth not faithfully in God. And natheless he will gladly hear speak of God: and he suffereth well that Christian men dwell in his lordship, and that men of his faith ben made Christian men, if they will throughout all his country. For he defendeth no man to hold no law other than him liketh " (*Voyages and Travels*, ed. by Hamelius, E.E.T.S., 1919, i., p. 162).

But the three events that perhaps more than any other disturbed the Church were: the contest between the Emperor and the Pope, Louis of Bavaria and John XXII.; the Captivity of Avignon; and lastly the Conciliar Movement. The effects of the Great Schism were undoubtedly lamentable though the Schism did not really divide the Church. It entailed, however,

---

[1] *Mandonnet*, under " Preacher " (*Catholic Encyclopædia*).

a loss of control by the centre, for the centre was at war within itself, and loss of central control meant lack of discipline everywhere and consequently corruption penetrated the Church at every point. Indirectly this contributed to the break-up of Christendom and the consequent rearrangement of the social ideals of the West. The community of Christendom was dissolved and common ideals, therefore, ceased to influence the Christian community as a whole.

But far more disruptive than the Schism was the quarrel with Louis, for it succeeded in enlisting against the Pope detachments of his natural supporters—for example, the Franciscans, religious who, being exempt from episcopal jurisdiction and both world-wide and yet subject to a Superior General, were by their constitution necessarily bound to the Papacy by closer ties than the rest of the clergy, and on whose loyalty consequently he could the more rely. Nevertheless during the struggle a portion of the Franciscan body, and that by no means the least active, went over to the side of the Emperor. The cause of their defection (1322) was their refusal to accept the Papal decision on poverty or to admit the right of the Pope to determine, and dispense from, the rule of St Francis. The " Spiritual " Franciscans claimed that no Pope could alter what St Francis had fixed, nor had any Pope the right to interpret the meaning of St Francis' words or practices. By the mediæval mind this attitude of the Fraticelli was judged to be heresy—that is, the denial of the primacy and determining power of the Apostolic See.

Thus at the moment of the attack of the Emperor on the Pope's claim to suzerainty the Franciscans, under Michael of Cesena, came to the former's aid. Their action had undoubtedly a very powerful effect on the ecclesiastical world, the more so since the " Spiritual " Franciscans, sheltering under the Emperor, were driven to fight on behalf not only of their own contention, but also on behalf of the Emperor's own claim of supremacy over the Spiritual Power. Michael of Cesena took up an Erastian position in ecclesiastical politics.

Moreover, the Emperor summoned to his aid the learning of his time ; his appeal of 1323 met with instantaneous success in legal and secular quarters. The great names on the imperial side were Marsiglio of Padua (*d.* 1342), who put forward his views in his *Defensor Pacis*,[1] and William Ockham, the Oxford Franciscan, who established himself as the Emperor's most brilliant pamphleteer. Neither Marsiglio nor Ockham, however, were so much supporters of Louis of Bavaria as champions of the Secular Power as such.

For curiously the claims of John XXII. surpassed the claims even of Innocent III. He began by demanding as his right to crown the Emperor; he ended by demanding as his right to appoint the king of Germany. On his side the main champion was Agostino Trionfo, whose book on the Power of the Papacy [2] was dedicated to John XXII. In it he placed the Papal power in the place of Christ on earth, and, therefore, as being in itself superior to the Angels and equal to the Saints.

First came then a spiritual quarrel between the Pope and a party of the Franciscans as to the limits of the ecclesiastical power of the Papacy, which developed, through the wild mysticism of Cesena, into a real schism. Into this ecclesiastical controversy was imported a secular quarrel as to the limits of the temporal power of the Papacy. Louis naturally retaliated on the extravagant claims of the Papacy by an equally extravagant assertion of the subordination of the Pope to the Imperial power. Marsiglio, Louis' Vicar in Rome in 1328, declared that the sovereignty of the state rests in the people, for the nation had become, in his much-quoted phrase, a faithful human legislator having no overlord (*humanus legislator fidelis superiore carens*). While limiting the power of the spiritual authority, Marsiglio would equally have restricted the power of the Emperor by denying the universal claims of Louis and substituting for them a purely German kingship based on election, in which the people were the fountain of justice, the makers of law, while the Emperor stood to the law only as its interpreter. Ockham was equally averse from any glorification of the Emperor; he subscribed to the ideals of Marsiglio:

---

[1] Cf. *E.H.R.*, 1922, pp. 501-518; and 1923, p. 8; also the *Defensor Minor*, ed. by C. K. Brampton, 1922.

[2] *Summa de Ecclesiastica Potestate* (1473).

a less ambitious Empire based on popular support, a national kingdom.

While the old " Kaiserthum " of Frederick II. had shrunk to the national kingship of Louis of Bavaria, the hegemony of the Papacy under Innocent III. had weakened under the effect of the French domination at Avignon. The struggle between the Imperium and the Sacerdotium was on a lower plane than in its earlier appearance not only in the personal character of the combatants, but also in their actual power. Louis had no influence outside Germany, and the Pope was politically an appendage of France. But while the circumstances of the present combatants were narrower than had been those of the great leaders of the Papacy and the Empire, their claims out-distanced those put forward by the earlier protagonists. They had less, and they claimed more. The captivity of Avignon, while it freed the Pope from dependence on the Empire, had freed the Emperor from much political interference from the Papacy.

Furthermore, the idea of nationality had come, and was invading even the Faith. The Pope had become all but identi-fiable as a French prince and the German spirit was in revolt against this. The captivity of Avignon had begun under Clement V. in 1307, the protest of Louis followed in 1323. The episode occurred at the very moment when nationalism as a new ideal was effervescing to a head. The consequences were obvious and immediate. St Catherine saw that the one thing that could save the Church was to bring the Papacy back to Rome, to establish publicly its international character. She was not thinking merely in terms of politics, but in terms of the Faith; she was thinking of the lost control of discipline; she was thinking of the visible break-up of the social ideals of Europe. The dyer's daughter had heard the spirit of revolt blowing through the narrow streets of Umbrian cities. She had heard of the *Populus Romanus*, whom Louis had flattered because he was a German, while the earlier and greater Emperor Frederick I., because he was a believer in universal Empire, had denounced it, and helped to depose Arnold of Brescia, its champion. She understood the mutterings that heralded the revolt of the Ciompi at Florence (1378), the Peasants' Revolt in England (1381), and the Maillotins in France (1382).

This new nationalism then (using the word "nation" in a sense wholly new and not to be paralleled to the old grouping of students into "nations" in the University of Paris) marks the difference between the quarrel of Louis of Bavaria and John XXII. and the earlier quarrel of Frederick II. and Innocent III.; it had been fostered by the Avignon captivity.

The final element that completed the break of the common unity of the Faith was the Conciliar Movement. Marsiglio had held that Papal authority was unscriptural and therefore it could only be derived from a General Council and from the legislature of the state. The community and the state were paramount; the Church had neither legislative nor judicial power nor property.

When the Schism came, and the difficulty presented itself of deciding which out of the two or three claimants was the true Pope, people began in despair to look for a tribunal which should be the standing committee of the Church. Various policies were suggested, and an immense literature survives of the proposals put forward for the healing of the Schism and for the future government of the Church. The necessity for some scheme that should put an end to the Schism, prevent its recurrence and reform the Church was generally admitted, but the precise means of securing these remedies was what baffled so many minds. There was no lack of plans, indeed there were too many plans, and each promoter held to his own.

One proposal for the solution of the problem was that the cardinals should withdraw from their various obediences, form themselves into a single body, and thus by depriving the two claimants to the Papacy of their supporters compel both to meet and settle their differences in such a manner as to make clear who was the undoubted Head of the Church. When this fell through—partly because the cardinals could not be persuaded to carry out their promises, partly because each claimant was prepared to create fresh cardinals to fill the vacancies caused by those who deserted him—the project of the Council of Pisa was introduced, by which it was claimed the two claimants could be deposed and a new Pope chosen. The Council met at Pisa (1409) to carry out this programme, but succeeded only in making confusion worse confounded by adding a third claimant to the two it had failed to eliminate. Moreover, the result of the proceedings was proclaimed with only half-hearted assurance, to the disappointment of the friends of reform who desired above all things that reformation should precede election, and that only after the reform had been accomplished should the election take place and an oath be exacted from the successful candidate, whoever he might be, to carry out the reform.

The discussions at Pisa make the ideas of the Fathers of the Council as to the government of the Church quite clear; only in the whole Church, they declared, did the plenitude of power reside, the Council was the representative assembly of that Church, possessing the same rights and subject to the same popular influences as national parliaments, the cardinals constituted the standing committee of the Church, and the Pope was President of the Assembly and the highest executive. Nevertheless the Council separated without achieving anything more practical than the addition of a third claimant to the Papacy.

The Council of Constance followed (1414-1418), and achieved unity on its own basis largely as the reward of the bustling activity of the Emperor Sigismund; but it failed to carry out the reform so much desired by the better minds. Above all, it developed and stiffened the nationalist organization of the Church. To begin with, at its meetings the nations were divided separately, each holding its own sessions composed of its bishops and theologians. When the nation had voted by a majority its own proposal it met the other nations in plenary session and sat in that plenary session as a national body debating as a single unit the various proposals and decrees. As a result, when, following the resignation of the Roman Pope, the flight of the Avignon Pope, and the deposition of the Pisan line, Pope Martin V. was elected, he proceeded to deal with the European situation as far as the Church was concerned by means of national concordats with the Holy See.

Nor was the end yet reached, for when the Council of Basel assembled (1431-1449) in accordance with the arrangement made by the Council of Constance, it came into conflict with the new Pope Eugenius IV., who dissolved it (1438). Æneas Sylvius Piccolomini, then a member of the Conciliar party, declared that this bull of dissolution attracted greater numbers to the Council than the original summons had done. Summoned primarily in order to reform the Church — for the essential condition, the ending of the Schism, had been already accomplished—reform was the immediate matter for its consideration ; indeed the argument in favour of Basel was : since a Council had succeeded in solving the problem of a disputed succession, why should it not be equally successful in solving the problem of reform? But the hostile attitude of the Pope drove the Council at Basel into the arms of a party who wished to settle the principle of Church government as well. The three points that had been in men's minds at Pisa and Constance were not yet completely settled. Only one, the union, had been accomplished ; the other two, government and reform, still remained. To a great extent the theories of Pisa were again brought forward : the Pope to be the first official of a constitutional assembly. Since Eugenius refused to accept this position it was resolved by the Council that he should be starved into surrender by the abolition of firstfruits.

Though great names are to be found among the members of the Council, the decrees of the Council were actually passed by people of no importance, officially or unofficially, little men impetuously passing resolutions on subjects baffling wiser wits. Moreover, since Eugenius proved obdurate and refused to withdraw his bull of suppression, the recalcitrants decided to go a step further and solemnly, at a session attended by only seven bishops, the Pope was deposed ; and at a subsequent session Felix V. was elected by one cardinal and eleven bishops. The Bishop of Tours voiced the principle of his party when he exclaimed — according to Piccolomini : " We must either wrest the Apostolic See from the hands of the Italians or else despoil it to such a degree that it will not matter where it abides." This pseudo papal election was a final blow to the influence of Basel. Henry VI. of England had already declared in a letter to the Council that he did not admit its right to be regarded as more than a "congregatio," and now Giuliano Cesarini, Archbishop Niccolo of Palermo, Cardinal Niccolo Cusa, and Sylvius Piccolomini passed over to the side of Eugenius. It was by that time clear to them that Basel was no longer animated by zeal for reform but rather by obstinacy and party spirit. The Council of Florence (Ferrara, 1438, Florence, 1439-1444) took over the work of Basel, and was rendered memorable by the presence of the Greeks, and possible by the munificent hospitality of the Florentine state under the Medici. Finally, in its sixteenth session (3rd February 1434) the schismatic Council was formally reconciled, and in its seventeenth session (26th April) retracted every utterance derogatory to the person of the Pope or the dignity of his office. Two years later a remnant still sitting at Basel made a forlorn effort to raise again the question of Papal government —it was the dying flicker of a conflagration that had threatened at one time to destroy the whole position of the Papacy as supreme authority over the whole Church. It now postulated that Papal decrees, to become possessed of dogmatic inerrancy, must have received the approbation of a Council; the executive power of the Papacy was to be limited to the carrying out of the acts of the Council. The attempt failed, and the revolution was over.

Nevertheless, the whole episode was symptomatic of the coming storm that should overturn the unity of Christendom. Religion might be the excuse, but the cause would be political. Already, in Bohemia, Hus had pointed the way. In agreement with the rest of Christendom on the doctrine of Transubstantiation, communion under one kind, and devotion to the Blessed Virgin, he had his own theories on the Dominion of Grace, as he had learned it from Wyclif, and also on the position of the hierarchy, and the use of the vulgar tongue in the Liturgy.[1] This last point, though the least doctrinal, was the most important. He became the symbol of a national revival. The Slav element of Bohemia had suffered under the Latin domination

---

[1] D. S. Schaff, *John Huss*, 1915.

introduced through the medium of the Christian missionaries. The new spirit in Germany quickened the new spirit in Bohemia; all that Louis of Bavaria had done for the Germans Charles IV. had done for the Bohemians. His Golden Bull had made the kingdom of Bohemia independent (1356); already Prague had become an archbishopric independent of its old metropolitan at Mainz (1344).

Hitherto German had been the language spoken in the cities and used by the preachers and the professors and in the official circles of administration and in the courts of law. The Golden Bull urged the teaching of the language of the people on the electors as honourable and useful. At Prague a new Slavonic town had been built by Charles, a new Slavonic monastery had been founded, and the old Slavonic rite restored. Popular Slav preachers, like Milicz of Kremsier, appeared. Further, a university had been established at Prague in 1347 and a Papal Bull approved it in 1348. The national literature had been developed by Sirril Flaska of Pardoubitsé (d. 1403); the Bible had been translated into the national tongue. The artistic genius of Peter Parhe of Poland proclaimed the power of Eastern Europe to achieve a civilization at least equal to the West.

This was the movement into which entered the new theories of Hus, influenced by, and influencing, the spirit of independence begotten of the new and rising nationalism. Moral in its beginnings, it grew dogmatic as it passed through the university, and political as it reached the people.

In every direction, then, forces were gathering to break up the common unity of the Faith. The only difficulty would be to predict where the rent would begin and where end. The country perhaps that seemed least likely to suffer from it was England with her close ties to the Papacy, her seeming docility, her comparatively scanty acquaintance with heresy, the apparent dying out of the Lollard movement.

But the forces were clear enough, and their course was shown by the triple movement:

First, the nationalist spirit which invaded religion when the Papacy established itself within French territory and lay exposed to the suspicion of being dominated by French influence. There was no reason why nationalism should not have remained compatible with a universal Papacy; but as soon as the suspicion arose that the Papacy had come into the possession of one nation and was being exploited by that nation in furtherance of its own political ends, then the whole national spirit of the rest of Europe was roused in opposition. The subsequent history of the difficulties of the Papacy must be written round that theme : the efforts of the French to secure their predominance, of the Emperors to establish their right of approval, of the Italians to convert it into a weapon for driving out the foreigner, of the Spaniards to link it to the fortunes of their new empire and to buy it with their new wealth. It becomes the centre of the new political intrigue. The kings and their great ministers of the next epoch endeavour to capture it, to secure election to it, in order that they may convert it into a political engine of national ascendancy.

Second, there was the revolt of the secular spirit against ecclesiastical supremacy. The learned world still followed Aristotle, but he was no longer the champion of the Guelphs as Aquinas had left him. Under the subtle commentaries of Marsiglio of Padua he had become a Ghibelline. The subordination of the Church to the State had indeed tempted all the great kings of the Middle Ages, but the subordination they desired was not in things spiritual but in lordship temporal and ecclesiastical—a lay censorship but not a lay interference with doctrine ; the more complete separation of the two respective spheres of influence. Pierre du Bois[1]—the most talented and judicious of the writers of the fourteenth century, the most original and the most akin to the modern mind, whose treatise might still find supporters and give birth to fresh schemes and new movements—admitted the right of the Papacy to all the kingdoms under the grant of Constantine, but he insisted that this right should no longer be carried into effect. The old view of Christendom as an assembly of princes under the spiritual hegemony of the Pope—whose power extended over temporal as

---

[1] *De Recuperatione Terre Sancte*, p. 33.

well as spiritual interests—had gone, he thought, as irrevocably as Dante's dream of a universal Empire sketched in the *De Monarchia*. He urged on the Papacy the surrender of all its temporal ambitions, of all its past powers, of all its territorial possessions. As he saw it, its future lay along spiritual lines only, a dominating moral force, teaching, reproving, inspiring the kings and peoples of the West, reaching out to the East in its influence, converting Palestine as well as Constantinople, gathering into one the forces that make for righteousness—a vision splendid not yet to be.

Third, the rise of the Conciliar movement, which, springing chiefly out of the reforming desires of the most devout, became insensibly merged in the larger problem of securing effective Church government. For a time it looked as though constitutional monarchy might take the place of Papal absolutism, or a republic even, on the most modern lines, be established round a Presidential Chair of Peter. Gerson and Niccolo Cusa had the same ideals[1]; they saw the Papacy, as it seemed to them, established by constitutional authority, no longer in a position to distract Europe with its quarrels with the Emperor, or its schisms within itself, or its failure to reform the Church. Only gradually, and out of the bitter experience of the three successive attempts at Pisa, Constance and Basel, was the lesson brought home that the results of the proposed change of government might be worse than the old government. The bishops found themselves subjected by the priests to the same theories with which they had tried to empty the popedom of its powers; and the priests themselves found the people as anxious to control them as they were eager to control their bishops: " We have seen at Basel amongst the bishops and Conciliar fathers, cooks and stable-boys judging the affairs of the world " (Mansi, *Pii II. Orationes*, vol. i., p. 231).

But while the Conciliar movement was thus defeated the impact of these three forces was destined to break Christendom, with whose fortunes were bound up the common social theories of the West. As the national bond tightened, as the royal power grew more absolute, as the spiritual power fell more and more

---

[1] J. N. Figgis, *From Gerson to Grotius*, Cambridge, 1907.

under secular domination, these social theories, lacking the support of a common headship and the defence of a common body of theological teaching, weakened, lost their force and vitality, and finally, so far as the greater part of the West was concerned, disappeared.

With the break-up of united Christendom faded the vision of a common Christian social polity.

CHAPTER IX[1]

ART

It is not least in the changing artistic conceptions of each generation that we discover how changing are their ideals of social life. Art responds very faithfully to the general outlook of its period. The artist is always a man of his own time.

Mediæval man was by nature a philosopher, by instinct a believer, by education a scientist, but by choice an artist. Every side of him then we shall expect to find expressed in his art. He was not an artist by accident; he had his philosophy of art. It was deliberately that he built or sang, that he produced beauty; nor was he in haste about it. He knew that time would be needed for his critical faculties to be developed. With an infinite capacity for taking pains, pains he took.

Consequently in the eleventh and twelfth centuries, which were the real formative ages of mediævalism, writings and criticisms on art abound. By the thirteenth century these were systematized. Elaborately fine-spun speculations on art—its purpose, characteristics, limitations and rules—were not the least of the subjects with which scholasticism busied itself, debating with abstract enthusiasms every point of view. Nor were the enthusiasms only abstract, for already the Greek artists were at work in Florence, and the Greek ideas of art had filtered through into Paris. Indeed, previous to that, Councils of the Church, while protesting against the Greek iconoclasm, had even decided what domain in art lay under the dictation of the Church. Of this rationalizing of art we can take St Thomas Aquinas as the most representative of thirteenth-century philosophers. He has given us a good summary of the thought of his time.

Art, in his concept of it, was the work of human reason, engaged not in mere thought but in practical action,[2] for the

---

[1] Throughout this chapter we have been guided by *L'Art et Scolastique* of Jacques Maritain, and though we have ventured to disagree with it at times, to anyone who knows the book the greatness of our debt will be obvious.

[2] *Cf.* St Thomas, in *Metaph*, Bk. II., lect. 2.

mind had open to it a triple possibility. First, it could speculate on truth, seeking truth for its own sake, as did the metaphysician. Little was he concerned with life, its hazards or its vagaries. His concern was only with the analysis of being, with abstract truth. Secondly, the mind could busy itself with a more practical subject; it could consider human motives and intentions, could sound the depths, the moods, and the conditions of the will. Thus engaged it had for its material to elaborate and to weigh up the moral sciences or ethics ; it had to decide the values of human conduct. Though this was more practical than metaphysics, it yet remained as intangible as metaphysics, since it dealt with what went on within the circumference of the man's being, his mind and will. It was a discussion of the right ordering of intentions, and not their ultimate issue in life. Thirdly, the mind could direct man in his actions outside himself—that is, beyond the sphere of speculative reasoning, beyond " doing " into " making," into the production of concrete things outside of himself.

This triple division of the power of the mind is to be found indeed before the thirteenth century[1] ; but in the thirteenth century it had become a commonplace, with every part of the division carefully distinguished. The speculative reason was spoken of as having truth for its object. The practical reason when *doing*—*i.e.* thinking and willing—was judged to have a universal, divine purpose. It determined the moral standards of life, and was, therefore, centred on man. The practical reason when *making*—*i.e.* producing things outside man—was, however, judged to have only a concrete human purpose. It was concerned not with moral life but with work. It centred on things, not on men.

The name art was given then to this making-business when properly governed by right reason. Art was the rightly reasonable way of making things and, therefore, a human virtue. An artist was a man who made things for concrete purposes and whose work when done corresponded to its purpose, and whose purpose itself was approved of by right reason. Only he had art, in the estimation of the scholastics of the thirteenth century,

---

[1] *Cf.* Aristotle, *Metaph*, I. ii., C. 1, 995, b. 21.

who produced things which right reason justified him in making, and which themselves fulfilled the purposes for which they were made.

It might seem that this view of the profession of art would be a very material one, since the artist was judged by the thing he had made. If the thing when produced did not fulfil its purpose, that would show that the man who made it did not possess or had not used art. The man was measured by the thing. But the scholastics replied to this accusation of degrading art by stating, that while it was true that art was to be condemned or approved by what it had made, this did not imply that art was not intellectual.[1] It could not be a mere mechanical act, for the artist had to begin his work with a purpose—that is, with an idea—and had to impress this idea on his material. He was performing, therefore, an intelligent action, for he was making something for a definite purpose, and this purpose, they argued, lifted his work up from a material standard to a human level.

On the one hand no one could watch the artist without noticing how much he was at the mercy of his material. It conditioned him, limited what he could do. The frailty of his material or its coarseness, its cheapness or preciousness, its endurance or evanescence, would have to be remembered all the time he worked and would affect his work itself. Yet on the other hand the opposite was true, for the artist was the master of his material. The paradox could be maintained both that the material governed the artist and that the artist governed the material. For art is always the triumph of mind over matter, though it is always also the triumph of matter over mind.

Art then was the quality of a man's soul which enabled him to " make " or produce under the governance of right reason. The capacity for this was inborn, but it needed art to bring it out. But it must not be thought that art corresponded to " skill "; St Thomas was most insistent on that point. Deftness and skill of hand enabled art the better to display itself, but they were not really conditions of art. They removed impediments to the full expression of art, but they were not

___
[1] *Summa Theologica*, I. ii. 58, 2.

necessarily included in a work of art. Art was to be judged by the conception of the artist and not by the execution.[1]

Again, the motive was also to be excluded from any judgment on art. The artist might have a low moral motive for what he did; but that would not affect the standard of his art. The purpose for which the thing was designed would in the eyes of the scholastics affect that standard, but not the motive governing the artist, for it was the thing and not the man that was the measurement of art, and purpose affected the thing while motive affected the man. The purpose, therefore, was to be scrutinized, never the motive. For example, there could be no art in making an idol to be worshipped, for right reason could not approve the purpose of the thing. A man's motive might be good and his purpose evil; the second was of more consequence than the first, for art was the rightly reasonable way of making things.

The motives then that governed the artist did not affect his art; they were part of that other domain of the practical reason, the domain of *doing*. They concerned the intention, were of moral value, and touched universal ends, divine purposes. Art on the contrary was human and concrete. What prudence was to the right doing of things, art was to the right making of things. Art meant that this making had been governed by right reason, prudence meant that this doing had been governed by right reason. To the scholastics this parallel and opposition between art and prudence was a constant source of interest. It was the type of problem they best loved to discuss. It was indeed the type of problem that Plato would have debated in a dialogue and Aristotle have subsequently analysed. St Thomas Aquinas could not let it alone.[2] He was fascinated by it. His style is enlivened when he comes to treat it. Epigrams break from his pen when he writes of it or refers to it. He found, for instance, that whenever prudence was called in to advise us about our actions, the end of those actions had already been settled by the moral law; prudence indeed dealt not with ends,

---

[1] *Summa Theologica*, II. ii. 47, 2, ad 1 m; I. ii. 21, 2, ad 2, and 57, 4, ad 3 m.

[2] *Cf*. I. ii. 56 and 57.

but with means to ends. The moral law, which fixed the ends of human acts, was established independently of us and we were ordered towards that moral law. The obligation to obey that law, therefore, possessed us. But prudence alone could determine whether this or that means were right for us in our fulfilling of the moral law.

Art on the other hand had the means settled for it already, for the materials carried their own laws, and were patient only of certain forms and uses. It was the end of his work alone that the artist could settle. Wood or gold or stone could be treated each only in their own way; but the purposes to which they could be put were various, and it was the province of art alone to determine which purpose should be chosen. Thus the precise business of art was to settle what end a given material could serve.

In art the object was outside the artist; in prudence it was immanent, within the moralist himself.

Because of these contrary qualities it so often happened that between art and prudence the artist found himself torn asunder. The outlook of the two virtues was so different that the genius of either seemed opposed. Art was to them so absolute, so scientific. It had laws that governed it, inviolable, fraught with disaster to whoever departed from them, inexorable, inevitable. But prudence was to the scholastic hardly scientific at all. It dealt with human individuals, with cases of conscience, with complications of detailed circumstances that could never absolutely recur. Nothing ever happened twice over in exactly the same way. That is why we needed prudence. We needed a virtue, delicate, sensitive, quick-witted, that would seize on the immediate problem in front of it, know which principles to apply, and be swift in discovering with what amount of modification one moral law deflected another. You could never lay down rules for prudence, for prudence was power or virtue which knew what rules to apply.

Art, so the mediævalist imagined, was far more rigid than prudence. Art was ruled by a code, prudence by case law. Prudence settled each thing on its own merits, art was itself settled by the thing it decided to make. The artist was dominated by the thing, the moralist was dominated by the man. Art was almost a science, prudence could not be.

Art was even infallible![1] It sounds a contradiction to our minds that anyone could ever have ventured on such a proposition. Art we think to be a matter of mood, of inspiration, the result of a temperament that is very far from infallible. Was there amongst the people of that time no such thing as an artistic temperament, we ask in astonishment. Were the scholastics so blind to these vagaries of the artists or were artists then too tame to have them? Which was at fault? Neither really, for the scholastic in his mind distinguished between the art and the artist. Art, dictated by right reason, could not err; the artist could certainly err. He could refuse obedience to his art. He could mistake what his art suggested to him. Art was present only when right reason governed the artist and directed him in what he made. This governance and this direction then were absolutely lodged in right reason; like right reason they could not err. Art could not fail the man; but the man could fail his art. Art was infallible, but not he.

In art then the result judged the man; in morals the man's intention judged the result. This point of view lies at the basis of all the mediæval literature on art. We must, if we are to judge them fairly by what they aimed at, look at their art through their own eyes. We may quarrel with their theories but without these theories we shall not understand fully what they were about. Of course we judge their achievements in the light of our own theories because we consider ourselves to have found the true light. We have a right to do that if we suppose ourselves to possess an absolute standard. Perhaps even without claiming to have discovered an absolute standard we yet must judge what they did by what we think they should have done. Yet also, in fairness to themselves, we must try to follow the working of their own minds and judge them as much by what they aimed at producing as by what they produced.

It will have been clear from all that we have so far said that all the arts were grouped together under a single label. An artist was the producer of any work. Nor would it be wrong

---

[1] *Cf.* Cajetan on *Summa Theologica*, I. ii. 57, 5, ad 3 m.

to apply this wider meaning to the word artist even in English.[1]
Thus Pope speaks of Vulcan (*Iliad*, xviii. 1, 479):

"Then from his anvil the lame artist rose"

—including smithy-work as a work of art. So again Shakespeare
used it of the professional arts (*All's Well that Ends Well*,
II. iii. 10):

"Relinquished of the artists, both of Galen and Paracelsus"

—and of any learned man (*Troilus and Cressida*, I. iii. 24):

"The wise and fool, the artist and unread."

Milton used it of the scientist, Galileo:

"The moon, whose orb
Through optic glass the Tuscan artist views."

"Artist" was then the common name given to the worker
who made any artistic thing. Christ to them was an artist. God
was the supreme Artist [2] since He was the world's Creator
and we "His workmanship," "His husbandry." This more
general use of the word was not thought to degrade the worker
in the fine arts when applied alike to him and to the labourer;
rather it lifted all up to the higher level and made each share
a common pride in the trade of every worker. The guild of the
painters in Florence was just one of many guilds of artists; so
too the guild of the doctors was another. The notion that
there were three separate types of life, commercial, professional
and artistic, would have astonished the thirteenth-century social
theorists. Every artist for them was an artisan, and every
artisan was an artist.

But looking back we can see that they were conscious of
some differences between the arts, because they recognized that
certain arts (we now call them the Fine Arts, Belli Arti, Beaux
Arts) had beyond mere artistry a further object: to give pleasure.
These were not only arts, but arts beautiful, arts of which an

---

[1] *Cf.* Murray's *Oxford Dictionary* under the word "Artist."
[2] *Summa contra Gentiles*, i. 93.

added purpose was to render things made beautiful. Gradually this was seen to be a more solemn business, an exalted form of life. By the fifteenth century the artist began "to give himself airs": "Your manner of life should always be regulated as if you were studying theology, philosophy or any other science— that is, eating and drinking temperately, at least (most?) twice a day, using light and good food and but little wine" (*The Book of the Art of Cernino Cernini*, 1372-1430, London, 1899, p. 83). There is in that sentence the first symptom of the Renaissance, the exaltation of the artist. He was ceasing to be an artisan, emerging into a separate caste.

But in the beginnings of mediæval art it was not yet like that: the fine arts were arts, like the work of the smith or the weaver, only there was an additional labour included. The things made were to be pleasing as well as useful, they were to be beautiful.

Beauty was a word that comes often into mediæval philosophy. Definitions of it were frequent. Sometimes they were traditional definitions that had been consecrated by a great master; it was felt sometimes that these traditional definitions could only with difficulty be properly explained and with still more difficulty be defended. But it was thought that by sheer antiquity they contained some magical virtue, if one had only the patience and genius to distil it out. Platonists were quoted as having defined beauty as "the splendour of truth"; St Augustine's phrase was perhaps even more quoted—"the splendour of order." Neither of these quite satisfied St Thomas Aquinas. He attempted many times to analyse the essence of beauty, and suggested several definitions of his own, but was not content with any. Every time he wrote on it he tried a new way of expressing its tenuous quintessence. His mind worked first analytically. He tried to disentangle the elements of beauty as he saw them, and in the first part of the *Summa Theologica* (i. 5, 4, ad 1 m) gave his simplest description of all: "That which, when seen, gives pleasure." Later on he refined upon this by showing that the word *seen* implied something intellectual: "that which gives joy in being *known*" (I. ii. 27, 1, ad 3 m). Both these really give the same idea, for he has only substituted *known* for *seen*, and *joy* for *pleasure*, in order to prevent his reader from looking upon beauty as a material trick appealing merely to the sense. Just as he had elsewhere insisted that the artist was not merely a materialist though his work judged him, but was a reasoning worker since he impressed an idea on matter, so here he would not consider beauty in its purely sensual appeal. Indeed he would have liked to limit beauty only to that which pleases the more intellectual senses. He would have denied that a fragrance or a delicious taste could strictly be beautiful: "Amongst all the senses, it is only with sight and hearing that beauty has relations, because these two senses are above others most knowledge-able" (I. ii. 27, 1, ad 3 m). But though a beautiful thing must be something that makes an appeal to the intelligence, it undoubtedly reaches the intelligence through the senses and must appeal to the senses as well as the intelligence—must please both. Perhaps beauty was of such a quality that it first satisfies the intelligence, but satisfies it in such a way as to make the satisfaction overflow into the senses; or perhaps it first pleased the senses and gave them a particular satisfaction capable of being presented to the intelligence in the form of an idea. Must all truths necessarily be beautiful? Must all beautiful things necessarily be true?

Once beauty was realized to be something that affected mind and sense, the question was raised as to how this were possible, since the mind worked discursively by way of argument and reasoning while the senses worked instinctively. Here was another problem which the scholastic delighted in. The analysis of thought was always his preoccupation, as the analysis of man is ours.

The production of a beautiful thing was the object of a particular kind of art, a fine art. Then the production of a beautiful thing implied a double purpose in the mind of the producer. As the effect of art, the thing must have fulfilled some useful purpose: as the effect of a fine art, it must also please. Professor Capito has given us an excellent volume on the *Sicilian Carretti* (Milano, 1924) which illustrates this point. From the days of Frederick II. the Sicilian peasant has insisted on having his cart elaborately painted at considerable expense. Nothing else than the pictures of the old heroes or heroines of chivalry will satisfy him. That is the convention which is handed down as a tradition from father to son. According to the professor, the structure and design of the carts is ancient and of noble origin, the arabesques between the supports of the carriage body being certainly Moorish, the carving of the rims and spokes of the wheels being Norman. Here then is a work of the fine arts : but originally the beauty of the thing never lessened its usefulness. Convention, however, has now decided that the decoration shall be an end in itself. The horse in consequence now groans under a load uselessly over-decorated. To St Thomas Aquinas a result like this could not be a beautiful thing. He never ceased to teach the principle that beauty must be the result of art and that art implied a useful object legitimately produced. For this reason the first object—the primary and measuring object—of the worker must be to produce something serviceable ; then the second object must be to make that effective thing beautiful. It cannot be beautiful—that is, cannot " please "—if the ornamentation obstructs the purpose. Were this to happen, the practical man would then want the ornamentation away ; and since the fine arts are arts, they must never prove a nuisance to the practical man.

All the arts are intended to be useful ; the fine arts are beautiful as well. Utility should not be injured by beauty, nor beauty spoiled by utility. A fine art is precisely the virtue in man which effects this union.

Our senses then carry the beauty of the thing made to the mind, and the result of this is delight in the will. The will goes out to the beautiful object, holds to it, clings to it or, as we say, loves it.

St Thomas, therefore, rejects the definitions of both St Augustine and of the Platonists, and seems to prefer " splendour of form " to " splendour of truth " or " splendour of order " (*De Divinis Nominibus*, iv. 5, and in *Commentary on Psalm xliv.*, lect. 2). Elsewhere he says " light beautifies since without light all things seem foul " (*On Ps. xxv.*, lect. 5.), and again : " Radiance is of the essence of beauty " (*De Divinis Nom.*, vi.).

In a treatise, *Opusculum de Pulchro et Bono*, attributed variously to St Thomas Aquinas and to his master, Albertus Magnus—which is so thoroughly of that period that it might have been written by any one of the newer school after the first half of the thirteenth century—we have more clearly perhaps than elsewhere the problem confronted and solved, as the thirteenth century saw the solution. There it is expressly stated that the essence of the thing (philosophically called the *forma*) beautifies it, and beauty is nothing else than the essence of the thing showing through its material, intelligently arrayed.

When you find out truth, you have toiled through matter and distilled the truth out of it by sheer labour; when you find beauty there should be no such toil. It should leap to your mind, please you at once : " Radiance is of the essence of beauty." The convincing quality of its own evidence is essential to it.

This does not mean that we should immediately be able to express or even grasp the concept of the artist, for it is not essential to the beauty of a thing that we should understand it, but it does seem essential to the beauty of a thing that it should be immediately recognizable as beautiful. The message of the artist, his idea, may reach consciousness only long afterwards, and may only dimly be discerned even by himself. Indeed often enough an artist may be a man of little intellectual power, nor need he have genius or intelligence. It is enough that he should have the art or capacity for expressing the beautiful.

In thought, we disentangle our universal concept from the individual object (so the schoolmen argued) : we see a house, or chair, or river, and have an idea of what a house is like, or a chair, or a river ; our mind by its native capacity is able to disengage from a unit its essential concept and to recognize the similarity whenever we see another unit of the same kind, however differently arrayed. We see a house, store in our memory what it essentially means, and apply the name at once to another house, differing though this second house may be in every apparent detail from the first. In knowledge the mind abstracts the essence from the individual ; in beauty the essence is still immersed in matter and recognized to be so. In knowledge the essence is universal, chair, house, river; in beauty it is individual, *this* church, *this* statue, *this* picture, *this* song. Consequently beauty is not a sort of truth, but a sort of goodness; in truth the image is carried from the object into the mind, in goodness the will goes out to the object. The will when loving has nothing in it to correspond to the idea in the mind when thinking. The mind's object comes into it, the will's object draws the will to itself. So was it of beauty, the scholastic argued: the mind went out to it, the will took pleasure in it, it ravished the will. " It is of its very essence that the recognition of beauty should satisfy the will " (*cf.* especially the *Commentary of Cardinal Cajetan* (1530) on this saying of St Thomas, *Summa Theologica*, I. ii. 27, 1, ad 3 m).

Yet, though beauty must in this way draw our hearts out of us and produce in its highest form ecstasy, and the raptures of the saints at the sight of Absolute Beauty were psychologically of the same nature as the thrill produced by the fine arts in a man sensitive to their beauty (" Out of the divine beauty are the essences of all things derived ": *De Divinis Nominibus*, cap. 4, lect. 5, 6), ecstasy is not the purpose of art. Art, that is, has not as its essential motive the production of emotion. Emotion will follow from beauty, for beauty will effect delight in the will since it must please. But an artist does not set out in art to produce emotion,[1] he sets out to produce a beautiful thing: " reason is the first principle of all the works of man " (*Summa Theologica*, I. ii. 58, 2). So logic is enthroned as the queen of the fine arts, and truth as essential to them. A lie cannot be good in the arts for it is opposed to the austere logic that ought to inspire them. Similarly, emotion cannot be their purpose. To write in order to bring tears by way of sentiment is to write ill.

Art must then be intellectual, since it is dominated by right reason and must be guided by logic. Beauty can never be used as an excuse to cover up a sham. There can be no beauty in what is only a pretence. Moreover, beauty itself though it be imprisoned in the material thing lifts that thing into a new

[1] " The exultation of the mind bursting into voice " (St Thomas in *Prologue super Psalmes*).

order, intellectualizes it, universalizes it. The beautiful thing is become through its concrete array of beauty a sharer in a wider life than its own. It has broken out of mere local conditions, it has touched the heart of the world.

Thus did the scholastics attempt to explain the apparent contradiction between national art and its universal appeal. Shakespeare is thoroughly English, we say: Dante is Italy articulate; in Homer we see the genius of the Greek; in Virgil all that made Rome great; in Racine the power of France, its grandeur, its heroic tragedy, its hard mirth. Yet though each of these is essentially of his own country and, indeed, of his own age, each is equally of all ages and all countries. We could, on the one hand, almost hazard the prophecy that cosmopolitanism will destroy art. Art needs to be localized in order to cross the world, to be individualized to appeal to all, to be nationalized to move all nations. Nor is the cause of this difficult to discover. Art, we began by saying, was to the schoolmen that quality whereby right reason governed men in the making of things. It governed them to produce outside of themselves a concrete thing. The purpose of this thing was the standard whereby we were to measure its success; the idea the author had in view in his " making " was to be considered in our judgment of it. What was he dreaming of when he made it?

Now each poet or artist, who had his purpose in composing his poem or work of fine art, must have had a concrete purpose to fulfil. He was making a thing. It was to be outside of him. It was to stand independently of the mind that made it. It was to be on its own. Hence a local habitation is of its essence, it must bear a name. On this account it must have been primarily intended to suit this mood or that, to effect this definite purpose, to relieve this or that pent-up feeling, or to be " a cleansing of the soul." Art was to the thirteenth century a deliberate thing, not the unconscious act of a mind in a trance; it was " a human act," not the mere act of a man. Reason must be in it. The artist made it for a definite time and for an immediate need, but the art that was in him made it for eternity— *i.e.* for the needs of all. The immediate need and concrete purpose ensured that the work should be localized and national, but the greatness of the art succeeded in giving it a wider application. Pindar sang the triumph of Sogenes, thereby singing for ever the gracious charm of the perfect athlete, the rhythm not merely of his motion, the ripple of his muscles, his ease, the curves of his lithe limbs; he was taking us through his champion with his delicate desires and wild youth into the beauty of the body in its disciplined and obedient service to the skill and prudence of a mind. We see not the hero only from Ægina of the boys' pentathlon at Nemea in the year 461 B.C. but the heroes of to-day's and to-morrow's contests, all the heroes of all games. Thus the fine arts share a double life—local and universal— are of time and of eternity. Thus they come to have a value beyond their immediate purpose, though fulfilling that immediate purpose perfectly. The value that they have is a spiritual value, and the immediate purpose is found after all to be merely a means to an end, the fulfilment of some nobler ambition than seemed apparent. The artist, therefore, may have a greatness which no one can measure, may be gifted with a power which seems to have no limit, reaching beyond his own time, influencing subsequent generations, a perpetual source of inspiration, guiding the taste of future artists and of those who see or hear or read the masterpiece.

Since, however, as we have several times repeated, art was objective, logical, intellectual, to the mediæval thinker; since beauty was "a species of good," we should expect to find that the mediæval artist considered his work almost an exact science: to admit this would not be an unfair representation of the views of that time. Art, they maintained, had "certain and determined laws" (*viæ certæ et determinatæ*). With all their hardihood of thought the men of the thirteenth and fourteenth centuries had enormous respect for custom. We have already seen in an earlier chapter how taxation depended for its validity on "customary" dues; the same was true of art. It had to follow customary laws. These were not the arbitrary choice of some theorist, but were discovered from actual use. They took the masterpieces of their own art, and thought they saw that though each masterpiece was different there were laws commonly observed in all of them, laws corresponding almost to a *jus gentium*, "the right found to exist in every nation." Nature never acts in vain, and nature in its art inspiration moved men along consistent lines and perpetually reproduced in every variety of expression fixed and definite laws. By induction these laws could be arrived at, and become the living logic dominating the intellectual side of art.

Ernest Mâle (*L'Art religieux du* 13*me Siècle*,[1] Paris, 1910) has shown how art was almost a liturgy with fixed rubrics of its own (p. 16) that at the beginning hardly ever changed, and how it was governed by almost mathematical rules. Thus, in the building of the cathedrals the north porch invariably was dedicated to the Old Testament, the south porch to the New Testament, the west to the Last Judgment. Everywhere was to be found symbolism of a most elaborate kind.

In some sense it is true these rules were imposed from outside. The Second Council of Nicæa (in 787, long before our period) had already decided that the artist was to paint indeed and so adorn churches and any place he willed, but that the principles of his art and the arrangement and disposition of his painting lay with the Fathers of the Church. Mâle holds (p. 406), against Viollet-le-Duc, that the artists were always taught by the theologians, and that the story of the former's revolt from Church authority gains no confirmation from the records that survive. Certain grotesques on gargoyles or on misereres, in spite of much that has been written about them, really do no more than give an amusing turn to the incidents of religious life, and in no way constitute an attack on the Faith.

An instance of this subordination of artist to theologian can be seen in the frescoes of the Spanish Chapel in the Green Cloister of St Maria Novella at Florence which were painted in 1350 by Andrea di Bonajuto under the direction of Fra Jacopo Passavanti. Another instance is given in Guignard's *Mémoires fournis aux Peintres* (Troyes, 1851, p. ix.) in reference to the church of St Mary Magdalen at Troyes in 1425: "Friar Didier, Dominican, having extracted and given in writing the history of St Madeleine, Jacquet the painter made

---

[1] *Cf.* also *L'Art allemand et l'Art français du Moyen Age* (1917).

a small pattern of it on paper. Then Poinsète, the tailor, and his maid assembled the great pieces of old cloth to serve to execute the patterns which were painted by James the painter and Simon the illuminator." There you have the assembling of the mediæval artist : first the theologian, then the designer, then the painter or craftsman. The theologian draws up the truth to be enunciated, the designer disposes of the " history " according to laws that custom has handed on to him, but in a way and style particularly his own, the painter then executes in colour and with skill the work confided to him. But it is the designer who is the real artist.[1] It is he who has the quality of soul which enables him to put outside of him a concrete thing fulfilling an intelligent purpose and governed by right reason.

There must indeed be in the artist a natural gift for this, which would seem to the scholastic to be due in great measure to his physical complexion. The tendency to art was to be found in his body (*Summa Theologica*, I. ii. 55, 2, ad 1 m), and arose from his sensitiveness to the beauty of the world about him. This was the groundwork, or more truly the condition without which no artist could finally produce great art. But the natural gift required development before it could be really great. It needed training and education. It was to be drawn out during apprenticeship to a more experienced artist who had the proper traditions, and who was to teach not by the exposition of merely theoretic principles but by the discipline of actual work. The apprentice went to him to watch, to be put through his paces, and to be corrected rigorously. There was no easy short-cut to achieve great art. Cernino Cernini lays down very positively that this need for apprenticeship was the considered judgment, not of St Thomas Aquinas only, but of the practical artist :

"It is the impulse of a noble mind which moves some towards this art, pleasing to them through their natural love. The intellect delights in invention ; and nature alone draws them, without any guidance from a master, through nobleness of mind ; and thus delighting themselves, they next wish to find a master and with him they place themselves in love of

---

[1] *Summa Theologica*, II. ii. 47, 8.

obedience, being in servitude that they may carry their art to perfection. . . . As soon as thou canst, begin to put thyself under the guidance of the master to learn and delay as long as thou mayest thy parting from the master " (*The Book of Art of Cernino Cernini*, p. 7).

Again : " Always take pains in drawing the best subjects which you can find, done by the hand of the great masters. If you live in a place where there are many good masters, so much the better for you. But I counsel you always to choose the best and the most famous. . . . Remember that the most perfect guide that you can have and the best course is the triumphal gateway of drawing from nature : it is before all other examples, and with a bold heart you may always trust it, especially when you begin to have some judgment in design " (p. 22).

Lastly : " Know that you cannot learn to paint in less time than this. In the first place you must study drawing for at least one year on tablets ; then you must remain with a master at the workshop, who understands working in all parts of the art ; you must begin by grinding colours, and learn to boil down glues, to acquire the practice of laying grounds on panels, to work in relief upon them ; and to rub them smooth and to gild ; to engrave well, and this for six years ; afterwards to practise colouring, to adorn with mordants, to make cloths of gold, and to be accustomed to paint on walls, for six more years—always drawing without intermission on holidays and workdays. And so, through long habit, good practice becomes second nature. Adopting other habits, do not hope ever to attain great perfection. There are many who say they have learnt the art without having been with a master. Do not believe them, for I give you this very book as an example. Even studying it day and night, if you do not see some practice with some master you will never be fit for anything, nor will you be able with a good face to stay among the masters."

Here at some length we have the theory of art from a practical artist. He admitted that some had not carried out this theory : but he thought badly of them and considered that either their work was, in spite of what they said, the result of some apprenticeship, or that it was not worth while.

The technique, as we would call it, had to be learned from a master; indeed it required a guild to teach it for it carried a tradition and was not to be acquired by mere instinct. The style was indeed subject to change, but even style must develop only by living continuity of theory: " A humble working member then of the art of painting, I Cernino, born of Drea Cernino of the Colle Valdessa, was instructed in these arts for twelve years [his practice, it will be seen, conformed to his theory or his theory was evolved from his practice] by Agnolo, son of Taddeo of Florence, my Master who learned the art from Taddeo his father, who was the godson of Giotto and was his disciple for twenty-four years. This Giotto changed the art of painting from the Greek to the Latin [manner] and brought it to the modern [style]; and he possessed more perfect art than ever anyone else had had."

Here you have all the theories of the schoolmen packed into the training of an artist: the natural gift, the long apprenticeship, the careful instruction, the " customs " of the guild, the personal direction of the master, the " certain and determined ways " to be learnt from the master, not as his imposed arbitrary rules but as discovered already existing in all great works of art. Style in this concept may develop and become " modern," yet in the end it will harden and die down. Then some new style breaks out from the old stem into bud and blossom, in its turn too to decay. The new style may not be as great as the old one, but it will have this in its favour, that at least it is alive. Perhaps it is only the herald of something greater, a style of transition, yet in it a genius may appear as great as the old masters, though it will not follow that his masterpieces will equal theirs. His manner, his style, may spoil or cramp him, narrow his expression, and deny him the opportunities that his power deserves. This does not necessarily degrade his art though it may hamper his capacity. Artists may yet be equal in greatness even though their works are by no means equal.

It may even happen that the greater artist has the less dexterity or manual skill. He tends to be busied over the ideas of his conception and has not perhaps been able to devote much time to mere power of hand. Indeed to the mediæval mind, dexterity in the fine arts could easily become a danger. It was at the most an external condition which did not affect art either way. A man might produce a masterpiece in which the anatomy was out of drawing, or he might be always true in his drawings to the exact proportions in nature and yet fail as an artist. No artist could, however, afford to despise exactness of drawing, though he was counselled to remember that mere skill might be his undoing, for he might become so set on the illusion of art as to produce something that was not art at all. The mediæval artist attempted to give not nature but a picture of nature, or even at times only a symbol of it (*cf.* St Thomas, *On Epistle to Titus iii. 9*).

No one who knows the mediæval artist in his work can doubt of his capacity to copy nature had he wished. Indeed we know that he did practise his hand at it and was trained to draw from nature. Witness the quotation we have already given from Cernino: " Remember that the most perfect guide that you can have and the best course is the triumphal gateway of drawing from nature: it is before all other examples and with a bold heart you may always trust it, especially when you begin to have some judgment in design." Moreover we have the note-books of Villars de Honnecourt,[1] with their carefully studied drawings to show us how he worked. Again he has copied skilfully the plan of a mechanical contrivance whereby an angel could be made to bow his head at the Holy Name. The man was dealing with his world intelligently. He drew for his own purposes the north-west tower of Laon cathedral, added sketches of Cambrai and of Meaux cathedral, and studies of the rose windows of Lausanne and Chartres and of parts of Rheims cathedral.

Nor should we think of this as a special characteristic of De Honnecourt. Professor Lethaby, in *Mediæval Art* (London, 1904), p. 215, quotes Dante's description of the images of the Virgin and the angel " wherein Nature's self was put to shame." " There, sculptured in a gracious attitude, he did not seem an

---

[1] *Album de Villars de Honnecourt*, 1906, pp. xviii, xxviii, xxx, xliv, lii, lx, etc. For an English example see *An English Medieval Sketch Book*, edited by M. R. James, Walpole Society, 1925, pp. 1-18.

image that is silent, one would have sworn that he was saying '*Ave.*' And in her mien this language was impressed '*Ecce Ancilla Domini*' as distinctly as any figure stamps itself in wax." And again, as an earlier example, Herimann of Tournay, who, describing the shrine of St Piat, says that on it were represented the five wise and the five foolish virgins, "who all seemed to weep and to be alive; these shed tears like water, those like blood" (*ibid.*, p. 216). The author of *Mediæval Art* also remarks: "That accurate portraiture was well understood at this time we may gather, if it needs proof, from the account that when Charles VI. was about to marry (1385) painters were sent abroad to bring him portraits of marriageable princesses. Isabella of Bavaria was approved as *belle, jeune et gente*" (*ibid.*, p. 241; *cf.* also the portraits of Louis IX. and the other royal portraits in the *Gazette des Beaux Arts*, 1903, pp. 177, etc). He adds that "Dante in two words defines the purpose of sculpture as *visible speech*" (*ibid.*, p. 216).

The mediæval artist as well as the modern knew and imitated nature. "Art's manner of working is founded upon Nature's manner of working, and Nature's manner upon creation" (*Summa Theologica*, i. 45, 8). This was a favourite saying of St Thomas, and one to which he frequently returned; he pictured God, nature and man as a triple set of workers, art following nature's way, and nature following God: "Art imitates Nature in her working" (*ibid.*, i. 117, 1). Art, however, does not copy, but carries on, the work of creation: "The procession of art is twofold—namely, of art from the soul of the artificer, and of works of art from art" (*Sentences*, I., dist. 32, ques. 3, art. 2). Art does not copy nature, but copies nature's works or nature's way. Man watches God in His Creation and learns His rules. Man was apprenticed to God.

Art then is not imitation of nature, though art cannot be divorced from nature. It watches nature, learns of nature, weaves nature's wreaths of flowers round the capitals of its columns, cuts into the bosses of its roofs the wild flowers of the countryside, yet makes no effort to paint nature in distinct resemblance, to trick you into a belief that you behold man " in his habit as he lived." At least the earlier mediæval artist had no such intention. For him creation was full of mystery, and each part of it hid some further mystery. He "moralized" the world about him. Vincent de Beauvais wrote his *Summæ* or planned them, if he did not live to complete them himself, with the deliberate intention of inducing Nature to disclose her secrets to him. Not for the service or comfort of man so much as for his instruction was he girdled with creation. He could find "sermons in stones and books in the running brooks "; indeed it was his religious duty to do so.

Nature then for the thirteenth and early fourteenth century artist was a fifth gospel, full of parables and miracles, and radiant with revelation. He considered himself at the best a commentator on this sacred book. Consequently he thought it his purpose, not to reproduce nature, but to reproduce a parable of nature. Text by text he unrolled it in front of the eyes of his audience, and at the same time as he provided it with a fragment of nature he tried to provide it also with the explanation of it. By itself nature was dumb; he would make it speak. Many eyes, all eyes indeed, saw it; how few understood it? He was determined on the other hand so to interpret nature as to help others for ever after to see it as he saw it.

First then he believed that nature had its own specific meaning. What that precise meaning was he waited for the theologian to tell him. He did not discover for himself, he was taught (Mâle, *L'Art religieux du* 13*me Siècle*, p. 456). Friar Didier, the Dominican, or his fellow-friar, Vincent de Beauvais, discovered that for him, or Fra Tomaso Aquino, or anyone else who had devoted himself to the study of these things. Then he took what he had been told and thought it to be his work to help others to know what he knew himself. He wanted others, whenever after they went out-of-doors, to see the same countryside they had always seen, but to see it with new eyes, to have not only sight but insight. So he had not only by his fine art to give a fragment of nature but the interpretation of that fragment of nature. Now of the two, the thing he had to devote most power to was not the fragment of nature, for after all however roughly it was done it did not very much matter as long as men saw what it was meant to represent; but he was determined that they should not mistake his interpretation of it. He would be content to give the symbol or sacrament just sufficiently to satisfy his purpose, but he would spare himself no pains to get the true interpretation of it into the mind of those who passed by.

Anything almost would do for a tree or a mother or a child or an angel, as long as it was suggestive vaguely of what he meant. Men had their own imaginations. He took that for granted. He relied on them to fill in for themselves his rough outlines. But he was most concerned to prevent anyone supposing that the tree was only a tree, or the mother or the child or the angel merely what they seemed. It hurt him that there should be folk for whom the world was only what it looked like and no more. Cernino speaks of his art as " painting for which we must be endowed with both imagination and skill in the hand, to discover unseen things concealed beneath the obscurity of natural objects and to arrest them with the hand, presenting to the sight that which did not before appear to exist " (p. 4).

Savonarola, who represented at the end of our period the ideals with which our period began, says the same of poetry : " The purpose of poetry is to persuade by means of the syllogism, called an example expressed in elegant language, in order to convince and delight at the same time : and inasmuch as our soul finds sovereign pleasure in songs and harmonies, so the ancients contrived the art of metrical arrangement the better by this means to urge men to virtue. But this metre is purely conventional and the poet can deal with his theme without the aid of metre or rhyme " (*Apologeticus*, pp. 38, 45-48, etc.). Any reader of the *Vita Nuova* or the *Convito* can parallel this passage with Dante's utterances, and in the *Divina Commedia* with his practice.

But, of course, once the artist or poet or sculptor began to describe nature for the sake of " an example expressed in elegant language," the chances were that he would be so enthralled with the joy of that which he gazed on as to forget the purpose of the description in the delight of the thing he had described. He would begin by drawing lions from life and then turn them into heraldic lions to show what lions stood for in his philosophy, their courage and noble-heartedness ; but it is hardly to be wondered at that after a while he became so absorbed in the lion he was drawing so carefully that he did not see so much what it stood for as what it was.

Historians of art have taught us that the English school of water-colour artists began with antiquarians who painted ruins to interest the learned and ended with artists who painted trees and fields to interest lovers of beauty. Such a fate too, as was to be expected, befell the artists of the early Middle Ages. They began as symbolists for whom nature was not so much a text as a pretext. Gradually symbolism lost its interest, or rather the interest in it was swamped by the greater interest in nature for its own sake. The study of nature for its own sake became a passion as men awoke to the beauties of the world. No longer was it a book of instruction but a book of pleasure. It was no longer a schoolroom but a playroom, where he came to find not lessons at all but delight.

The Mother and Child were painted as before ; but the divine light that the artist had striven to give to the features of both was waning, it was not the Mother and the Child now so much as any mother and any child. Move from Giotto to Andrea del Sarto and you have the whole pageant of art from the thirteenth to the fifteenth centuries, the attempt passing from a representation of a divine thing to the representation of human things.

Such charm as the primitives have lies there, in their asceticism, in their desire not to flaunt beauty in front of you but to let you discover the beauty about you for yourself, and to find in it a reflection of the endless beauty of God : " God is the most beautiful of all " (St Thomas in *De Divinis Nominibus*, cap. 4, lect. 5), for He is absolute beauty, the pre-existing beauty, the giver and sharer of beauty, " from the divine beauty is derived the existence of the world."

Art had, therefore, in so far as it was fine art, to imitate, not in order to reproduce a thing, but only to manifest a form.

For this reason there was always a subordination of matter to form ; consequently the qualities of mediæval art that were most dominant were purity and calmness. The subordination of matter to form entailed a ruthless sacrifice of every irrelevant fact; nothing superfluous was allowed to obscure the message —that is, the lesson. There was to be no lingering over unnecessary details. Sensuous delectation was essential to fine art, since the purpose of beauty is to please and man is compacted of body and soul, and gets his ideas—said the schoolmen— through his senses; but sensuous delectation was allowed to enter in only ministerially, to minister a pleasing idea to the mind. Fine art, since its purpose was the reproduction outside man of an idea which pleased, must produce emotion; but it was not for a moment considered that emotion was its aim. Emotion followed from it, could not be kept out of it, but was not the purpose for which any art-work was to be done.

Since man was body and soul, he could never exclude sensuous feelings from following any of his ideas; the influence of each on the other was so subtle, so universal, that it was impossible to have the one and exclude the other. Nevertheless the mediæval moralist who tried to dominate art as well as life, thought that nothing should be done in order to produce sensuous feelings, though things could be done from which sensuous feelings would be sure to follow. It was not the presence of sensuous feelings but the direct intention of arousing them that seemed to him weak alike in art or life.

This has made his art as objective as his life was. His cathedrals are not built to impress the beholder but were the spontaneous expression of his own worship. He did not build for edification but for art: " Art demands much quietness and to paint the things of Christ you must abide in Christ " is the only critical remark of Fra Angelico which Vasari has recorded. This is not pietistic, but artistic, criticism. Any sinner of the Middle Ages would have agreed with it as well as any saint.

After 1350 the serenity of mediæval art began to be lost. Emotion now overpowered ideas, symbolism gave way to nature, the body outweighed the soul. Before that, the only expression of violence that the mediæval artist ever allowed himself was in depicting vice; evil was not calm, he thought, was unbalanced, lacked rhythm and harmony; he was an

Aristotelean before he could read Aristotle, he had caught, or rediscovered for himself, the classic theory of the Poetics and of Plato, or inherited it from Byzantium.

Moreover, it would seem that about that date there entered into art a new note, the note of the pathetic, the gift of tears (Mâle, *L'Art religieux de la fin du Moyen Age en France*, 1908, p. vii. *et seq.*). Was it St Francis and the Fioretti that begot this movement? Was it the inevitable result of so much beauty brought fresh before man's eyes? Was it a luxury that his century of peace bequeathed to him, the relaxation of his feelings after the terrible years of the Dark Ages? What brought it? Here you have a very interesting and perhaps insoluble problem. Walter Pater has attempted to describe the problem but not to answer it in the pages of *The Renaissance*; the difficulty is to trace the beginnings of the new movement. May it not even go back to St Augustine? Is it not to be found in his *Confessions*, and even in his *City of God*? (*cf.* Book XIX., cap. 15, vol. ii., pp. 323 and 452). At least the name of Abelard, "the great clerk and the great lover," seems to be linked with it, and the unknown author of *Aucassin and Nicolete*. In any case, we can almost fix the year 1350 as about the time when this new element had attained a dominant position in the art schools. The *dolce stil nuovo* was already tremulous with emotion. The shadows of the Black Death had given a touch of melancholy to the century or driven it to hectic jollity. Chaucer was about to write, in France there were the earlier chansons of the soldiers, Boccaccio was telling his tales.

While the north retained a longer fidelity to the old tradition, the south had renounced all asceticism and restraint in art and had begun to riot. The classical rebirth of Europe was producing the classical " machinery " of sibyls and nymphs and triumphs, but not yet the perfect balance of the classics.

The reign of the theologians over art was ended ; the reign even of morality over art was done. Art had in mediæval eyes no rights against God, no " good " could be opposed to Him, " all beauty was derived from the divine beauty." Apart from Him and against His law no beauty could be found : " If an art turns out objects which man cannot use without sin, the artist who makes such works sins himself, because he offers directly to others the occasion of sinning; it is as if one made idols for idolatry. As to the arts of which the produce can be used by man well or ill, they are lawful, and yet, if there are any of which the works are put to evil use in the greatest number of cases, they ought, though lawful in themselves, to be extirpated from the city by the office of the prince, according to the teaching of Plato " (St Thomas, *Summa Theologica*, II. ii. 169, 2, ad 4 m).

There were, it seemed clear to them, certain moral concepts, which though extrinsic to art had yet to be considered by the artist, since he was not only an artist but a man. As an artist he had to consider beauty as well as purpose; but as a man, if he were living under Christian inspiration, he had also to consider its higher light that he might be helped to direct his own natural light. Nothing could be really beautiful if it were not in accord with the divine order.

It is of particular importance to notice this, for the influence of the artist is beyond our measurement. The power of the writer, orator, painter, musician, sculptor, poet and architect to move their generation, and indeed subsequent ages, can be guessed at but not measured, for it is an elusive power, escaping observation, doing far more effective work than appears. These subtle forces affect the leaders and thence soak through to the lowest strata, the people. The work then of the artist in the state is far more subtle than, and as potent as, the work of any other member of the community. To the mediæval thinker the artist was the teacher of human knowledge; wherever his work was to be seen was the real school in which were trained the younger generation. He touched the life of his neighbours and of his nation not at one point only but at all. The other workers produced this thing or that, and so helped forward in piecemeal the good of the community. But the artist was conceived of, with his genius to create or discover beauty, as urging forward and upward, at once the general good of all.

Of course no one supposed the artist to be merely a seeker

of beauty. He was a worker, who needed support in very material ways for existence. He worked for a wage. But the schoolmen made note of a distinction, between the purpose of the workman and the purpose of his work. We have already explained (p. 239) that the motive of the artist did not fall under art, nor however low that motive might be did his art necessarily suffer degradation in consequence. They had instances innumerable to confirm them in this belief. There were great masters who were little men. So here again they carefully separated the workmen's aim and the aim of his work. The purpose or motive of the workman might be his fee, but the purpose of his work might yet be to please, to discover and reveal beauty. It might well be that an artist whose whole energies were set on making money would lose his appreciation of beauty; or rather that he might under such conditions succumb to the flattery or persecution of society and produce work not really beautiful. But this need not be.[1] Fra Lippo Lippi might rival Fra Angelico in depicting the beauty of the spiritual life, even though he could not rival him in living it: "There are some," says Cernino, "who follow the arts from poverty and necessity, and also for gain, or for the love of the art; but those who pursue them from the love of the art and true nobleness of mind are to be commended above all others" (p. 7). They are to be commended, but not necessarily their art. To work in order to live is the lot laid by God on man. But to produce the fine arts, the purpose of the work must be beauty, the discovery and revelation of "that which when understood gives joy."

The moralist, looking behind art and man's endeavours to produce beauty and discovering as he thought the passion that must drive man for ever in that direction, saw the explanation of it to lie in the fact that he was a creature of God: "To tend to progress is to tend to the Beginning" (St Thomas in *Sentences*, II., dist. 18, q. 2, art. 2), Who is also the End. Thus man was led upwards to the most perfect. The appearance of beauty was merely a sacramental and outward sign. Within was the invisible grace. Man had to pass through appearance

---

[1] *Summa Theologica*, I. ii. 57, **5,** ad 1 m.

before he could touch reality, had to be lifted up from what he saw to what he could not see, to pass from sense to reason, and from reason to spiritual insight. The effect of true culture then must be to make a man more spiritual.

Yet the life of art seemed to be the very reverse of this, for man, straitened between beauty and its appearance, so often halted at the sensuous and never reached through to the heart of beauty. " Concupiscence is infinite " (*Summa Theologica*, I. ii. 20, 4), yet " no man can live without delight " (II. ii. 35, 4, ad 2 m ; cf. *Ethic. Nic.* viii. 5 and 6 ; x. 6). If he lost the spiritual, he drifted to the carnal ; one or other he must have for the fulfilment of the desires of his nature. Art indeed, despite all the mischiefs of which history might accuse it, enabled man to have this nobler concept and to pierce with keen eyes to " the splendour of the form intelligently arrayed in matter." Art even was a pledge of the complete fulfilment of this in the life beyond. The artist was a prophet, a priest, a seer : " To this therefore all other human operations seem ordered as to an end. For to the perfection of contemplation is required security of body, to which is ordained every expedient for making obtainable the things necessary to human life. Calmness also is required, from the disturbance of the passions, to which a man comes through the moral virtues and prudence ; peace also is required from external disturbance to which is ordained the whole governance of civil life. Thus rightly considered all human duties seem intended to present truth to those who wish to contemplate it " (*Contra Gentiles*, iii., cap. 37, § 6). So was the purpose of the artist declared by the scholastics to be the purpose to which the rest of life converged. The artist was the priest of natural religion, its preacher, the expounder of the hidden beauty of God. Mysteries were in his keeping. He was the dispenser of these mysteries of God. But to accomplish his destiny the artist needed asceticism. No less than the priest of supernatural religion, the priest of natural religion could lose the sense of his greatness, degrade his high office, be corrupted by passion or greed. Temptation beset him, he must fight with it (*Summa Theologica*, I. ii. 43, 3) ; distraction must be carefully rejected if he was to be dedicated to his single purpose (I. ii. 42, 3) in austerity, in carefulness, in prudence, zealous, high-minded and high-resolved.

"There is a false race," says Savonarola (*Apologeticus*, pp. 45-55), "of pretended poets who can do naught but run after the Greeks and Romans, repeating their ideas, copying their style and metre, even invoking the same deities—almost as though we were not men as much as they [the classic authors], with reason and a religion of our own. Now this is not only false poetry, but likewise a most hurtful snare to our youth. Were this not already as clear as sunlight, I would labour to prove it; experience, the only teacher of all things, having so plainly manifested to all eyes the evils born of this false kind of poetry, it is needless to pause to condemn it. . . . Even the pagans condemned poets such as these. Did not Plato, whom now all praise, declare the necessity of making a law for the expulsion from the city of those poets who, by the example and authority of most iniquitous deities and the allurements of most shameful verse, filled the world with ignominious lust and moral destruction? . . . Even amongst the ancients, some condemned vicious things and extolled the generous deeds of the great. By these poetry was turned to good use, and I have neither the right nor the wish to condemn them."

Again, in his *Prediche sopra Amos e Zaccaria* (Florence, 1497), he urges that the beauty of holiness is a real and attractive beauty : " And the reason of this is because the untainted soul shares the beauty of God who lends His divine charm to the body." In his Sermon xxviii., *On Ezechiel* (Venice, 1520), he repeats this : " The beauty of man and woman is the greater and more perfect the more resemblance it has to primary beauty. What then is this beauty? It is a quality that results from the proportion and symmetry of the members and parts of the body. . . . What is the source of this beauty? You will see that it emanates from the soul. . . . Take two women of equal beauty, let one be good, modest, and pure, and the other be a prostitute. You will see the good one shine with a more than earthly beauty, and the other, however handsome she may be, is in no way comparable to her. . . . Note some devout person, boy or girl, who has the divine spirit within ; note that youth, I say, when engaged in prayer and in the flush of the divine beauty, and on his return from prayer you will see the beauty of God reflected in his eyes, and his countenance radiant almost as that of an angel."

On the Saturday before the Third Sunday of Lent, Savonarola, the last voice of the Middle Ages, made his appeal to the artists of his beloved Florence : " These young men go about saying of this woman or that, here is a Magdalen, here the Virgin, there a St John ; and then you paint their faces in your churches, which is a great profanation of divine things. You painters do very ill. Did you know, as I know, the scandal you cause, you would certainly act differently, you fill the churches with vain things. Think you the Virgin should be painted as you paint her? I tell you she went clothed as a beggar, she went in rags."

A scholastic would have told Fra Girolamo that his own St Thomas, whom he quoted so frequently, would have refused him the right to speak as to what was good and what was bad in art. He was a moralist, a preacher ; his virtue was prudence, and prudence may not judge art. Prudence might be more truly a virtue than art in so far as it made men good simply (I. ii. 66, 3 and II. ii. 47, 4), but art was more truly a virtue than prudence in so far as it was more scientific and had more of the intellectual splendour of an authentic habitus (I. ii. 66, 3, ad 1 m), and " life in accordance with thought is better than life in accordance with man " (II. ii. 47, 15). The prudent man, even the preacher, lived in a different world from the artist ; each found it hard to understand the other. The artist and the mystic were nearer akin, for the mystic had wisdom " architectonic to all the intellectual virtues," and had prudence " only as the doorkeeper to the King " (I. ii. 66, 5).

God alone to the mediævalist was equally great as Doer and as Maker, alone could harmonize art and prudence. The ages have sacrificed one to the other in action and reaction, swaying violently from side to side. The Renaissance sacrificed prudence to art in the name of beauty, the Victorian era sacrificed art to prudence in the name of respectability : the Middle Ages seem more nearly to have balanced either of them, the modern schools to have flouted both.

For expression in art was thought to proceed both from the work itself and the means employed, and not from the subject chosen; art resulted in emotion, but emotion was not its aim.

As we have said already, mediæval art did copy nature: the local flowers are to be found carved in the churches; the vintage capital in Rheims, the centre of the wine district, is evidence of this. But the sculptors strove to make the cathedrals into encyclopædias, not so much to please as to teach. Victor Hugo's idea that the sculptors were anti-clerical is not borne out by facts: the caricatures begin in the fifteenth century and are never malicious. The convinced believer could afford to indulge his sense of humour without any loss of faith.

The earlier Middle Ages made no effort to produce emotion; and it was the evils of the search after emotion which Savonarola denounced, for he was defending the older theories of art. No sufferings are ever depicted in the primitives, except the sufferings of the damned. Every early Madonna is smiling and gracious. There is no early representation of the Madonna at the foot of the Cross, nor of Our Lord shown as suffering. If He is shown suffering, He is shown serene. There is the Beau Dieu of Amiens, the royal figure at Chartres: these are not even tender in their beauty but majestical. It is the Christ, not of devotion but of theology, love incarnate, not a human friend.

Finally, it would be false to think that the artist of the Middle Ages loved to be anonymous and so escape renown. The architect, for example, or mason or *cementarius*, was one who made profession of the art of building; and often he is represented in the very church he built (Lethaby, *Mediæval Art*, pp. 244 and 598): Amiens Cathedral in 1220 was built by Master Robert of Luzarches, master of the work, as the inscription, let into the pavement of the cathedral, states. He was followed by Master Thomas de Cormont, and he by his son, Master Reynault, who "put the writing" in 1288. In Rheims Cathedral is the finely engraved grave slab of Hugo Libergiers, holding in his hands a model of the church and his measuring rod, and on the field are shown his square and callipers. Round the border runs this inscription : CI GIT MAISTRE HUES LIBERGIERS QUI COMENSA CESTE EGLISE EN L'AN MCCXXIX ET TREPASSA L'AN MCCLXIII. He also built Notre Dame at Rheims, as his grave slab at St Denis in the same town shows. Notre Dame of Paris, below the sculptures on the doorway in large raised letters, exhibits its own founder, MASTER JEAN, and the date 1257; we know too of Pierre de Montreuil (1265), Eudes de Montreuil (St Louis' favourite master), and Pierre de Chelles (1307) as part workers in the glorious fane. Over the central portal of St James of Compostella is an inscription eighteen feet in length to the effect that the building was completed in MCLXXXVIII. by Master Mathew. Over the tympanum of the doorway of St Ursin at Bourges (twelfth century) is this, GIRALDUS FECIT ISTAS PORTAS.

In Westminster Abbey on the cornice of the shrine of the Confessor in letters of blue mosaic, dating from 1279, was the name of the artist who made it, PETRUS ROMANUS CIVIS, with the name of Henry III. as having ordered the work ; while in the mosaic pavement was the name of Odericus of Rome, 1268.

The artist, whether architect or sculptor or worker, was duly honoured at his trade. After seven years of apprenticeship to his master, he claimed to be recognized as a man of skill. Even then he was only a " bachelor " or " companion." It was only for some great work, a thesis, that he was made a master (cf. C. Bouchal's *Biographical Dictionary of French Architects*, 1887).

The mediæval theories of art help us to understand the social theories of the ages in their appreciation of the artist as a teacher like the theologian or the philosopher or scientist, the holder of an intellectual talent or habit, superior in some ways to the merely prudent man. He sought balance and restraint, he did not aim at emotion, he honoured work as giving him almost the prerogatives of a creator. Symmetry he valued and the hierarchic organization of the world, which he thought extended beyond the borders of sight into the invisible kingdom, order reigning in fullest perfection in the splendid courts of God.

Not visible things but what they stood for was, at the beginning, the object he had in mind, only gradually he gave this up under pressure from the new Renaissance spirit. The Middle Ages had definitely ceased when art became so busy with the visible as to forget the invisible beyond.

This is what Savonarola saw and feared. Himself an artist, he would have been able to reply to the critic who forbade him to judge art, by quoting great names amongst the artists whose judgments agreed with his own, the Michael Angelo of *The Last Judgment*, and the Botticelli of the latter period of his art.

Definitely indeed Botticelli fixed on the year 1500 as the ending of the glories of the Christian greatness " three and a half years " after Savonarola had been hanged and burnt. His mature judgment is inscribed in Greek characters over that picture of the Nativity in our National Gallery which shows him no longer negligent of the ecstasy of spiritual things. In this picture angels and men are in harmony, the Child is born, happiness is seen in the Mother, even in bleak nature, under the stars, over the sky :

" This picture I Alessandro painted at the end of the year 1500, during the troubles of Italy in the half time after the time of the fulfilment of chapter eleven of St John in the second woe of the Apocalypse when Satan was loosed upon the earth for three and a half years. Afterwards he shall be chained and we shall see him trodden under, as in this picture."

Afterwards we shall see him trodden under . . . afterwards . . . but for the present Satan was let loose.

BIBLIOGRAPHY

WITHOUT intending to supply a general bibliography, it may be suggested to a reader who desires to know the life of the mediæval period to make trial of some of these volumes, in addition to those quoted in the preceding pages :

G. B. Adams, *Civilisation during the Middle Ages*, 1894.
E. L. Cutts, *Scenes and Characters of the Middle Ages*, 1911.
E. K. Chambers, *The Medieval Stage*, 1903.
L. Thorndike, *Medieval Europe*, 1920.
C. R. Beazley, *Notebook of Medieval History*, 1917.
Brentano, *The Middle Ages* (trans. E. O'Neill), 1921.
M. Bateson, *Medieval England*, 1903.
D. Hughes, *Illustrations of Chaucer's England*, 1918.
K. H. Vickers, *England in the Later Middle Ages*, 1920.
J. J. Jusserand, *English Wayfaring Life*, 1921.
J. H. Flemming, *England under the Lancastrians*, 1921.
J. D. Thornley, *England under the Yorkists*, 1920.
E. Benson, *Life in a Medieval City* [York], 1920.
A. Tilley, *Medieval France*, 1921.
J. Evans, *Life in Medieval France*, 1925.

THE "SUMMA THEOLOGICA" OF ST THOMAS AQUINAS

ITS PARTS AND CONTENTS

<table>
<tr><td colspan="2" align="center">First Part   (Pars Prima)</td></tr>
<tr><td>QQ. i–xxvi.</td><td>Of the Sacred Doctrine: of God and the Divine Attributes.</td></tr>
<tr><td>QQ. xxvii–xliii.</td><td>Of the Blessed Trinity.</td></tr>
<tr><td>QQ. xliv–xlix.</td><td>Of the Creation.</td></tr>
<tr><td>QQ. l–lxiv.</td><td>Of the Angels.</td></tr>
<tr><td>QQ. lxv–lxxiv.</td><td>Of the Work of Six Days.</td></tr>
<tr><td>QQ. lxxv–xciv.</td><td>Of Man.</td></tr>
<tr><td>QQ. xcv–cxix.</td><td>Of the Divine Government.</td></tr>
</table>

<table>
<tr><td colspan="2" align="center">Second Part   (Prima Secundæ)</td></tr>
<tr><td>QQ. i–xlviii.</td><td>Of the End of Man: Human Acts: Passions.</td></tr>
<tr><td>QQ. xlix–lxxxix.</td><td>Of Habits: Virtues and Vices.</td></tr>
<tr><td>QQ. xc–cxiv.</td><td>Of Law (De Legibus): Grace.</td></tr>
</table>

<table>
<tr><td colspan="2" align="center">Second Part of Second Part   (Secunda Secundæ)</td></tr>
<tr><td>QQ. i–xlvi.</td><td>Of Faith, Hope and Charity.</td></tr>
<tr><td>QQ. xlvii–lxxx.</td><td>Of Prudence: Justice.</td></tr>
<tr><td>QQ. lxxxi–c.</td><td>Of Religion: The Interior and Exterior Acts of.</td></tr>
<tr><td>QQ. ci–cxxii.</td><td>Of Piety: Observance: Obedience, Gratitude and Contrary Vices.</td></tr>
<tr><td>QQ. cxxiii–clxx.</td><td>Of Fortitude: Temperance, its Parts and Contrary Vices.</td></tr>
<tr><td>QQ. clxxi–clxxxix.</td><td>Of Gratuitous Grace: The Contemplative Life: The Active Life: States of Life.</td></tr>
</table>

<table>
<tr><td colspan="2" align="center">Third Part and Supplement   (Pars Tertia: Supplementum)</td></tr>
<tr><td>QQ. i–xxvi.</td><td>Of the Incarnation.</td></tr>
<tr><td>QQ. xxvii–lix.</td><td>Of the Blessed Virgin Mary: The Christology and the Mariology.</td></tr>
<tr><td>QQ. lx–lxxxiii.</td><td>Of the Sacraments: Baptism: Confirmation: The Holy Eucharist.</td></tr>
<tr><td>QQ. lxxxiv–xc.
Suppl. QQ. i–xxxiii.</td><td>Of Penance: Extreme Unction.</td></tr>
<tr><td>QQ. xxxiv–lxviii.</td><td>Of Holy Orders: Matrimony.</td></tr>
<tr><td>QQ. lxix–lxxxvi.</td><td>Of the Last Things.</td></tr>
<tr><td>QQ. lxxxvii–xcix.</td><td>Of Purgatory: The Beatific Vision: Damnation.</td></tr>
</table>

INDEX

ABELARD, Peter, 6, 32, 59, 260 ; Aristotle re-
born, 6 ; his method, 35 ; *Sic-et-Non*, 35
Accomplished Damsel of Florence, lament of a
girl in a series of sonnets, 78
Agricola, anti-scholastic, 49 ; *De Formando
Studio*, 49
Albert the Great, 175 ; on Aristotle, 36 ;
approves slavery, 100 ; *Opusculum de Pul-
chro et Bono* sometimes ascribed to, 246
Aldobrandino of Siena, his governance of the
body, 49
Alexander de Villa Dei, *Doctrinale*, 34
" Alliances and Covines " of town labourers,
116
Ambrose, Bishop of Milan, St, 122
Amiens Cathedral, its builder, 266
Ancren Riwle, 79
Angelico, Fra, 262 ; remark of, 259
Angelo, Michael, his *Last Judgment*, 268
Anglo-Saxon Chronicle, 134
Anglo-Saxon law, 104
Anjou, Charles of, brother of St Louis, 27,
199
Antonino, Antoninus, Archbishop of Florence,
St, 27, 60, 64, 148, 181, 189, 206, 207,
208, 209 ; theory of law, 28 ; disapproves
of competitive methods in education, 58 ;
commends readiness of speech, 60 ; definitions of *servus*, 103 ; miseries of the poor,
107 ; attitude to slavery, 121 ; on property, 127 ; on trade, 156 ; on dishonest
practices in trade, 159 ; on just price,
161 ; economics a moral question, 164 ; on
different trades, 178 ; on soldiers and soldiering, 194-200 ; clerical fighting, 201 ;
deceptions in war, 202 ; reprisals, 203-4 ;
" mystical body " of nation, 203 ; *Summa
Moralis*, 28, 58, 155, 156, 159, 161,
172, n.1, 175, 178-80, 189, 209, 210
Aquinas, St Thomas, 6, 11, 13, 14, 17, 19,
27, 32, 33, 35, 49, 53, 61, 99, 124, 125,
126, 127, 144, 170, 182, 183, 184, 197,
206, 210, 217, 221, 231, 265 ; on law, 12 ;
defines law, 12, 14 ; function of law, 12 ;
divisions of law, 12-16 ; four essentials of
law, 17, 30 ; on taxation, 18 ; on women,
20, 84 ; teleological view, 71, 73, 75 ; on
sin, 97 ; on slavery, 100, 107, 121 ; definition of slavery, 101 ; degrees of authority,
101 ; on absolute rules, 101, 120 ; on property, 121, 124 ; man's right to possess,
125 ; on politico-economic science, 151-4 ;
on usury, 155, 167, n.1 ; on middleman, 161 ; on legitimate and illegitimate
trading, 162 ; on honesty in art, 178 ; on

Aquinas, St Thomas—*continued*
peace, 182-185 ; on just war, 188 ; on the
spiritual supremacy, 189-90 ; on pagan
rights, 190 ; on heresy, 217-8 ; on lapsed
heretic, 219-220 ; on art, 236, 238-9,
255 ; defines beauty, 243-5 ; essence of
beauty, 246 ; *Commentary on Canticle of
Canticles*, 6 ; *On the Sentences*, 10, 262 ;
Summa Theologica, 12, 15, 16, 17, 35, 36,
71-4, 97, 102, 121, 124, 125, 127, 172,
176, 178, 182, 183, 184, 185, 187, 188,
191, 192, 193, 210, 216, 220, 247, 251,
255 ; *Commentary on the Ethics* (Aristotle),
15, 263 ; *Treatise on the Governance of the
Jews*, 17 ; *Commentaries on De Anima*, 35 ;
Metaphysics, 36 ; *In Cælo et Mundo*, 36 ;
Summa Contra Gentiles, 61, 263 ; *De Re-
gimine Principum*, 99, 101, 102, 104, 189 ;
On the Politics (Aristotle), 100, 101, 151 ;
De Usuris, 167, n.1 ; *Commentary on Divine
Names of Dionysius*, 183, 245, 246, 258 ;
On St Matthew's Gospel, 183, 184 ; *On
Epistle to Hebrews*, 184 ; *Treatise on War*,
188 ; *De Regimine Hebræorum*, 190 ; *Contra Errores Græcorum*, 215 ; *On Psalms of
David*, xxv. and xliv., 245 ; *Opusculum de
Pulchro et Bono* (attributed to), 246
Aristotle, 6, 15, 35, 36, 96, 155, 181, 182,
233 ; theory of slavery, 10 ; the slave soul,
100 ; " private possession and public use,"
128 ; contemptuous of trade, 176 ; *Politics*,
25
Art, artist, qualities requisite in, 177 ; fraud
demands restitution, 178 ; crimes of artists, 178 ; musicians, 179 ; actors, farmers,
husbandmen, 179 ; reflects social ideas,
236, 267 ; mediæval man artist by choice,
236 ; art criticism systematized by thirteenth century, 236 ; definition of Aquinas,
236-7 ; purpose primary consideration, 238 ;
not to be confounded with skill, 238, 254 ;
purpose affects art, motive the artist, 239 ;
corresponds in " making " to prudence in
" doing," 239 ; ruled by law, 240 ; art
infallible, not artist, 241 ; added purpose
to give pleasure, 241-2 ; fine art, 243-4 ;
dominated by reason, 247 ; national art,
248 ; double life of fine art, 249 ; laws
of, 250 ; involves natural gift, 251 ; long
apprenticeship, 251-3 ; nature the best
model, 254 ; does not imitate nature, 255 ;
but interprets, 256-7, symbolism of, 258,
268 ; subordination of matter to form,
259, no appeal to emotion, 259-60 ; characteristics of mediæval art, 259 ; later

S

273

INDEX

East, Emperor of, 215 ; Eastern schism, 215

Education, scholastic argument for, 33 ; divisions of curriculum, see *trivium* and *quadrivium*, 34 ; aim of educational training, 35 ; Abelard's idea of, 35 ; method, 35 ; villeinage a bar to, 38 ; neglect of English in system, 43-5 ; centres in Middle Ages, see Schools ; Roman theory of, 49 ; older methods discarded, 49 ; new methods, 49 ; war of pamphlets, 49 ; Mafeo Vegio's work on, 51-68 ; earlier methods fostered individuality, 53 ; disapproved competitive inducements, 58 ; encouraged ready speaker, 59-60 ; set accuracy and precision above rhetoric, 61 ; vocational training in fifteenth century, 64 ; not how to live but how to make a living, 68

Eleanor of Aquitaine, queen, patron of letters, 86

Election, system extolled, 102 ; John succeeds to throne by, 102 ; custom on " democracy of Tuscany," 102 ; praised by St Thomas, 102

Emperor, Holy Roman, the, 22, 26, 129, 130, 184, 189, 190, 198, 199 ; Emperors : Frederick I., Barbarossa, 20, 130, 227 ; Frederick II., 27, 130, 220 ; Sigismund, 130, 229 ; Henry VII., 198 ; Louis of Bavaria, contest with Pope John XXII., 224-5 ; Charles IV., 232

Empire, Holy Roman, the, 25, 130, 189 ; law of, 19, 20, 21, 27, 137

England, kings of, Richard I., 7, 130 ; Henry III., 8, 169 ; Henry IV., 24, 38 ; Henry V., 24, 38 ; Edward I., regard for law, 94 ; ideal of justice, 95 ; new army, 115 ; encourages trade, 173 ; method of campaign, 195, n.1 ; Edward III., 115, 177 ; Henry II., 132 ; John, 132 ; William the Conqueror, 132 ; Edward II., 195, n.1

English, prejudice of scholarship against teaching of, 43-5

Equality praised as principle of social life, 102 ; equality of citizenship in burdens and honour, 102 ; principle exalted, while slavery accepted, 103

Erasmus, Desiderius, represents parting of the old and new ways, 50

Eymeric, Nich., his *Directorium* for the use of Inquisitors, 218

Felix V., anti-pope, elected by extremists of the Conciliar party at Basel, 230

Feltre, Vittorino da, new educationalist at Mantua, 49

Feudalism, origin, 7 ; double-edged, 7 ; national and international force, 8 ; amalgamation of Roman and barbaric customs, 110 ; nearest approach to practical Com-

Feudalism—*continued*

munism, 132 ; contractual principle of, 133 ; duty of vassals under, 134 ; incidents, 135 ; *Curia Regis* partly a feudal assembly, 135 ; relation of vassals to lesser tenants, 136 ; immunities, 136 ; involves question of suzerainty in England and Scotland, 136 ; definitions of system, 140 ; break-up of, 140. See Property

Feud-letters, or challenges of fifteenth century, 191, 192

Florence, war with Pisa, 205 ; Council transferred to, 231 ; triumph of Council, 231

Fortescue, Sir John, his *Commodities of England*, 180

France, 24, 25, 27, 32 ; kings of, Philip Augustus, 7 ; Louis IX. (St Louis), 9, 21, 22, 24, 27, 75 ; Philip IV., 22, 23 ; Charles VI., 24, 255 ; Philip VI., 24 ; Charles VIII., 24, 25 ; Charles V., 85 ; Louis XI., 115 ; Henry IV., 115 ; law derived from Rome, 21 ; participation of the nation in government, 24, 25

France, Marie de, her legend of *Guigemar*, 86

Francis, St, the Poverello of Assisi, 144, 146 ; condemns idleness, 156 ; orders his followers to work at a trade, 157 ; his Testamentum, 157 ; Brother Giles of Order of, 157 ; *The Mirror of Perfection*, 157 ; *Regula Prima*, 157 ; *Little Flowers of St Francis (Fioretti)*, 157, 260

Franciscan " Spirituals," Fraticelli, denounce private property, 146 ; condemned by the Papacy, 146 ; adherents of the Emperor (Louis of Bavaria) against the Pope, 225-6 ; led by Michael of Cesene, 225

Frescobaldi, Italian moneylender, 172

Galileo, 242 ; love of his nun daughter, 83

Gaunt, John of, friendly to Wyclif, 145

Gerson, John, his ideals of Church government, 234

Gesta Francorum et Germanorum, 100

Gherardina of Florence, account of, 78

Girls, same faults as boys, 38 ; advice for boys applicable to girls, 65 ; married for money, 77 ; letter on behalf of girls to Savonarola, 83 ; sermon of Humbertus de Romans : *For Girls and Maidens who are in the World*, 87

Glanvill, 111

" Grandes Compagnies," devastations of, 116, 117

Gratian, 30 ; codification of, 6 ; develops theory of Property from the Fathers, 122 ; the *Decretum*, 13, 177, 181, 188

Grotius, his international law not the *Jus Gentium*, 15, 206

INDEX

Libell of Englishe Polycye, 180
Libergiers, Hugo, builder of Rheims, 266-7
Liberi-tenentes, or *socemanni*, compose class of manorial dependents, 138
Liberty, freedom, not an end in itself, 94, 95 ; not the object of *Magna Carta*, 95 ; essential freedom of the will, 97 ; problem of realization, 99 ; races fit for, 100 ; basis of distinction between freedom and subjection, 100 ; definition of a freeman, 101
Lippi, Fra Lippo, 262
Lollardy, Lollards, social theories subordinate in Rising of (1381), 118 ; Poor Preachers of, 145 ; denounce property and wealth, 146
Lombard, Peter, Master of the Sentences, 10, 77
Lorraine, Duchess of, her *Romance of the Countess of Vergi*, 87
Lucca, Tolomeo de, 27 ; part author of *De Regimine Principum*, 33, 96, 122 ; on education, 33 ; on riches, 96 ; on dishonest trading, 158
Luzarches, Master Robert of, builder of Amiens Cathedral, 266
Lyra, Nicholas de, *Gloss*, 192

Maggi, Sebastiano dei, 148
Mahomet first a trader, 176
Maillotins, revolt of, 228
Mâle, Ernest, *L'Art religieux du 13me Siècle*, 250, 256 ; *L'Art religieux de la fin du Moyen Age en France*, 260
Man, destined to live in community, 98 ; in state of nature, 98 ; effect of sin, 98
Mandeville, John, description of Great Chan of Cathay, 224
Manicheism, Manicheans, view of marriage, 91 ; heresy, 217
Manor, manorial, the outward sign of feudalism, 110 ; smallest territorial unit, 137 ; organization of, 137 ; classes of dependents on, 137-8 ; manorial courts, 139
Marcel, Étienne, 24
Marcia, younger daughter of Cato, her remark, 77
Markets and fairs, 151, 164
Marriage, indissolubility of, 34 ; instituted by God, 76, 91 ; lower state than virginity, 76 ; marriage act not sinful, 76, 77, 91, 92 ; ideals of, 77 ; low motives in, 77 ; choice in marriage, 78
Marsiglio of Padua, 233 ; adherent of Emperor, 226 ; *Defensor Pacis*, 226
Mary, Blessed Virgin, cult of, 92 ; influence on art and chivalry, 92
Medici, Lorenzo dei, tribute to his mother, 83
" Merrie England " becomes " sighing or sorrowful England," 148
Meung, John de, misrepresents women, 86

Midi, heretics of, 126, 208
Milan, 26, 27
Modus Tenendi Curiam Baronis, 38, 159
Monderville, Henri de, his study of surgery, 49
Moneta, *Adversus Catharos et Valdenses*, 70
Money takes place of land, 141, 142 ; affects attitude to land, 143
Money-making, trade, commerce, based on absolute ownership, 147 ; benefits, 150 ; evils, 151 ; a practical science, 154 ; illimitable nature, 155, 168 ; sinful motive for, 155 ; lawful motive for, 155 ; judged by purpose, 156, 157 ; Antonino of Florence on, 156 ; honest trading commendable, 156; problem of motive, 164 ; profits, 167 ; increased interest in, 173 ; object for taxation, 173 ; royal trade policies, 173-4 ; necessary to moralize, 175 ; origin in fallen human nature, 176-7 ; subject for denunciation, 177
Monica, St, 50-1, 66
Montfort, Simon de, 8

Naples, 26
Nationalism, nationality, effect on war, 181 ; a political force, 212 ; rise of, 227-8 ; expression in Hussite movement, 231 ; quickened in Bohemia, 232 ; in Germany, 232 ; its part at the Council of Constance, 229 ; contributed to break-up of Christendom, 232, 233
Nations, law of, conclusions from law of nature, 15 ; arrived at by experience, 16 ; identified with the *Jus Gentium*, 16, 121, 124
Natura corruptæ (fallen nature), 9
Natura institutæ (original nature), 9
Nature, law of (*lex naturalis*), natural law, 9, 12 ; confers natural right, 12, 100 ; definition of Ulpian, 13 ; primary and secondary principles of, 13, 14 ; principles of, immutable, 14 ; conclusions from, mutable, 14 ; all human law derived from, 16 ; freedom and, 100 ; property and, 123, 124
Nature, supplies art with principles, 152 ; way of, 152 ; vital impulse to artist, 251, 253 ; the best model, 252 ; art interprets meaning of, 255-8
Norman law, 104

Ockham, William, Franciscan, 11, 20 ; pamphleteer in support of Temporal Power 226
Oresme, Nicholas, Bishop of Lisieux, *De Mutatione Monetarum*, 175
Orleans, Charles, Duke of, *Debate of Heralds*, 180
Oxford, university of, 46, 47 ; specializes, 46

276

INDEX

INDEX

Property—*continued*
permeating, 133, 134 (see Land-holding and Land-ownership) ; owners enjoined to give alms, 143 ; influence of trade and idealism on, 147 ; disappearance of old ideas on, 148 ; need the first claim on, 148 ; converted into power, 149

Prudence, corresponds in "doing" to art in "making," 239 ; concerned with means, 240 ; ruled by case law, 240

Pythagoras, 39

QUADRIVIUM, second part of the educational curriculum, 12, 35

RACINE, Jean, 248

Rastell, John, 45

Reiner, converted heretic : *Contra Waldenses Hæreticos*, 220

Renaissance, 30, 61, 93, 115, 147, 148, 268 ; worship of the individual, 147 ; age of refinement and exquisite torture, 210 ; art contrasted with Mediæval and Victorian, 265

Representative assemblies, origin of, 22, 23, 24, 25 ; method of, 25 ; not found in Italian city-states, 25, 26, 28

Rolle, Richard, of Hampole, 5, 12

Roma, Egidio de, schoolman, 27

Roman Emperors, 208 ; Constantine, 189, 233 ; Empire, 3, 4, 5, 6 ; law, 6, 13, 21, 73

Romans, 101, 102, 189 ; king of, Henry VII., 21

Romans, Humbertus de, fifth Master-General of Order of Preachers, 31, 32, 40 ; on education, 31 ; on girls, 38 ; advice to preachers, 40, 41 ; on things required in novices, 64 ; on prerogatives of women, 71-2 ; on feminine qualities, 81, 82 ; encourages learning among women, 87 ; examples of learned women, 88 ; preaches on living on usury, 163 ; on living on labour of others, 163 ; on extortionate innkeepers, 163 ; on evils of markets and fairs, 151, 164 ; on tournaments, 192-3 ; on peace, 211-12 ; recommends works of mercy, 222 ; on defects in hospitals, 222-3 ; advice to doctors, 223 ; Sermons : *Ad omnes litteratos*, 31 ; *Ad omnes scholares*, 39 ; *Ad scholares in grammatica*, 39 ; *Ad omnes mulieres*, 72 ; *Ad mulieres pauperes in villulis*, 82 ; *Ad mulieres religiosos quascunque*, 82 ; *Ad juvenculos sive adolescentulos seculares*, 87 ; *Ad mulieres burgenses diviteo*, 90 ; *Ad mulieres nobiles*, 90 ; *In nundinis*, 150 ; *Ad laicos in villis*, 163 ; *Ad operarios conductivos*, 164 ; *In merchatis*, 164 ; *In Inquisitione Hæreticorum*, 214 ; *De Eruditione Prædicatorum*, 31 ; *Summa Præ-*

Romans—*continued*
dicantium, 211 ; *De Eruditione Religiosorum Prædicatorum*, 213

Rome, 4, 6, 7, 19, 27, 99

Roselli, Nicholas, 27

Ruskin, John, inscription in church at Venice, 158

SACCHETTI, Franco, on women, 82

Salerno, university, specializes in medicine, 46

Salisbury, John of, attitude towards Aristotle, 6 ; and Abelard, 6 ; *Policraticus*, 182, n.1

Savonarola, Giovanni, 27, 67, 68, 90, 148 ; distrust of parliaments, 28 ; on education, 49 ; letter to, 83 ; his letters to Countess of Mirandola, 83 ; sermons, 148 ; *Life* by Burlamacchi, 150 ; on art, 257, 268 ; last voice of Middle Ages, 265 ; *Apologeticus*, 257 ; *Prediche sopra Amos e Zaccaria*, 264

Schism, schismatics, Great Schism, 47, 224, 225, 228, 230 ; Eastern Schism, 215 ; sin against charity, 216 ; not necessarily heresy, 220 ; under Church's jurisdiction, 221 ; sacramental powers not lost but abused by, 221

Schoolmen, scholastics, idea of law, 8, 9 ; education, 33 ; rise of anti-scholastic educationalists, 49 ; on position of women, 70, 73, 74, 75 ; on slavery, 97, 99, 100, 101, 102 ; on property, 122, 123, 124, 125, 126, 129 ; on trade and commerce, 154 ; on wealth, 155 ; on war, 181 *et seq.* ; borrow from Stoics, 210 ; on unbelief and schism, 216, 217, 218, 219, 220 ; on art, 236, 237 *et seq.*

Schools in mediæval period, 45 ; grammar schools, choir schools, song schools, schools attached to hospitals, guild schools, chantry schools, independent schools under laymen, 45-6

Scotus, John (Erigena), scholastic, 55, 210 ; defends private property, 124

Sens, Council of, 6

Seville, Isidore of, 30

Shakespeare pictures mediæval attitude to usury, 170 ; thoroughly English, 248

Shepherds voice discontents of the unfree (*The Shepherds' Play, The Towneley Plays*), 107, 108

Sicilian Carretti, 244, 245

Siena, St Catherine of, 27, 227

Sin, justifies law, 9 ; the cause of authority, 10 ; origin of slavery, 10 ; all sin slavery, 97 ; begat government, 98 ; origin of private property, 122 ; private property treated under, 123 ; unbelief, sin against faith, 216, 217 ; schism, sin against charity, 216 ; guilt of, 219 ; punishment due, 219

278

INDEX

Slave, serf, villein, definition of, 101 ; ambiguous use of term *servus*, 103 ; three meanings of, 103 ; manumission of, 103, 105 ; generic term, 104 ; hard life of, 105 ; general rising of, in fourteenth century, 107 ; extreme interpretation of, 109 ; disabilities of, 109 ; favourable influences on, 110-11 ; villein main representative of unfree, 111 ; improved conditions of, 112 ; effect of Black Death on, 112 ; slave only to a personal master, 113, 114 ; approaching enfranchisement of, 115 ; grievances of, 118 ; primary cause of Rising of, 118 ; *servi* of Domesday, 138 ; villeins comprise large class of dependents on manor, 138

Slavery, serfdom, villeinage, bar on education, 38 ; institution due to sin, 97 ; origin in Fall, 97; causes of, 99-100; by natural right, by legal right, 100 ; necessary to society, 102 ; devised by human reason, 102 ; accepted as normal, 103 ; serfdom based on land tenure, 104, 120 ; improving conditions, 105, 110 ; effect of commutation, 110 ; unalterable character of status, 112 ; effect of Black Death on, 113 *et seq.* ; slavery and *Jus Gentium*, 121 ; decay of villeinage, 141, 144

Sorbonne, Robert de, on boys' education, 39, 59 ; denounces proud masters and preachers, 48 ; *De Conscientia*, 37, 40 ; *De Confessione*, 166, n.1

Spynk, Richard, claimed as a villein, 112

State, the, 128, 188, 192, 219, 233 ; its end the Vision of God, 184 ; " mystical body," 203, 207 ; has power to kill, 207 ; Marsiglio's theory of, 22, 226

Stoics' ideas borrowed by Church, 98, 122, 210

Subjection, of man to man necessary for restraint of evil, 9 ; due to sin, 9, 10 ; for the common good, 11 ; of a slave, 72 ; of woman to man, 72, 75 ; twofold nature of, 72

Suit and service, duty of vassals and tenants, 143

Susa, Henry de, Cardinal (Ostiensis), *Summa Aurea*, 190

Tacitus, 224

Taxation, Aquinas on lawful, 18 ; justification of, 135 ; kings dependent on, 135 ; for benefit of trade, 173 ; moral justifiability, 180

Thaon, Philippe de, his computation, lapidary, bestiary, 49

Tournaments, forbidden by law, 192 ; Humbert de Romans on, 192-3

Tours, Oriental MSS. in library of, 48

Tractatus Novæ Monetæ, 175

Treaty, treaties, 211 ; observance among *jura gentium*, 16 ; of Etaples, 24 ; of Troyes, 24

Trionfo, Agostino, *Summa de Ecclesiastica Potestate*, 226

Trivium, first part of educational curriculum, 12, 34

Truce of God (*Treuga Dei*), 210

Turks, 189, 208, 209, 214

Ulpian, law of nature, 13

Unbelief, sin against faith, 216 ; three classes of unbelievers, 217. See Heresy

University, universities, origin of system (*Studia Generalia*), 46 ; spread, 46 ; preeminence of Paris, 46, 47 ; four great centres, 46 ; degrees, 47 ; deterioration in fourteenth century, 47 ; study of Oriental languages, 47 ; diffuses learning, 114 ; " nations," 228 ; established at Prague, 232. See Bologna, Oxford, Paris, Salerno

Usury, labour demands condemned as, 117 ; De Romans on, 163 ; treatise attributed to Pope Celestine, 165 ; Aquinas, *De Usuris*, 167, n.1 ; forbidden in Scripture, 167 ; first usurer, 168 ; cause of hatred of Jews, 170 ; Church's interpretation of, 170 ; view of Eastern Church, 170 ; English law stricter than canon, 170 ; Bromyard on, 171 ; lenient interpretations of, 171-2 ; risk justifies compensation, 173 ; dividends, 173

Vanity, responsible for human arts, 177 ; in dress, 177

Vegio, Mafeo, of Lodi, career of, 50 ; Thirteenth Book of *Æneid*, 50 ; combines old and new theories of education, 51 ; citations from, 51-58 ; treatment of child from birth, 51 ; food, clothing, discipline, 52 ; training, 53 ; punishment, 54 ; individual treatment, 55 ; school life, 56, 57 ; competition, 58 ; distrusts readiness of speech, 60 ; allows ornament in speech, 61 ; stresses individuality, 63 ; games, 63, 64 ; advice applicable to girls, 65 ; personal habits, 66 ; delights of country life, 67-68 ; *De Liberorum Eruditione*, 51

Velluti, Donato, account of two unmarried women of Florence by, 78

Verona, Guarino da new educationalist at Ferrara, 49

Vicenza, Giovanni de, inaugurates Crusade of Peace, 186 ; failure, 187

Vienna, Council of (1312), enforces Oriental studies on universities, 47 ; decree enforced by Council of Basel, 48 ; remains inoperative, 48

Virgil, 62, 66, 67 ; stands for Roman greatness, 248

279

INDEX

Virginity higher state than marriage, 76

Vittoria, Francesco, on war, 206-11; influence on Suarez and Grotius, 206; fresh statements of old points, 207-9; idea of mercy, 210; *De Jure Belli*, 206; *De Potestate Civili*, 206

Voragine, James of, 72

WALTER, Hubert, Archbishop of Canterbury, 111; exacts oath from John, 132

War, 100; new art of, 115; influence of French War on labour discontent, 116; justifies taxation, 135; consistency of, with Gospel, 181, 185; Christian theory of Augustine, 181, 187, 188; quoted by Gratian, 181, 187, 188; fresh problems of, 181; miseries of, 185; to be avoided, 185; Lombard wars, 187; Aquinas on three conditions of just war, 187-8, 193, 201; Aquinas' definition as defence of peace, 188; how just war may be waged, 188, 190, 191; Antonino of Florence on, 194; on hired soldiery, 197, 212; degradation of war, 195; defensive, 196; non-combatants in, 196-7, 203; Crusades justifiable war, 198, 205; public authority in, 198; conduct of, 199; reasons against clerical fighting, 200-1, 206; morality of stratagems in, 201-2, 206; of reprisals, 203-4; wars of aggression, 204; civil war, 204-5; wars of freedom, 206; offensive and defensive, 207; new statement on just war, 207; motives for, 209; geographical discoveries lead to, 208; a scourge of sin, 211; alien to spirit of Christ, 211; futility of, 211

Wealth, riches justified by distribution of superfluous, 145; power of, 147; new culture built on, 147; opposed to old idea, 148; not to exceed need, 158; W. Langland on spending of, 158; made evil by evil production, distribution or consumption, 164; the *Jus Pauperum* in, 168; fraught with peril, 180; pursuit of, continues, 180. See Money-making

Wessel, John, opposes scholastic education, 49

Westminster Abbey, 94; the artist of the Shrine of the Confessor in, 267

Women, boys taught reverence to, 65; subject to men, 69; Aquinas on, 70-3, 84; De Romans on, 71-2; place in society dictated by her purpose, 75; unmarried, 78; active life of, 79; power in the home, 79-80; critical attitude to, 81-2; love of, 83; neglect of, 83; ironical references to, 84; protest against popular view of, 84-5; literary women, 86-7; learning encouraged among women, 87-8; position determined by individual achievement, 89; common failings of young, 89; denunciation of fashions of, 90; position influenced by cult of Blessed Virgin, 92; Pierre du Bois on education of women, 92-3

Wyclif, John, theory of " Dominion," 10, 145, 190, 231; throws over private property, 145-6; his Poor Preachers, 145; copies the friars, 145; not a clear thinker, 145; disowns communism, 146; popular as champion against papal taxation, 221; as apostle of disendowment, 221; loses influence as heresiarch, 221